China Spicy and Salty

2006

Did you eat?
Book 2

Virginia Heslinga

3clocks
publications

Also by Virginia Heslinga

Memoirs
Grace Interlaced
Gracia entrelazada

Historical Novel
Wounded Dove

Did You Eat? Series
China Sweet and Sour: 2004
China Spicy and Salty: 2006
China Sharp and Zesty: 2009 *(available spring 2026)*

China Spicy and Salty

A Few Views on Learning

Learn the good that you can of the foreign people and reject the unsuitable.
　　Pearl S. Buck

Teachers open the door; you enter by yourself.
　　Chinese Proverb

As long as your horse is strong, travel and learn to know different places.
　　Mongolian Proverb

Studying and learning are a lifelong road from Grandmother's lap to the grave.
　　Hui Proverb

Without experiencing setbacks, one cannot gain knowledge.
　　Chinese Proverb

Published by 3clocks Publications, LLC

China Spicy and Salty: 2006

Book 2 in the series, **Did You Eat?**

Copyright © by Virginia Heslinga, 2025

eBook ISBN: 978-1-964590-05-9

Paperback ISBN: 978-1-964590-04-2

Audiobook ISBN: 978-1-964590-06-6

Cover and interior design by Gordon Saunders

Publisher's Note: This is a work of creative non-fiction. The author has presented the events accurately and fairly to the best of her ability. Although all the incidents in the book are based on fact, names and some identifying details have been changed to protect privacy.

In addition to telling a story of challenges in remote regions of China, this book aims to provide insight for reflections and to stimulate actions of cross-cultural communication, respect, service, and appreciation. The author and publisher make no claims to provide any type of professional advice expressed or inferred.

Contents

Characters

Virginia's American Team

Virginia: Worked in Amity's Summer English Program (SEP) as a team member in 2004.
Jerry: Virginia's husband, since 1972, was ordained as a minister of the gospel in 1973.
Trudy: A registered nurse, who trained and mentored nurses.
Danielle: A family friend who had a variety of jobs from flight attendant to tennis coach.
Jim: Danielle's 10-year-old son.

Left Banner Participants in the Summer English Program

Principal Chimeg (Chuh meg): Host administrator.
Vice Principal Guo (Kwaw): Secondary host administrator.
Gladys: Head teacher of English and our team's official translator.

Sally: Gladys's 11-year-old daughter.

Anu (Ahnuh): a twenty-two-year-old Mongolian teacher from a small desert village.

Solomon: a 25-year-old Mongolian teacher and camel rancher.

Zaya (Zahya): a young English teacher of sixth-grade-level students in our host school.

Beijing Guide

Naomi: Beijing friend since 2004, as well as a translator and interpreter; an English major.

Amity Staff

Jessie: Goes with teams to locations that host a SEP team for the first time.

MeiLi (MayLee): Amity staff member who leads practical cultural classes in Nanjing for the SEP teams.

Wuhai Residents

Principal Chen (Djden): Principal of the 2004 school for Amity's SEP.

VP Zhu (DJu): Vice principal of the 2004 host school for Amity's SEP.

Emily: Head of the English department at the 2004 SEP school.

Thomas: Once a science teacher, then a senior middle school English teacher.

Penny: Taught at a vocational school, wife of Thomas.

Ye (Yay): A college age student who becomes a friend.

Characters

Erdeen: A Mongolian woman, Virginia's 2004 teaching assistant.

Jeff : A friend of Terry's who teaches with Terry at a vocational school.

Jason: A junior middle school teacher with energy and excellence in English.

Terry: A Christian who attended the church nearest the 2004 host school.

Kent: One of the lead teachers at the host school in 2004; older sister of Autumn.

Marge: A lively young teacher at the host school for the Amity 2004 SEP.

Autumn: Younger sister of Kent and an avid learner of English teaching at a junior middle school.

Pastor Samuel, his wife Ruth, and daughter Deborah: new to Wuhai in 2006.

Ying Yue (Ying Youway): A translator and English teacher born and raised in Wuhai, away at college in 2004, translates a conversation for Jerry and a local pastor in 2006.

Chapter 1

Lost at the Start

"Virginia, I've lost my carry-on bag. My medicine and glasses are in it!"

"What?" I looked at her oversize purse that hung on one shoulder. "You don't have your carry-on bag?"

We'd collected our luggage at the Beijing carousel assigned to our flight. Jerry and Jim were our alert hunters standing at the edge of the conveyor belt to snatch our cases. We'd traveled for twenty three hours and an adrenalin surge with the end of flights had given them energy. I was watching them when I felt someone else next to me and turned to see Trudy. She had tears in her eyes.

"It's not here. It won't be on the carousel. I think I left it in the Shanghai international airport!' And then our team nurse had tears spill out of her eyes.

Jerry and Jim heard Trudy and turned as if to say with alarm, 'What?'

Danielle, the fifth person of our team, approached and put an arm around Trudy.

I thought back to when we shouldered our small bags while we rushed to get our suitcases from the luggage

1

carousel in Shanghai. Distracted, I'd been looking from the luggage up to a high walk way. I had hoped to see the friends who were going to take us to the Shanghai domestic airport. I did recall that Trudy had moved back just enough to put her pink carry-on case on a chair next to where we stood.

"Trudy, you're are exhausted. You hardly slept on any of the flights. We're way off our normal time zone and routines. We'll figure it out. I'll report the missing bag here. It was pink, like a cherry blossom, right?"

"It will be okay," Danielle added, arm still around Trudy.

"What was in your carry-on Trudy?"

"Extra reading glasses, sunglasses, medicine, and personal items."

"As soon as we get our bags, I'll find the baggage claim. China takes helping foreign guests seriously. We'll report your case. If that office doesn't have anyone who speaks English, they'll still be able to read English if it's printed. Remember not to use cursive when you write anything or fill out forms in China." Trudy nodded and took the tissues Danielle offered.

All the checked bags arrived. We loaded them on a convenient free cart and followed signs to baggage claim. Down a level, in a far corner, we found the baggage claim office. Cases of different sizes filled the space so that the small gray haired man who took the information barely had room to sit in the office. He spoke some English but had me print the information. I gave our Beijing address for the dates we would be in Beijing and then the Nanjing address for the Amity Foundation in case it took them days to find the case.

By the time we returned to the main level, it was nearly

2

one in the morning. The travelers who had arrived on the late flight with us had disappeared while we were at baggage claim. My team followed me without complaint as I led the way to the main level and front exits. How many school trips did I lead in my past twenty-eight years of teaching without having students lose backpacks, lunch bags, or jackets? Now, with three adults and one child, an important item had gone missing on our first day in Beijing.

At this middle-of-the-night hour, in the area where taxis, shuttles, and reserved limos formed lines for travelers, no vehicles were in sight except one taxi. The driver was asleep, his head on the steering wheel. Had the vehicle I had reserved waited even an hour for us?

I saw two young men in uniforms with airport logos and asked in my meager Mandarin if they spoke English. One did, and he understood I wanted a van that could take all of us to the Beijing Guesthouse. I showed him the name and address written in English and Chinese. He said he would make a call and walked away.

In minutes he was back. "A van will come soon."

"*Xie xie*," I said. My team knew I'd said thank you, but I could see their energy fading.

The van arrived in fifteen minutes. It looked like a white delivery van to me, but it had six passenger seats and room behind the last row of seats for our luggage. No identifying transport company name appeared anywhere on the vehicle or in it.

I suspected that the airport employee called someone he knew with a van. I asked the price and hoped not to have to bargain. The cost seemed fair. I agreed to the price and turned to my overtired team. "Go ahead. We can get in."

Weary but trusting, they let the driver load the luggage in the back and climbed into available seats. Though my

Chinese was minimal, I sat up front. I knew that I could at least say, stop. I'd say it in English too so my team would know we had a problem with this driver.

Dear God, I prayed silently. *We have come to try to help people. Please get us to our hotel safely.* We were not going to a typical large and modern tourist hotel on one of the large brightly lit avenues. To experience Chinese culture right from the start, we'd be going away from the main avenues into a warren of narrow streets rarely with any street lights.

Chapter 2

Hutong Arrival

The van jolted over some bumps, but the driver seemed cheerful even now in the middle of the night. He had spoken quickly to the young man who had called him, too quickly for me to understand any of it. Probably they talked about sharing the payment. What I thought reasonable compared to the costs of taxis in the US could be high pay here.

In 2004, my Chinese and Mongolian students had explained the guanxi system to me. Guanxi existed as a network of mutual trust, obligations, and exchange of favors. I told them that the US, and every country I had visited, had guanxi in some form. Growing up with my Italian family I saw active connections and favors because of guanxi.

I had *yuan* with me. Yuan, the Chinese renminbi, *RMB*, their version of currency, had been with me since 2004. I had kept the money rather than changing it with the hope that I would meet the goal of returning to China. Even when the exchange rate went down from what it had been, I held onto the yuan as a tangible connection to my hope to return to China.

It had seemed like an act of faith to keep the paper money. Getting into this unmarked van at 1:30 a.m., with only windows in the front, without knowing the driver's language, and with three tired adults and a sleepy child depending on me also seemed like an act of faith. I'd find out soon if it was faith or foolishness.

Our middle-of-the-night Beijing van driver leaned over his steering wheel as we left the airport. We passed through a toll and entered the center of Beijing on a wide avenue. The van driver had a heavy foot, but we didn't take any corners on two wheels. In 2006. The streets seemed eerily empty.

When we entered the narrow streets of historic old Beijing I listened to the van driver make a call on his cell phone for directions. He turned into a narrow lane, then another. He needed help to find our accommodations.

Beijing won the honor of hosting the summer Olympics for 2008. Modern, high tech, and luxury accommodations dominated China's plans for opening the city to the world. Hutongs as ancient homes, walled, on narrow streets, and in small neighborhoods, were being torn down.

The van driver slowed as he entered a long narrow alley of a street. I recognized it from 2004, but it looked different at night. I could barely see the closed shops lining the edge of the road in front of the ancient walls of the general's courtyard.

The van's headlights gave the only illumination of the street. No one was on the street. The headlights showed a cement wall in front of us topped with wooden arches stretched across the road creating a dead end. In the center of the wall ahead was a tall red wooden gate. It looked like a feudal door. I guessed that if it opened wide, the van could squeeze through into the guest property.

A rope dangled beside the red door. The driver stopped in front of the gate, exited the vehicle, and using both hands pulled down hard on the long rope beside the gate. We heard a sound somewhere between a gong and a bell.

"Where have you taken us?" Danielle asked as she hugged a sleepy Jim.

"I know it looks scary now but wait until we are inside. It's special."

Even with the dim light in the van, I could see Danielle's concern. The gates opened. Our driver returned and got behind the steering wheel. Through the gates we saw tiny white lights strung over the curved upward edges of the Chinese style eaves of the buildings surrounding a courtyard. An array of lights also draped through limbs of slender trees in the courtyard presenting a fairy land beauty.

I paid the driver the agreed upon price and supervised the unloading of the luggage by the driver and Jerry. We didn't need to lose any more bags. Small smiles appeared on my team's faces for the first time since we had arrived in Beijing. The tiny white lights twinkling in the courtyard gave a gentle beauty, but the sight could not remove our blanket of exhaustion. We carried our luggage inside to the dimly lit office and up to the reception desk.

I leaned against the welcome desk in the Beijing Hebei Hutong Guesthouse and handed all our passports to the desk clerk. At least Trudy had kept her passport, money, and a few days of medicine in her shoulder bag. My head ached just thinking about the difficulties we would have faced if she didn't have those items.

Trudy leaned on the counter near me and Jerry. Her

eyes filled with tears again. "I'm sorry. I'm so tired. I can hardly think straight. I've never traveled for so many hours. I do remember that I put my carry-on case on a chair at the International Airport close to where we waited for the checked luggage."

"Trudy, we've reported it." I should have made sure to check on all the bags before we moved to the domestic airport. I should have looked before we even met Ruby's parents. I could feel my heart clutch with concern. Making sure my team had all their luggage should have been a priority for me because they had never taken a trip like this, and I had.

Trudy continued, "I have some of my medicine in this shoulder bag, but I brought enough to get through all the weeks here in my carry-on. My special skin cream, eye drops, and an extra pair of glasses, too. Do you really think they'll find my bag?"

I did not remind Trudy about the number of people passing through Shanghai's international airport. Anyone could have picked up the bag by now, an airport guard or someone who decided to steal it. Because it was an unclaimed bag, it could even end up being destroyed.

"I don't know Trudy, but if it doesn't appear, we can figure out how to get another spare set of glasses, even prescription sunglasses if you need those, and a refill of your medications in a couple of days. My young friend, Naomi, arrives this morning. She will help us figure it out."

"What if she can't?" Trudy asked.

"What if who can't do what?" Danielle asked. Ten-year-old Jim leaned back on the lobby couch and closed his eyes.

"We're talking about Trudy's carry-on bag," Jerry answered.

"Virginia, don't you think that they'll find it? I heard the

Chinese are very efficient." Even at home, Danielle always seemed to think optimistically. I gave thanks again that Danielle was on our teaching team.

"It is a very busy airport. I am sure they'll look for it."

We stood silently. We had three days to be tourists in Beijing. Then we would travel to Nanjing for the required Amity orientation, being trained by the Non-Governmental Organization to prepare us to live and teach in a remote area of China.

"And if the airline finds my case after we leave Beijing? Trudy asked.

"I gave Amity's headquarters in Nanjing as the second place to reach us. We'll be in Nanjing for at least five days."

"That's good." Danielle said. She gave Trudy another hug.

"Danielle is right, Trudy. Don't worry. We'll do what we can and ask the Lord to help us. Something will work out." Jerry said as he put his hand on Trudy's shoulder. She seemed comforted. He had been her pastor for twenty years when we lived in New Jersey.

The hotel desk clerk spoke. "Here are your passports."

"Thank you." I turned to the reception desk to get them from him.

"Be careful with the yellow paper." The desk clerk's voice was low. He handed me Jerry's passport last.

I remembered showing the yellow paper and Jerry's passport to my Massachusetts friend, Ruby, who had grown up in Shanghai. Ruby had translated the words. "It says, 'This individual is not to preach anywhere in China.' Virginia, the hotel staff will see the yellow paper and the pronouncement. You will have to submit your passport everywhere you stay in China."

"I know."

"They will watch and listen to make sure Jerry does no preaching. He doesn't intend to do that, right?"

"No, not at all. He will use the Amity textbook and give practice for comprehension and speaking in conversational English activities. That's all."

"Still, be careful, even in casual conversations. No evangelizing is allowed. Even casual phrases or informal words can be misinterpreted." Ruby paused. "Why did you put pastor as his job on his passport application?"

"The application required that we list his job. Being a pastor is his job."

"Pastors are also counselors and managers of an organization. You could have put non-profit manager or counselor. His passport would not be marked in this way."

"Yes."

"Next time, talk to me before you fill out any papers."

"Next time?"

"If Jerry and your friends like the Amity work in China as much as you did, they will want to return with you."

"Ruby, I don't expect anything from them except this year. My first experience was made special by more than the work. It was the people and the changes that occurred in my heart and attitude that made me want to return to China. I feel like an unfinished work. With Jerry and people I know well as a team, I think the time and work here will change me and them in ways I can't imagine."

"Including the ten-year-old?"

"You've met him. Jim is like a little old man except that he looks like a ten-year-old and also like a Northern European Cupid."

"Jim's looks will be like a magnet for attention in China. People do not see many blonde, blue-eyed, fair skinned children anywhere in China, not in the biggest cities and not in the remote places where Amity sends people. I hope he is not shy. Honestly, I am surprised that he was given a visa by the government since you will not be in a major city."

"I think the Amity staff was surprised by the approval for Jim, too."

"I am happy for you, and I can help make your arrival easier. My parents-in-law will meet you at the international airport and drive you to the domestic airport. Where is your assigned location this year?"

"Farther south and west than where I was in 2004."

"Is it a city?"

"Not by China's standards. The Left Banner of Inner Mongolia seems to be an area with a small city surrounded by a desert, plains, and some mountains."

"They cannot have many teachers of English, and yet they will have a Summer English Program?"

"Amity said teachers will come from small towns all over the Badain Jaran and Gobi areas. Some teachers will come from towns that have only one school building for all ages. Some of the teachers have not attended college."

"The program may be more difficult than your first year."

"Different, but at least this summer I know the team. The pressure I feel is because they trust me for whatever we do as tourists and in the Amity work."

Ruby said, "I think you will adapt as a team of adults, but I feel concern about Jim." Ruby had a son around Jim's age. She frowned and said, "Jim will feel so alone when you are all busy with your classes and meetings. What are you planning for him?

Chapter 3

Selfish or Broadening?

I slept from two a.m. until seven. Then the phone beside the bed rang with a chirping sound.

Around and over the queen size bed, rosewood carved with birds, flowers, and vines encased the bed with a headboard, footboard, and sides, but huge circles in the sides allowed a person to climb into the bed. I reached through one of these carved circles and picked up the phone.

"Yes?"

"Virginia, it is Naomi. Shall I come to your hutong now?"

"Naomi, I am so glad to hear your voice. We arrived much later than expected and I think everyone will sleep longer. Why don't you arrive here at eleven. Jerry and I will meet you then, at the reception area."

"Yes, I will be there at eleven. I am glad you have arrived. I am excited to see you again."

I knew Naomi would be on time. One habit of China that I enjoyed was that people arrived on time as a mark of respect. Usually they were even early. I slept a couple more hours, but with daylight, I just lay still awake looking at the lacy side carvings beside me, especially at a large butterfly.

Why had the longing to return to China taken ahold of my thoughts and dreams? I certainly had wrestled with frustration and anger in my first summer teaching in a remote area of China. Conflicts came each day via coworkers' actions and my own inner battles.

Dissonance between the life lived in a region of China compared with the life I had in Massachusetts struck daily chords of disquiet. I felt like I had gathered one hundred pieces of a thousand-piece jigsaw puzzle. The compulsion to find more pieces remained in my dreams and in my waking hours. Somehow, I felt sure the other pieces could only be found in China.

I had never felt this pull to return to any of the other countries I had visited to see friends, to teach, or to explore as a tourist. Living in the simplicity and communal culture of remote China and going to work each day helping teachers entwined my mind and heart. The teachers I worked with had long hours and outrageous class sizes yet exhibited obvious devotion to helping their students. In such a different culture, I found much in common with my own career and daily life challenges. I also found caring teachers who became friends.

Five weeks in the summer program on the other side of the world needed months to reflect on and sort the tumult of thoughts and actions I experienced. Comparisons surfaced like puzzle pieces floating toward me on peaks of waves that I couldn't place because I couldn't grab them. Ideas swirled through my long-held beliefs on culture, personal identity, individualism, family prejudices, relationships, and life purposes. I saw similarities between the Inner Mongolia culture and the Mongolian people and my father's family, immigrants from Italy. How could this be? Did it go back to Marco Polo's connection to Kublai Khan, grandson of Genghis Khan?

The ideas would not stop. Life at home did not remove or even dim the questions and memories from China that had reshaped so many of my ideas. I felt like I experienced an interruption of a transformation. Cocooned in a culture that had for millennium held high respect for teachers, and removed from the daily distractions at home, I had reflected on my life looking for insight into the patterns of my choices.

What happens if a chrysalis cocoon that a caterpillar enters for transformation is pulled away from the twig or leaf where it had spun its silk pad, a protective shell? I felt like that had happened to me. My chrysalis, spun with the exceptional silk of China, had been pulled away from an attachment that supported transformation. I hadn't emerged. I'd been pulled away, interrupted in discovering something I needed to know about myself when I returned home.

The only way I could see to quash the incomplete feeling was to return to China.

But how?

I couldn't give up my marriage or my job. I had family responsibilities that would make a long-term job overseas impossible. Amity's Summer English Program required only four and a half weeks; a sliver of time that included training, travel, teaching, and debriefing. Would that be enough time to resume the transformation?

Working with a non-governmental organization like the Amity Foundation provided weeks of challenges for volunteer teachers in its Summer English Program (SEP). It wasn't the summertime teaching that caused me to hesitate.

I had never felt as valued as a teacher as I had in China. Hospitality and grace toward cultural behavior differences appeared each day toward the team of volunteers.

The trouble came because the team I had worked with had been misaligned. We had gathered first as a full team in the impersonal sprawl of Los Angeles International Airport (LAX). We had never worked with one another before the Amity program. Only when we arrived in China for the Amity training did we learn that most SEP groups were teams of people who knew one another, and who prepared goals, supplies, activities, plans, and were in prayer before they left for China.

I had applied as an individual, as had the other four people on my team. Amity grouped us by the commonality of our Baptist church affiliation. Had Amity considered that the United States has over sixty-five registered Baptist denominations, and more unregistered Baptist denominations? Our meeting was polite and reserved. The only male in our group had experiences in several short-term overseas jobs, taught at a small college in Boston, and, at six foot three, towered over the four women in our group. We had not even arrived in China before he spoke to us as if he was the team leader.

Discomfort with one another created shells of reserve around each of us. In the training time, I remember watching the other teams who knew one another. I envied them the ease and humor they showed. They had relaxed attitudes toward trusting one another and God. That came through clearly in group prayer times when all the Amity teams were together.

My team experience improved as we began to openly share concerns with one another, but that came slowly and not at all with one team member. I vowed that I would never again work with Amity as a random individual to be placed with a team.

If I returned to China, to work with the Amity NGO, I needed my own team. So I talked. I planned. I presented. I prayed. I scouted out friends, relatives, and colleagues. I knew people who had the qualities of friendly confidence, communication, generosity, flexibility, resilience, and a heart for service, but the costs in time and money caused many to say no.

Not everyone could get four and a half weeks of vacation time. My husband, Jerry, had three weeks of vacation time, and two weeks for continuing education. He is a pastor, and because Amity is a Christian organization, taking his vacation time and continuing education time together was approved by the church of which he was the pastor.

On his own, Jerry would not have chosen to go to China. Asian food and oppressive heat are two things he does not enjoy. But he had noticed a positive change in me when I had returned from my first trip and told him about the surprising and amazing experiences in the Summer English Program (SEP). The disappearance of bitter anger in me led Jerry to think he wanted to be a team member and learn for himself how the SEP experience in China had changed my attitude. Jerry even worked with me to find others who would join us as a team.

It took almost two years to find two other adults who would be able to afford the time away. They had an attitude open to adventure, plus the flight fare and donation amount to cover the Amity and host school expenses. The first person who said she wanted to be with me on an Amity team was a recently retired nurse we had known for fifteen years.

Trudy wanted to have an unusual adventure to start her retirement, and she felt as comfortable with Jerry and me as she did with her family. Trudy explained that she had first considered going to China in 2005. Only in spring 2006 did she make her decision.

While working as an RN, Trudy had also taught and mentored new nurses. Now she decided it would be rewarding to work to help teachers of English in China improve their listening comprehension and speaking skills. Trudy was an answer to a prayer because Amity encouraged teams to include a nurse or an EMT. There was no guarantee of what medical facilities would be near the remote teaching locations.

The second person to say she wanted to go to China and work with Jerry, Trudy, and me was a stay-at-home mom. Danielle had been a flight attendant, a horseback-riding teacher on a dude ranch, and a tennis coach. She often made me feel like a slug because she loved to bike, ski, or work for hours in her garden. She had traveled widely but had not taken any big trips since the birth of her only child.

Jim was a late-in-life baby, born when Danielle was forty-four. He was ten years old in 2006, popular in school, as polite as an adult, good at sports, and observant.

"Danielle, you are good at so many things that are qualities Amity teams need. You're friendly, energetic, and well-traveled. You'll be a great team member. I'm so happy you want to join us." I told her when she came to tell me her decision.

"There is one problem, something I have to have if I really am to go on this trip."

Chapter 4

Beijing, How Great Thou Art

"Are you awake?" Jerry asked as he got up out of the bed.

"Yes. I was thinking about what went into getting the team together and the crazy arrival here in the middle of the night."

"I heard the phone earlier."

"It was Naomi."

"She's still coming to help us get around the city and go to the Great Wall?"

"Yes. She'll be here at eleven, and I know she'll be on time, probably early."

"I'm hungry." He looked around the room and found what we needed to make tea or coffee, plus a basket of fruit and cookies. After we were dressed, we took tea and fruit and sat at one of the wrought iron tables in the courtyard.

"It seems gray today," Jerry said as he looked around the courtyard.

"That could be good for us. It gets so hot in the bright sun, that maybe today will be a better temperature for sightseeing. I'm going to knock on Danielle and Trudy's doors, to make sure they're awake."

I had met the young woman, Naomi, who would be our Beijing guide, in 2004. She had a translating job in Beijing. Jerry and I had reserved a family suite that had a separate little bedroom so Naomi would be able to stay right at the guest house with our team. She would be our guide for the time we had in Beijing because she could have a few days off from her job.

When Danielle, Jim, and Trudy appeared, they each carried a piece of fruit too, but Danielle and Trudy also had tea cups. They pulled over chairs to sit with Jerry and me, but Jim kept standing looking around and asked. "What's this area called again?"

Guest House courtyards have greenery and areas to relax and visit.

"*Siheyuan*, and it means an open green area for family and guests. It sounds like sih-hyeh-yuen."

Jim repeated, "*Siheyuan*."

"Good work, Jim. You know, you will probably learn more Chinese faster than any of us because the younger a person is, the faster they can learn a language by hearing, repeating, and using it."

"What are the plans for today?" Danielle asked.

"I feel like I am barely awake." Trudy added.

"My friend, Naomi, will take us to do necessary errands, like going to the bank, getting the layout of this hutong and the closest tourist sites to us, but if possible we should go to the Great Wall today. It's in Beijing's area but almost fifty miles from here. Naomi will be here shortly after 10:30."

"That's soon." Jim announced.

"Yes it is, but we only have three days here in Beijing. We will learn some cultural practices before we go to Nanjing for the orientation. Doing tourist activities before our weeks of teaching is something I didn't do in 2004, but it makes sense to be tourists first. After the weeks of teaching, the volunteers usually feel tired and ready to go home."

"But you did tourist activities after your teaching time in 2004," Danielle remarked.

"I didn't know better. Now I am hoping this arrangement will work better for us."

"So remind me again, home is twelve hours behind us here?"

"Yes."

"I should go email Greg that we are here and safe. They have that little corner that is like a business center off of the lobby."

"Jerry and I have been up for a while. I already went and let my family, Greg, and the church Trudy attends in New Jersey know we have arrived safely."

* * *

20

We were all in the guest house lobby when Naomi arrived. She took my hand in both of hers, then bowed toward Jerry, Trudy, Jim, and Danielle. To me she said, "*Huanying jie jie.*"

"What did she say?" Jim asked immediately.

"She said welcome older sister."

"You're not her sister."

"It is just a greeting of respect for an older woman who is also a friend."

"Am I your little brother then?" Jim asked Naomi.

"You may be. I would say, *Huanying xiao didi.*"

Jim smiled. "My name is James, but my nickname is Jim."

"*Huanying* Jim. Nicknames are not common in China. In fact, people use last names when they give their name."

"Is Naomi your last name?"

"No, it is my chosen English name. When we study English here, our teachers ask us to choose an English name. That name is used in our English classes."

"Are you going to have brunch with us?" Jim asked.

"Brunch?"

"It's a word that mixes breakfast and lunch. You have it when it is late for breakfast but early for lunch."

"It is almost midday. I can take you to a good breakfast place near here."

"Is Jerry your big brother?"

"I can greet him as big brother out of respect for his age, and because I am also a Christian, he is my brother in Christ." To Jerry she said, "*Huān yíng gegē.*" Welcome older brother.

"*Xie xie*, Naomi." Jerry replied.

Immediately, Jim said, "This is my mom. Her name is Danielle."

"*Huanying*, Danielle."

"*Xie xie.* I learned that much, plus *Nihao.*" Danielle looked alert and energetic.

Trudy stepped towards Naomi. "My name is Trudy."

"*Huanying*, Trudy."

"I've learned the same few words as Danielle, but I am shy about using them."

"Did you eat?" Naomi asked, and I surprised everyone by laughing.

"What's funny?" Danielle asked.

"Did you eat? I heard that so often the last time I was in China. Now Naomi has brought back those memories with that question. That question is as common here as, 'How are you?' in our country. A difference is that they actually wait to hear your response to their question."

"Did you eat? It's a good question. I'm hungry. Mom doesn't have any more snacks."

I told Naomi, "They have a breakfast buffet here, but we missed it. We had some fruit and tea. We are ready to go with you to have a meal."

"Trudy and I had Nescafe instant," Danielle said. "We needed coffee."

Naomi led us through the big, red, now open gates into the narrow alley. We saw people in tiny shops, cooking on low brasiers, and selling items like baozi. The scent of the steaming buns filled with pork, beef, or red bean and lotus seed paste, spices, and onions drew us to a man cooking baozi on a brazier beside the street. I gave the man some yuan to match the price on his cardboard sign and let the team each take one.

"What is this? It's good!" Jim announced.

"*Baozi*," Naomi told him.

22

"Don't talk with your mouth full," Danielle reminded him.

"*Baozi*." Jim said it after her.

"Baozi," Naomi continued, "is a steamed bun with a filling. The dough is light. Sometimes they are fried but steamed like this, they are light."

"They are like mini pillows that taste good." Jim laughed and ate another one.

To the obvious delight of the man making the baozi, we bought everything he had. He served us a variety of baozi on bamboo plates the size of teacup saucers. Even with no English, he could tell we enjoyed the tastes.

After many *xie xies* and Naomi teaching *hao chi* (delicious), we said *zàijiàn* (goodbye) to the man. Then we followed Naomi for three more blocks through a colorful stream of people, sounds, scents, sights, carts, cats, elderly men playing chess, people on scooters, and buyers and sellers of vegetables, other *baozi*, and calligraphy. Sounds included vendor's calls, bicycle bell chimes, and music. Scents included roasted street food, smoke from brassieres, spices, animals tied and penned for sale, the heat of the day, and humanity.

Naomi stopped at a small local restaurant. "Are you still hungry for a brunch?"

Red and yellow lanterns hung from the doorway. Bicycles leaned against the plain cement front wall. Through the large front window we saw the light inside came from lightbulbs in red and yellow lanterns, mismatched wooden tables, and walls plastered with menus and pictures.

"I can eat more," Jerry announced and we all agreed.

Before we entered, Naomi asked, "Do you need to email home? There's an internet café across the street."

"No, thank you, Naomi. I contacted family and friends

to let them know we had arrived safely. We will all be able to email easily when we get to Nanjing." I did not mention that my rare experiences in internet cafes, in 2004, had shown me dark and dirty interiors. Often the printed letters and numbers on keyboard keys were obscured by dirt or missing.

We entered the restaurant. It had cement block walls and a cement floor. The roof looked like corrugated tin. The interior had room for six tables. Naomi led us to the only table that had eight stools around it. The wooden table seemed worn smooth by use. Steam clouds rose from the area behind a wide counter that had a foundation of wood but was topped with linoleum. The counter separated the cooking area from the customers. Other diners made some noise with chatter, laughter, eating their noodles, and the tap of their chopsticks on the porcelain bowls.

"Why don't you order, Naomi? Order something not spicy that will give us a good meal."

"Not spicy?"

"I think I am the only person on my team who has had lots of spicy dishes over the years. My Italian grandmother made spicy hot dishes for our family. Jerry does not eat spicy food."

"Jim and I like Mexican food, and that can be spicy." Danielle said.

Bù là," Naomi said. "It is good for you to know for 'no spice.'"

"Bu la?" Jim and Jerry repeated.

"*Bù là*, means not with hot spicy flavor. It is good for you to know how to say it because dishes in every province have some high spicy, chili dishes."

"*Bù là*," we all repeated. Naomi nodded and went to order a meal for us.

"I'm not very good at remembering foreign words," Trudy said.

"I have to think of some association to remember foreign words and phrases," I replied. "Actually, *bu la* is great because it reminds me of the French '*Ooo la la*,' which is about a different kind of spicy hot, but it makes the connection I need."

"'Ooo la la' and 'bu la,' I will remember that now," Trudy said with a laugh.

"When our students struggle with English words, we need to remember to see if there are some connections to help them remember the sounds and meanings. They love idioms and will have studied many. We need to help them make connections with those too."

A few minutes after Naomi put in an order, inexpensive bowls in a white and red pattern, about five inches tall, and six inches in diameter were brought to our table by two smiling young women. Noodles, broth, and vegetables filled the bowls. A peeled hard-boiled egg topped the other contents of the bowls. Two pots of tea arrived with small handleless cups.

"I think I'll need some water too," Jerry mentioned, and the rest of my team agreed. Naomi nodded and went back to the counter. We watched and listened to her speak to one of the two cooks. She returned to the table with bottles of water for all of us. Naomi knew that foreigners needed bottled or boiled water.

"We can be thankful to the Lord for this meal," Naomi said. We all nodded. Her words were not a total surprise. We knew Naomi was a Christian. She told me in 2004. With her eyes open and looking at all of us, Naomi said as if conversing, "We are thankful for this food and time together. May we grow in strength in all ways."

We nodded in agreement. None of us said an Amen aloud.

Now we looked at our bowls and at the implements we had, *kuaizi* the Chinese word for chopsticks. Even though we had practiced using *kuaizi,* I could see the confusion of my team.

"How are we supposed to eat soup with chopsticks?" Jim asked.

"*Kuaizi,* chopsticks, can you say that word, Jim? Kwai zi." It has a w sound after the K."

"Kwai zi," Jim repeated with a smile, and we all said it.

"Pick up your bowl and drink the broth," Naomi said with a smile.

Only I moved to follow her direction, so she said it again. "Pick up your bowl and drink the broth. Then it is easy to eat the egg, noodles, and vegetables with your *kuaizi.*"

I paused to watch my team. They sat still.

"We can pick up the bowl?" Jim asked, his eyes wide. He looked at his mother for confirmation. I guessed Danielle had taught him to never pick up a bowl to drink the liquid, especially in front of other people.

"Yes. It is the easiest way to eat this meal. Virginia did it. Do just like me." Naomi picked up her bowl. I tipped mine up again. Jerry went next. The broth was hot, but drinkable. Still, Trudy, Danielle, and Jim sat still.

"And do not worry about making noise while eating. Noise shows enjoyment of the meal. You can suck in the noodles even if you make noise. Go ahead. Try."

Jim needed no further encouragement. His eyes sparkled. He picked up his bowl and drank most of the broth as fast as if trying to win a contest. When he set the bowl down, he said, "I love China." Then he picked up the hardboiled egg, ate it in a few bites, and started eating the vegetables and noodles with his *kuaizi*. He did well. I could see Naomi liked Jim's enthusiasm.

By the time we finished our meal, we all had learned the meaning of *tang, dan, miantiao, shucai, shui, cha, and yi dun fan* (soup, egg, noodle, vegetables, tea and meal). I had not foreseen how easily my team would learn from Naomi.

Next, we walked to a bank. We did not exchange money at the airport, and we needed some cash. The relief I felt after the happy mood and walk to the bank ended when we stepped into the bank. Individuals stood before every teller. Rows of chairs were filled with people waiting for their number to be called. A machine for people to get a number was near the doorway. We each took a number and went to find seats in the rows of straight chairs.

We had only two goals after our late breakfast today. Exchange money and go to the Great Wall. Anything else we fit into the day would be extra treats. We had such a short time in this huge historic city that we had agreed ahead of time to have full days. We could sleep on the plane to Nanjing on Monday.

Naomi maintained her smile and enthusiasm but the glitches we encountered at the bank, even with Naomi to help us, made me wonder again at the challenges of leading a team of naïve Americans in China, especially when we had to show passports to conduct business at the bank.

Jerry's, with the yellow slip, increased the bank teller's curiosity. A bank manager came out to examine it and stared at Jerry. Money seemed to be counted out in slow motion compared to how we saw it counted for the Chinese people at other windows.

An hour later, we rushed to the large central bus station. Though Naomi herded us well, we missed the bus she had planned for us to take. We also missed the second bus we could have taken to a special section of the Great Wall called 'Mutinanyu.' It was forty-two miles away.

Finally, a bus we could take arrived, and we found some seats when three Chinese stood and offered us seats. Jerry, Jim, and Naomi stood, but Naomi told Danielle, Trudy, and me to take any seats offered. It would be rude to reject the offer.

We rode to Huairou District, about 36 miles away, but still part of Beijing. The shift from the bustling city sprawl became more of a landscape with mountains in the distance. We passed farms that Naomi said grew corn, apples, and chestnuts. We also saw greenhouses.

No bus went directly to the entrance area for the Great Wall. We switched to a van that could hold eight people. Naomi had booked this from our hutong this morning. The terrain had tree covered hills, streams and small rivers. And then we had our first glimpse of the Great Wall, snaking along the mountain ridge in the distance.

When Naomi told me she had booked a private van to take us directly to the Mutianyu section of the Great Wall, I was concerned that she does not use any of the money we paid her as a guide. I had given her extra money for transportation.

"Naomi, is all of this covered by the money I gave you?"

"Yes." She smiled and nodded. Her petite size and sweet appearance hid her determined and skillful bartering. She said she had gotten a good price for the private van. We would have it as long as we needed it for the rest of the day.

In my research about the Great Wall, I had learned that Mutinanyu had cable cars to the top of the wall and optional toboggan rides down from the top. If we hiked to the top, we would be so tired we might not walk far on top of the wall. I had asked Naomi to find a way for us to go to the Mutianyu entrance for the Great Wall.

The van zipped upward on roads with hairpin turns. Jim, Jerry, and Naomi smiled as if they were on an amusement park ride. The ride stopped at a narrow, black-topped road. Parked cars were off on either side of the road. Our driver parked in a tree shaded spot away from the dozens of vendors who looked at the van as if it would deliver treasure. Even Naomi seemed daunted by the horde of hawkers lining the roadway to the Wall.

Naomi had never been to the Great Wall. The expense of such a day trip was beyond her budget, as it was for many Beijing residents. Yet, with determined steps, she took Jim's hand and moved forward. We followed them. Some sellers had booths and tables filled with wares beside them or behind them. Banners and flags decorated every area. Some vendors had goods in baskets at their feet. They all waved at us. Others shouted invitations walking alongside us coming out from their colorful tents with folding tables, boards over cement blocks, and displays for every kind of souvenir marked with the Great Wall: shirts, scarves, jackets, hats, socks, slippers, pet collars, flip flops, cups, plates, mugs, bowls, jewelry, toys, flags.

Scents that wafted to us came from meats flavored with garlic, soy sauce, or sesame oil marinated and roasted on skewer sticks longer than popsicle sticks. Some booths and tables offered peppers, sticky fruit treats oozing sweetness, lotus root, popcorn, and roasted ears of corn. The near chaos of sights and scents was mixed with the sounds of persistent loud calls to buy the wares.

The people selling items easily blocked our way because we walked slowly in the heat, and the road toward the cable car seemed steep. I heard Naomi saying something loudly to the hawkers that approached us. Soon Jim repeated the same words in Chinese just as loudly with her. He smiled as if participating in a game.

Whether someone chose to climb to the top of the wall or took a cable car, they would have to run this gauntlet of aggressive salespeople. I paid for our tickets for the cable car, round trip for Trudy and me, but one way for Jerry, Jim, Danielle, and Naomi. They wanted to ride the toboggan almost a mile down the mountain to the level of this narrow road.

We would have to make sure that they found towers five or six for the toboggan gate. The cable car would take us up to tower fourteen. I guessed they would have a substantial walk to get from our arrival point to tower five or six.

Entering the cable car, we escaped the hawkers. Salespeople were not allowed to push their wares near or on the actual top of the wall.

"What were you saying to the people trying to get you to buy things?" I asked Naomi as the cable car with just our group started the ascent.

Jim, flushed with the excitement of the whole event, answered, *"Tài guile!"* Too expensive! That was fun!"

"He says it well," Naomi added. Her smile showed happiness with Jim's enthusiasm and relief that we had done well through the noise and aggressive sales tactics.

From the cable exit point, we still had to walk up a dozen steep steps and climb a metal rung ladder to get to the very top of the wall. We stepped over a stone rim and took a few steps to stand on the wide top of the Great Wall.

We adults stood in quiet awe. This part of the wall with thick forested slopes on both sides offered views in each direction to a great distance. On one side we could look west into Inner Mongolia, and on the eastern side we saw the wall itself, dense with watchtowers continuing on the main ridge, diminishing into the distance.

Jim only stood still for a minute before whooping with delight and running out away from us, then back to hug his mother.

"What are all these mountains?" Danielle asked Naomi.

"Here they are the Yan mountains you see. Only small villages and farmland with orchards exist to the east, but we cannot see them from here."

"I have a panorama view on my camera," Trudy said, "but nothing could capture this. It's like a dream of layered mountains. The ridges blend into one another and the wall tops all of it."

"Let the view sink in," I said. "The views we will have on our assignment in the desert region won't have anything as spectacular as this."

A view of mountains in Inner Mongolia from one of the towers atop the Great Wall

Naomi explained this view gave us a clear way to see the wall's defensive purpose. We all walked at different speeds as we wandered along the top for an hour. Since we had arrived late to ascend the wall, our time was limited since the toboggan ride was not open in the evening.

At the highest point where Jerry and I stopped, he leaned forward against the wall looking into the west. I stood beside him, leaned against him, and said, "I think we should top off this moment by having you sing something from here."

"Sing?"

"You have a great baritone voice. I always love to hear you sing. How many people around here do you think would recognize anything you sing in English, and no one is near us except our group. Don't sing about a wall. Sing about the beauty we can see from this height. Sing something to praise God."

We looked around. Danielle, Jim, and Naomi were farthest away. They had walked in the direction of the toboggan ride. We could barely see them or anyone else. Jerry would have to jog to catch up to them at Tower Five. He stood facing west.

"All right," he said and sang the first verse and chorus of *How Great Thou Art.*

Oh Lord, my God
When I, in awesome wonder
Consider all the worlds Thy hands have made
I see the stars, I hear the rolling thunder
Thy power throughout the universe displayed
Then sings my soul, my Savior God to Thee
How great Thou art, how great Thou art
Then sings my soul, my Savior God to Thee

How great Thou art, how great Thou art!

I saw Danielle and Jim turn to look back down the long stretch of wall toward us at the sound of Jerry's strong baritone voice. Looking in the other direction I saw Trudy. She had walked back toward the cable car tower. She looked over the wall, down the mountain. I didn't know what she thought she saw, but when she looked back at us, she made a motion as if whacking her head with the palm of her hand. It was an 'Oh no!' gesture.

Chapter 5

More Guanxi

Trudy and I reached the low road moments after the toboggan riders skidded in, laughing hard and exclaiming breathlessly about the ride. Trudy turned from looking at the happy riders and said to me, "I still haven't calmed down from hearing Jerry's voice fill the air with *How Great Thou Art.* No preaching and no evangelizing, remember? My heart was beating out of my chest!"

"He was singing and I doubt anyone in hearing distance knew the English words."

"Too bold. I knew you were brave to come to China on your own, not knowing anyone back in '04. But brave and bold can have different results. Those words echoing across this ancient wall, it worried me."

"We're fine. Jerry won't preach or evangelize, but he might sing." I was partially joking trying to ease her worry. We watched our group arrive, still filled with exhilaration from their twists and turns down the wall. The toboggan run needed many curves because even with breaks on the carts, if the run was straight it would be too dangerous.

"I can't believe we just zoomed down this boundary between China and invading tribes."

"It seems like a different planet from Beijing." Jerry commented.

"I walked and jogged on the Great Wall and drove a toboggan down from it." Jim sounded thrilled and proud. "I don't know if my teacher will believe me when she asks what we did over the summer."

"I can't believe we're out having these experiences," Trudy said. "Wouldn't most people be resting at the hotel to get over jet lag?"

"Being active until bedtime will help us to sleep better than sitting still feeling jet lagged," I responded.

Naomi pointed to the road ahead. "There's our driver."

We could see the van and our driver looked like he had rested well in the shade of overhanging trees in his waiting hours. Naomi walked quickly ahead of us and toward him. They talked and when we joined them, she told us. "There's a family owned restaurant nearby. They have special fish dinners. Guests can catch the fish from a pond next to the restaurant."

"Is this restaurant owned by his family?" I asked because in China if there were any family or friends with businesses, people tried to send business to those connections.

"Friends of his family own it," Naomi told us.

"Guanxi then," I nodded.

"What's guanxi?" Jim asked, quick as ever pouncing on a new word to learn.

Naomi smiled."Guanxi is doing a favor for someone and knowing they will also do a favor for you." Jim nodded but already was looking ahead at the pond.

"Jim will love fishing for his dinner, but do we all have to do that?" Danielle asked.

"No. You can select something already caught."

The full dinner cost 321 yuan, roughly thirty American dollars. For that we had five dishes, drinks, and Jim's fishing adventure. He leaned far over the low pond wall, angling his rod with obvious experience and concentration. Naomi jumped and caught the back of his shirt. In one swift move she pulled him upright at the moment he raised a fish he'd caught.

A waiter appeared, bowed slightly and whisked the fish away. When Jim saw it next, the scent and look made his mouth water. We enjoyed our dinner and the breeze that came across the pond. Here, as in Beijing, weeping willows added delicate beauty to the scenery.

Jim, ever curious, asked Naomi, "Is your family in Beijing, Naomi?"

"My mother lives far in the south, a city known as one of the furnaces of China."

"'Cause it's so hot there?"

"Hotter than Beijing," she answered.

"What about your dad or do you have a brother or a sister? I don't."

Danielle said, "Sorry, Naomi, Jim always asks questions."

"I don't mind. I do have a brother, though I was not supposed to have one."

"Not supposed to?" Jim pushed back a bit from the table giving Naomi full attention.

"In China, since 1979, we have a law, one child per family. I am the first child, but my parents did not want to abort their second child. To keep the child they had to pay a large fine. It took years for them to pay the fine."

Jim looked at his mom and I wondered if he understood abort. I saw Danielle reach out and give his hand a quick squeeze.

Naomi continued, "My brother has started college this year. He lives at home with our mother and commutes to his school."

"What about your dad?"

"My father is dead." Naomi answered with her usual calm. "He died eight years ago. He worked two jobs and one required hours late at night. He was robbed one night when he walked home. He resisted the robber and was stabbed."

I shivered. It felt too cool under the willow trees. The pond seemed a dull satin mirror.

"I'm so sorry," I said. Trudy reached out to touch Naomi's arm.

Naomi continued, "When my father died, my uncle called my mother. In China guanxi is strong. People who are helped will help in return. My father helped pay for his younger brother to go to college. My uncle is a successful architect. He told my mother he would pay for me and my brother to go to college."

Jim looked around at our faces and asked. "Do we have guanxi too?"

"Yes," we said in unison. Satisfied with that group affirmation, Jim asked another question. "When do you get to see your mom and brother?"

"I travel home every year for Spring Festival. People do that all over China. That is our biggest holiday so people try to go to their home city and spend time with their family. I do talk with my mother and brother on the phone each week."

Jim nodded and studied Naomi as if he wanted to memorize her. The mealtime wound down to focus on the dishes of steamed spiced fish, dishes with bitter cabbage, pickled vegetables, sweet savory pork, and stir-fried eggplant.

"Naomi, this meal reminds me of a lesson about Chinese dishes that I learned from a teacher in Wuhai. She said China's essential flavors for a good meal were sweet, sour, bitter, salty, and spicy."

"There can be many varieties, but she is correct. Those five flavors are important."

On the return trip to Beijing I could feel and see the tiredness setting in, but we still chatted with Naomi. I told her about Trudy's lost carry-on case.

"Do you think the airport staff will find my case?" Trudy asked Naomi.

"I don't know. Shanghai is the busiest airport in China, but they will look for it."

Naomi went with us to the hutong guesthouse. She walked hand in hand with me. I noticed that Jim saw Naomi take my hand. Jim took Jerry's hand. That made Danielle smile and she reached out to hold hands with Trudy. I had told the team in one of our pre-trip meetings that in China, friends of the same gender often walked holding hands demonstrating closeness.

At the large red gates, still slightly ajar since it was not dark, I said, "I'll go with Naomi to the front desk. I need to remind them that we will have one more person at breakfast."

"And I will need to show them my ID to stay here." Naomi said.

"I will explain you are a friend and our guide. It works well that our room is a suite with an extra little bedroom."

"We have that too," Jim said. "I sleep in it. Mom and

Trudy share the big bed. Did they make the little bedrooms so people could have their kids stay with them?"

Naomi said, "It goes back to the time when people who were rich traveled with a servant."

"We're not rich," Jim said.

"Actually Jim, we are," Jerry remarked kindly. "What we have and how we live make us richer than eighty percent of all the people in the world."

Jim looked amazed, but also like he gave that view serious thought.

"Let's all go into the lobby," Trudy suggested. So that's what we did. This day a bond had formed with Naomi and a stronger connection amongst all of us. We had shared curiosity, frustration, amazement, fun, enjoyment, family news, and the challenging journey in and out of one of the mega-cities of the world.

We entered the small lobby. Again only the receptionist was at the large welcome desk. When he looked up, he surprised us with a beaming smile. He came quickly out from around the desk. In his hands was Trudy's pink carry-on case. "Your bag has arrived."

Chapter 6

Guanxi, Church, and Palace

A small card in a blue envelope was taped to the top of the case. Trudy went to the nearest chair, sat down with her pink carry-on in her lap, and opened the card. Even the receptionist stood with us watching and listening.

"Please read the card out loud, Trudy," I asked. She nodded, took a slow breath and then read the card.

Dear friends, I saw this pink bag, no one was near it. I checked for a name.

To my surprise, I saw the name of a person my cousin Ruby told me was coming to China as a volunteer to help teachers of English. I called Ruby.

She told me where you were staying.

It is a privilege to help you on your way to work with teachers in China.

Your friend, Lu

Such a matter of fact, kind, and affirming note. We looked at Trudy, at one another, even at the receptionist who looked happy even though he did not understand how remarkable it was for us to have this bag delivered.

"Wow, I'd say it was guanxi from Lu to Ruby, and now it includes us. We owe Lu and Ruby in a big way." Danielle said.

"What are the odds that Ruby's cousin arrived in Shanghai, that huge busy airport, shortly after us, and spots this pink case all by itself, checks for a name and sees it is Trudy's carry-on?" Jerry asked.

"That he went over to the case to even look for a name tag? And he recognized Trudy's name on the tag, called Ruby to get the address of where we are staying in Beijing, and then sent it here? Incredible." Danielle said aloud what had gone through our minds and silenced us.

"You are lucky to have your case," the receptionist said.

"*Xie xie*," we said again to him.

"We can give thanks," I said.

Naomi took my hand and Jim's. With strength she pulled us out of the reception area. Everyone followed. She walked us into the courtyard and farther away from the reception area. Naomi stopped when we stood near the table where we had gathered in the morning.

"It is good and right to give thanks," she said, "but the receptionist was watching. You told me Jerry has the yellow paper in his passport. I think the office people in China do not recognize the difference between preaching, evangelizing, and prayer. You need to take care. Remember, in China, outside areas are better for sensitive discussions.

Naomi joined us in a circle of giving thanks with our eyes open and our heads unbowed. We sat around the table to be less conspicuous if the receptionist was still watching. Now, seated around the table, we looked from Naomi to Jerry.

He said, "Let's give thanks to the Lord. Whenever we are nervous about anything while we are here in China, I hope we can remember this amazing gift from Lu, Ruby, and the Lord. Ginny calls events like this God-incidences."

The arrival of Trudy's carry-on case, such an unexpected answer to prayer, totally surprised me. Why could I pray about something and then be shocked when a quick answer arrived?

Because it didn't happen all the time. That's why, I told myself. We prayed but could not know what, how, or when our prayers would have an answer. Often, we just waited, sometimes for years. Sometimes the answer to a prayer was obvious. Sometimes it wasn't. I believed God heard every prayer, but as much as I wanted to, I couldn't predict His timing or the way in which he would answer.

Tired physically, but renewed with relief for Trudy, we went to our rooms. The next morning early, which was evening of the previous day back in the US, I emailed Ruby about her cousin's sharp eyes and thinking. She admitted to having been surprised when Lu called her. I thanked her and asked for Lu's contact information so I could thank him directly, too.

After enjoying a generous selection in the guest house buffet breakfast with western and Asian options, we set out for another full day as tourists. Out in the hutong, the smiles of the roadside cooks and scents of their wares led to stopping for a few baozi. They had such a delicious scent and flavor, it didn't matter that we'd already had breakfast.

Naomi led us to the largest bus station near us. We traveled an hour before changing to another bus. The second bus, larger than the first, had air conditioning and a full load of tourists. The bus emptied almost completely at the Summer Palace.

"This is like Disney World!" Jim announced as we ascended the first of hundreds of staircases people could use in the palace grounds that stretched around a lake. The buildings near the water had offered breezes for the emperor and royal family.

Naomi spoke to us like a tour guide. "The Summer Palace of the Emperor and Empress had been in use since the mid-1700s up until the time of the last emperor of China. Europeans attacked this palace and did damage once in 1860 and again in 1900. After each attack, the palace and gorgeous gardens were repaired and enlarged. Now the grounds have almost three thousand special features, buildings and gardens, opened to the public. It is a UNESCO World Heritage site."

"What's UNESCO?" Jim asked.

"It sounds like a word, but it is an abbreviation for United Nations Educational, Scientific, and Cultural Organization," Danielle said.

"Because it is a UNESCO site, the Summer Palace and all its grounds are preserved as a special part of human history," Naomi added.

"Did you know all this before you brought us here?" I asked Naomi. "You definitely sound like a tour guide." My team agreed.

"I knew some facts, but I studied more to give you a full picture."

Maps of the grounds appeared on paths, at the top and bottom of staircases, by each gate, near the temples, houses, and bridges. Some of them had English on them, but with Naomi's help we easily found our way to major sites. Jim had questions about the dozens of animals and bird sculptures decorating the edges of the flying eaves. He asked more questions about the arched bridges, the towers for Buddhist incense, and the marble boat on the lake.

In the five hours we had for wandering before closing time, we could not see everything. High on a marble balcony, we stopped for the views, breeze, and taking pictures. Jim stood a bit apart from us. While we watched, he was approached by a Chinese girl about his height.

"Do you speak English?" She asked in clear English.

"Yes. I'm from America," Jim answered.

Her smile equaled a ray of sunshine. She obviously felt thrilled to practice English with Jim. They had a conversation that excluded any awareness of the adults around them.

We listened and when their conversation paused, we commended her on her mastery of English and asked her name.

"My English name is Bella." She blushed, and her parents, who had been standing a short distance behind her came forward. Naomi translated our comments to the girl's beaming parents. The parents told Naomi it was a reward for all their daughter's studying and the extra English lessons they paid for to see her having an easy conversation with an American.

We adults conversed and did not notice that Jim and Bella were no longer right next to us. The young Chinese couple looked as concerned as we felt while we tried to see the children through the crowd.

"Jim?" Danielle called loudly. She pushed her way with Naomi through a group that had just arrived in our area beside the balcony overlooking the lake.

"I'm sure they are together," Trudy said. We followed Danielle and Bella's parents looking past people, statues, and corners of buildings.

"There, on the left," Jerry said.

"By the small pagoda," Naomi added.

Even just two minutes of a missing child caused fear in the couple and my entire team. Surely every parent in any country would feel momentary panic if they could not see their child in a large crowd in an unfamiliar city, especially a city with a language they didn't know.

Jim and Bella had not even thought about how they wandered. When we showed up, Bella and Jim were exchanging email addresses. She tried to explain qq, the email system in China. Jim told her he never heard of qq email. Bella said that she had never heard of gmail.

We adults shared relief and appreciation for the challenges of parenthood with Bella's parents. Then we said *zai jian*. They said goodbye and took Bella back up to the balcony where we had met. We continued our meandering back down staircases and white stone paths toward the exit.

I had blisters on my heels by the time we left the Summer Palace. I realized then that I'd better be careful and switch to my sandals. Every day would include lots of walking and stairs. Amity required any volunteers to be able to walk at least a mile in high temperatures and to have the ability to ascend multiple flights of stairs in a row. Schools were commonly multi-story and not air-conditioned.

Dusk had settled as we arrived at the neighborhood around our hutong area. Jim said he was hungry, so Naomi led us to the little restaurant where we'd had our first breakfast. We ordered baozi, pork fried rice, and dumplings. There was little conversation on our walk back to the big red gate that stood ajar. I wondered what time of night it was shut tight.

When we paused outside the long low building where all our rooms were located, Naomi said, "We should get up earlier tomorrow for breakfast. I think we need to leave by 8:30 for church. You do want to go to a church service?"

"Yes," we adults replied together. Jim nodded as he yawned.

"Isn't that early for a worship service? We weren't planning on going to Sunday School," Danielle said. 'We have Sunday school before our worship service at home. Jim and I go to both, but we didn't plan on doing that here."

Naomi explained, "The bus will take at least forty-five minutes. I thought we could attend the ten a.m. worship service. The service is about two hours long. The church I will take you to has four services. There are long lines of people waiting to get into each of the services."

"Long lines of people? Why?" Jim asked with surprise.

"Why what?" Naomi responded.

"Why are there long lines of people waiting to go into the church?"

"The building has seats for two thousand. Many people want to attend. Even if we get there early, we will have to wait in line."

"Two thousand?" Trudy asked.

"Our little church has 80 people on a good Sunday morning," Danielle said.

Jerry added, "We have some large churches in the US, churches that have a thousand or more in a Sunday service, but it would be rare to have people waiting in line early."

"Are we going to your church, Naomi?" Jim asked.

"No. My church meets in a house. This large church where we will go tomorrow is long established. It started in the 1800s by Methodists. It is the Chongwenmen church."

"Is your house church close to this hutong?" Jim asked.

"No. It is far, on the other side of the city. Foreigners do not go to house churches. But you will all feel welcome at the Chongwenmen church."

"And we'll leave early to get there?" Jim asked as he yawned again.

"Yes, we will leave early. Thank you, Naomi," Danielle said as she put her hand on Jim's shoulder, perhaps to guide him to their room, perhaps to quell the questions. It didn't work.

This interest and importance placed on going to church amazed Jim. He had grown up in New England where the joking term for Christians was *'God's frozen chosen.'*

Jim turned to look at Naomi and Jerry and asked, "Why would so many people want to go to church?"

Chapter 7

Sunday, Steady, or Summer Faith

J im did not get a long answer to his question about why so many people wanted to go to church before he went to bed. He seemed ready to sleepwalk to their room. I remembered the full attendance at Chinese churches in 2004. I had asked the same question to myself. The desire to attend church seemed so strong among Chinese Christians. At breakfast Naomi and Jerry tried to give Jim answers.

Jerry started, "Jim, in China there are not many buildings where Christians can gather. The government requires special licensing and supervision for churches. People who want to gather with other Christians for singing, sermons, prayer, baptisms, and special events know that getting to church earlier than the service time will mean they can probably get a seat."

Naomi continued, "We have a large population in Beijing, and people remember when all the churches were closed for some years. They value meeting together."

"All the churches were closed?" Jim asked.

"Yes, but since I was born, they have been open. Christians in China think time with other Christians is special. Don't Christians in America feel like that?"

"I don't know, but my mom and I like our church." Jim answered.

Naomi added. "When a person joins a church here it is a serious commitment." Then Naomi looked at Jerry. "Isn't this true in the US?"

Jerry answered, "It is true for some churches that have membership classes and that mentor new members, but not all churches do that." Then he spoke to Jim. "Jim, you know we have many churches in every town in our country. People take church services for granted. They almost look at churches like any club or group that interests them. We have multiple churches in every town. People can church shop."

"Church shop?" Jim and Naomi asked together.

"If they don't like the way something is done in one church they look for another one. Some people look for what makes them feel good. They do not want membership that requires much participation. People do not feel they are taking any serious risk by attending a church gathering or by becoming a church member."

"Why do they have risks here?" Jim asked looking at all of us.

"The government here does not encourage belief in God." Jerry said.

"The government doesn't?"

"No. People who join a church here risk having problems with the government." I added. "It was the government that closed all the churches for about ten years."

Naomi looked into Jim's face. She seemed to decide he had enough details. She finished, "Christians who worship together, who get baptized and join a church need faith and courage."

Jim's face looked more serious than I had ever seen. He took his mother's hand.

* * *

Sunday morning and forty-five minutes on a bus with standing room only took us to the church. I still could not imagine figuring out the buses to take to lead the group around the city. We had told Naomi that even if it took longer than the metro, we wanted to see the city, so we preferred to stay above ground in transportation.

Maybe, if I stayed in Beijing for months and had no one to help me, I'd figure it out. Having Naomi's help us was a gift each day. Meeting her in 2004 had been another God-incidence that helped me then in transportation and sight-seeing. With their qq email communication system and by using my college email, rather than gmail which China did not encourage, we built a friendship over the years.

As we neared the church on the number 111 bus, a young woman noticed Jerry's Bible. She asked, in English, if we were going to the Chongwenmen church.

"Yes. We are." Naomi answered. Then she said more to the young woman in Chinese. I heard the words *Měiguó rén* which I knew meant American. The young woman nodded to us as the bus stopped. "Come with me. I go to this church every Sunday."

She led us toward a long line of people, two and three people deep, waiting to go into the church. To our surprise, even while she greeted people in line, she led us past the line to the entrance to the church. "Because you are foreign guests, you do not have to wait in line."

Naomi explained, "You can follow her right in. The other service has just finished. There are seats. They have a special section for foreigners. I do not want to sit in the foreign section. This church has headsets you can put on that will translate everything into English for you. I will sit just behind the section for foreigners."

I didn't ask any questions but wondered if Naomi would feel nervous about escorting foreigners to a church. Did she fear being noticed with foreigners by cameras that focused on the doors to the church. The cameras were not obvious, but we had been warned that China had started to gather images of the people who attended churches.

In our foreign section we met a woman from Kansas who had been teaching English in Beijing for twenty-six years. She was married to a Chinese man. We met tourist couples, and two American college students studying Chinese in capital universities. A couple from Spain was in our row. I could talk to them, and I did. They would listen to the service in Spanish on the headsets. The row in front of us had a team of American college students who would help students with English as a month-long service project their school had arranged.

Music started the service. I didn't need the headset to enjoy the instruments and voices sharing traditional hymns, and my headset had an annoying buzz anyway. Jim sat between me and Danielle. He wasn't using his headset either. When we all sat down after the singing, we put on the headsets. Information was given about church programs, and an offering was collected by baskets passed along the rows while a choir sang.

When the sermon started, Jim listened for a few minutes but then stared down at the Bible his mom had handed to him. He could read the English columns, but his frown said this wasn't enough. I helped Jim write some simple Chinese characters in a notebook I had with me. He alternated between watching the pastor and practicing the characters.

Trust God in all circumstances, the pastor proclaimed. God knows your needs even before you do. God will provide what you need, maybe not everything you want. Maybe God's timing won't be the timing you choose, but God loves you, knows you, and will take care of you.

I glanced sideways to my right at Jerry about the time he looked at me and smiled. He knew trust did not come easily to me, not for people and not for God. He also knew that my first summer in China had eroded some of the wariness I felt toward trusting God. I returned a slight smile toward him about the time I felt Trudy, on my left, bump my side with her elbow.

"Such a good reminder, isn't it?" I looked at her as she whispered, "I can't believe how worried I was about my carry-on and look at the amazing way it came to me in just a day."

The pastor concluded the sermon and noted that communion would follow. Jim gave the notebook back to me. He put his headset on and sat forward on the edge of his seat as if he didn't want to miss anything. I knew Jim had been baptized in May. June was the first time he had communion in our church. Now he could have communion with believers in China.

The pastor explained that anyone who had been baptized could take communion. Jim turned to his mother with a big smile. Then he turned to me and said, "I'm baptized."

"Yes, I was there when Jerry baptized you."

An immediate distraction came as people who had not been baptized left the sanctuary. The worship time was finished for them. The rows of foreign visitors stayed.

We also saw sixteen people leave the sanctuary with communion cups and bread. I turned around and wished I could ask Naomi where they were going. The woman from Kansas leaned toward me and said, "There are people in the overflow rooms. They have been watching the service on television in different rooms connected to the sanctuary, and they will take communion in those rooms."

People stood and walked to the front of the church in orderly lines to receive the small cup of communion wine and a piece of bread. After receiving these elements, some people stood in prayer for a few minutes. We left the sanctuary quietly as the other people did. Outside voices of people rose in appreciation for the time of worship, the unifying experience of communion, and enjoyment of one another.

I hadn't realized how cool it was in the building until we stepped into the bright sun. Naomi came to join us and experienced Jim's delight.

"I could take communion here, Naomi. I was baptized this spring. Pastor Jerry, I mean Mr. Jerry baptized me. Mom, didn't I take communion because I was baptized?"

"Yes, you did." Danielle turned to Naomi and Trudy and said," Only two months ago Jim was baptized. He had to meet with Jerry for a few weeks to talk about faith, why he wanted to follow Jesus, and describe why he wanted to be baptized. He had to explain what baptism meant. Then, at the baptism, he gave a testimony of his faith to the church."

"That's wonderful, Jim." Naomi gave him a hug.

"It has been a special morning," Jerry added. "What could we do now, Naomi, that could be special for you and Jim?"

"I think Jim has been very good with the food here, but he probably would enjoy going to Pizza Hut. There is one near here. Maybe a fifteen-minute walk."

"Pizza Hut? Really? Yeah! Let's go!" Jim took Naomi's hand as if he would follow her anywhere. We walked to a shopping mall that seemed like the huge modern one I knew from Paramus, New Jersey. It had just as many deluxe department stores.

The Pizza Hut had Roman columns, small statues on pedestals, plants hanging from the ceiling and live trees in huge ceramic pots. None of us had ever visited such a Pizza Hut in the US. Naomi knew about western fast-food restaurants in Beijing, but prices were far too expensive for her to ever eat in one. We let Jim and Naomi order the meal. The bill was 330 yuan. Naomi's wide eyes showed concern.

"Don't worry Naomi, we are sharing all our costs. This amount is a total of about forty dollars. We cannot have such a lovely pizza meal with salad and beverages at home for six. This has been a great way to treat you and Jim." I didn't want her to have any concern about prices.

* * *

Naomi guided us to Tiananmen Square. We had all seen it, even Jim had seen it in his social studies book at school and in posters about China. She led us to the middle of the Square and suggested we look in each direction while she told us about the buildings. We turned around slowly and saw the Great Hall of the People on the west. It is a legislative building and used for ceremonies Naomi said.

To the North, the Tiananmen Gate had a huge portrait of Chairman Mao. Behind that gate was the Forbidden City, a palace complex from the days of the emperors. Tomorrow the plan was for us to tour that national symbol.

To the East Naomi described the National Museum of China.

"What's in that?" Jim asked.

Naomi answered, "Ancient items, history of our revolution, and different kinds of art."

"We had a revolution too, a long time ago. What's that way?" Jim asked as he pointed to the huge building in the south.

"That is the Memorial Hall for Mao Zedong, Chairman Mao. You know of him?"

"I've heard of him. The museum is about him?"

Naomi paused and looked at me and the team. Then she answered. "Mao Zedong's body is on display, and there are rooms filled with showcases of his achievements."

"His body? Gross! Isn't it rotting?" Jim's expression looked as if he could smell the rotting body.

"His body has been preserved somehow." Naomi looked at me not realizing I was a person who could explain. She had no idea that my brother was an undertaker.

"Jim," I said, "After a person dies, there are ways to slow the body from decaying. There is a special liquid they can put in the body. What undertakers do is called embalming. People also can slow or stop a body from decaying by keeping it in cool or cold temperatures, like when we put stuff in a freezer."

Naomi chimed in, "Yes. They did that embalming. Then they had to keep Chairman Mao's body cold and in a low light chamber."

"You've seen it?" Jim asked as if he was seeing Naomi as a whole new person.

"Yes. Once. That was enough."

"Mom, I don't want to see the body."

"That's fine Jim. None of us planned on it."

We had been so focused on Jim and thinking about Mao's body that we did not realize a crowd that had gathered around us. Elderly individuals, young parents with a baby or a toddler, and teens. Looking beyond them, I noticed a man at the edge of the crowd who had a camera aimed on us. Was he just a Beijing resident noticing the foreign blonde child? I couldn't know.

"We've drawn an audience," Jerry said.

Naomi turned and spoke to some of the people closest to us. It was Jim who drew their attention. Elderly people asked if they might touch his bright blonde hair. Jim said yes and they gently patted his hair. Parents asked if Jim could hold their baby and let them take a picture. Teens wanted to practice some simple English with him.

The discussion of Mao's body was erased by these people who had never seen a blonde blue-eyed western boy. When Naomi told him the requests, he acted like a little movie star. For twenty minutes, he looked happy giving people what they asked for. Danielle helped him figure out how best to hold a baby or a toddler while the parents took pictures. Some parents wanted to be in the pictures, so Naomi took family pictures.

Trudy, Jerry, and I stood aside and watched Naomi, Jim, and Danielle act as ambassadors of friendly goodwill. When other Chinese senior citizens and families realized Jim allowed pictures, a steady stream of socializing and picture taking continued.

Jim had shown many times that he had maturity beyond his years. It came from the way his father and mother modeled kindness. I thought about this day, of the willingness Jim had to spend time with adults in this overwhelmingly huge city. In the church I had seen a child who needed some entertainment like writing characters through a long sermon. I also saw his joy in his choice to follow Jesus, to have affirmation of his choice to be baptized by taking communion.

I couldn't tell if he had realized today that he had a real international faith family. Jim amazed me with how he seemed at ease laughing, talking, posing, and smiling at strangers who wanted to meet him, talk to him, have a picture with him.

We finally said goodbyes and walked toward the Forbidden City. A huge billboard size digital clock caused us to stop in the square and stare at it counting down.

"Why is the clock counting down, Naomi?" Jim asked.

"Beijing has the Summer Olympics coming on August 8, 2008. The clock is counting down until o8/o8/o8. Eight is a special number in this country."

"For two years this big clock will just count down?"

"Yes, Jim."

"Why is eight so special?"

"Do you know how to say any numbers in Chinese, Jim?"

"Ms. Virginia taught me zero to ten."

"How do you say eight?"

"Ba"

"Yes, and *ba* sounds like *fa* which is like a blessing to prosper, to become rich, so in China, eight is thought to be a lucky number. All over China people believe this."

"Do you believe in luck, Naomi?"

"I believe in God working to guide us. I like Ms. Virginia's word, *God-incidence*."

Jim nodded as if he understood that. Maybe he did. For a ten-year-old, Jim seemed too good to be true now. Could he continue this behavior for the rest of our summer weeks?

Chapter 8

Heavenly Square, Gate, Gardens, and Roast Duck

How many visitors to Beijing, in 2006, started a Sunday with time in church and ended by staying until closing time in the Forbidden City? I couldn't guess. Naomi had explained since we only had three hours after our Pizza Hut lunch, we could see a little of the huge complex home of emperors for centuries. People could easily spend a whole day in the Forbidden City.

We walked from Tiananmen Square through the visitor's gate known as the Gate of Heavenly Peace. Although Naomi had lived in Beijing for years, she had not been in any of the sites. Their entrance fees were far beyond her survival budget. I saw Naomi looking at the way the sunlight glowed on the gilt-edged carved rooftops.

Once inside, Naomi said, "It would take more than a day to see all of this city."

"Have you been here before?" Danielle asked.

"This is my first time to be inside. The entrance fees are high."

"It's a city?" Jim asked.

"Yes, a city for the emperor. It is six hundred years old.

59

Parts of it have been rebuilt or renovated, but the style is still from ancient days."

"Should we wander at our own pace and meet back here at closing time? When is closing time?" Jerry asked.

"Five in the summer hours." Naomi told us.

"I'd be nervous to go anywhere except with Naomi," Trudy said.

"I'll be glad to stick with Naomi. Since she is seeing all of this for the first time, it will be fun to go where she goes," Danielle said.

That's what we did. Naomi chose the places to explore. The Hall of Supreme Harmony had golden dragons. These impressed Jim because below its glowing richness he found information that said over 10,000 dragons were in the hall and the connected terrace below. Dragons appeared in elegant power poses from the top of the golden roof tiles to dragons designed as waterspouts for drainage of the hall area.

"The dragons are on the roof, in the waterspouts, around the stairs, in the walls. It's like a dragon heaven."

Naomi moved him from dragons to lions. "Look, Jim. See the lions."

Jim stared at the lions and made a face. "Are they supposed to be scary?"

"Yes, very frightening," Naomi answered.

"They look like big scary dogs." Jim said as we encountered the first huge pair of lions. I thought he was right. The Chinese lions looked like fierce dogs with manes.

Naomi said, "You're not wrong, Jim. They are called foo dogs in English, but they are guardian lions. Probably their model was one of our strongest dogs maybe a Tibetan Mastiff.

"The Himalayans Mastiff, that looks like these lions, is a

special creature. Long ago, people designed these statues with the faces of other Chinese dogs, Chow Chow dogs."

**Bronze Statue of a male lion in the
Forbidden City, Beijing, PRC**

Jim said, "Foo dogs? Chow chow? Those names aren't scary for guard dogs."

"Maybe not in your language, but these are meant to be mythical beasts, not just plain lions. These are powerful. The artist who designed these probably never saw a real lion. People believe these guardians are creatures that have the spirit of magnificent courage. People believe these guardians could stop evil spirits and intruders."

Jim walked close to the statue. "This one has a ball under his paw."

"Yes," Naomi showed happiness with Jim's comment, "As people face the lion, the male is usually on the right. See how he holds a ball under his right paw? Sometimes it looks like an embroidered ball. That represents a globe or power. His mouth is open.

"The female lion has a cub under her paw. Often her mouth is closed. The lions together represent balance."

"Yin and yang?" Trudy asked.

"Yes. Harmony. I did not think you would know about Yin and Yang. Do you also learn about Feng Shui in your country?"

"We've heard of it, but don't understand it clearly," Trudy replied.

"Naomi, do you believe these special creatures can protect people from evil?" Jim asked as he stepped back to take in a wider view of the male and female lions.

"No. I believe only Jesus can protect us from evil," Naomi had moved closer to Jim. She gave her answer softly in English. I realized Naomi had concern about stating her faith out loud. Many people in China knew some English even if they did not try to speak it.

We walked to the moat-like river that ran as a defensive barrier around the city. Every part of the wall on each side of the moat had carvings that connected to symbols and legends. Naomi pointed out the massive vats made of bronze that also symbolized protection. Filled with water, they stored water for the city's use or to fight fires. Faces of more mythological guardians decorated these gigantic vats.

Then Naomi took us to the palace gardens. In these gardens we stepped into yet another world. Shade cooled the air beneath cypress trees. Blossoms like confetti appeared on some paths. Flowers, trees, small pagodas, and cleverly designed rock gardens filled the air with sweet scents. The air felt cooler than in the full July sunshine. Pagodas of different sizes hid among rock formations. We walked curved paths. Everything felt quieter in the gardens.

Once Naomi stopped and touched the branch of a flowering tree. "I never imagined such a place of peace in this city."

Jim appeared less affected by the gardens. As we turned

to walk toward the main Tiananmen Gate, he asked, "When will we eat supper?"

Naomi asked, "Where would you like to have a meal?"

I said, "You have been such a wonderful guide. This is our last day with you. We would enjoy going someplace special with you. Is there a restaurant you think we should visit? If this was our only time to ever visit Beijing, and we wanted a memorable place, where would it be?"

Naomi's beautiful brows pulled together in a frown. Then she asked, "Probably you would like to visit the restaurant where some of your presidents and other famous leaders and movie stars have had special meals?"

"It will be expensive." Jerry said

"Jerry, this is a once in a lifetime and will be a treat for Naomi too," I responded. Sometimes he needed to be reminded not to let his Dutch view of finances affect vacation trips.

Naomi led us to Quanjude, a famous roast duck restaurant. Even approaching the doorway we could smell scents rich and spicy. Inside looked grand with the Chinese red lacquer, gold trim, wall hangings, and colored glass. We followed a uniformed maître d' past private dining rooms set like secrets into walls. Since we had not made a reservation, we ate in the larger hall. When we were seated, the gentleman in his white and gold trimmed jacket gave us menus that seemed like storybooks. They had large glossy pages of photos, calligraphy and color.

**Outside and in Quanjude, a restaurant chain
in cities of China, this is in Beijing.**

"I am amazed they had a table for six without reservations," I said to Naomi.

"This is still an early hour for dinner in Beijing," she replied.

My eyes practically glazed over from the fullness of the day, but I noted the waitstaff in silk jackets that brought refreshing hot towels to us also poured passionfruit juice and stayed just a step away from our table. Naomi gave our order in Mandarin. Her voice seemed respectful and sure. It was a relief to listen to her order. I noticed she indicated Jerry when she said, *"Bu la."*

The décor had purposeful similarity to the Forbidden City with colors of red, black, gold, white, and gray. I saw a bar area that looked like an aluminum sculpture, blue bookshelves filled some nooks, and at the end of this grand room was a glass fireplace. On this hot day it held a gigantic arrangement of flowers. The arches created a feeling of entering through a gate into history. I don't know how a place could be modern, majestic, and cozy, but glances into the private rooms showed this mixture.

Would I see the important flavors that I had learned about in 2004 when I taught in Wuhai? Multiple appetizer dishes appeared in what Naomi had ordered as a full dinner. We would take our time consuming these dishes that looked as wonderful as their scents implied.

We had steamed tofu with eggplant and celery. A platter of steamed cabbage with garlic sauce and a dish of spicy asparagus and cauliflower also arrived in a generous portion. Our glasses were refilled with passionfruit juice even before they were empty, and a server came with pots of hot marigold tea. Naomi said the duck would come with a sweet sauce.

"I like lots of flavors. I even eat hot sauce, spicy sauce, the kind in Mexican restaurants," Jim said with pride.

Naomi responded, "In China, wherever you go will probably have at least five different healthy flavors."

"Why?"

"I learned sweet helps people to appreciate what is sweet on this earth. Bitter is to remind people of fire that we need, but it is dangerous. Sour reminds people of precious wood. Salty makes us appreciate water that relieves thirst. Spicy reminds people of the warmth they need."

The main dish, the duck arrived on a cart. It appeared as a whole golden bird. It gleamed with a caramelized glaze. Naomi spoke to the meat carver and the waiter who stood by the carver's side. Naomi told us she had ordered duck bone soup. It would be made from roast duck bones and would be served at the end of the dinner.

Like magic, the carver's sharp slim knives flashed over the bird until thin slices had spread in a fan pattern over two porcelain plates. Waiters moved a plate to each end of our table. Then the carver worked on dicing the crispy skin. That went onto two smaller plates, and they were placed near the platters of sliced duck.

"Mom, we have to ask Dad to carve our turkey like that," Jim said. We laughed.

Danielle answered, "Not likely."

Naomi showed us how to eat this dish of Peking Duck. "There are specific standards for this dish. Take the pancake..."

"We call this thin style of pancake a crepe," Trudy mentioned.

"Thank you, Trudy. I am glad to expand my English. Take the crepe pancake and smear on the sweet dark sauce. On top of it put thin slices of duck and crispy skin if you like that. Add cucumber, scallion, fold it up and enjoy it." My tastebuds had the best food treat of the day.

"Is it good?" Naomi asked.

We all answered with words like wonderful, amazing, delicious, superb.

Jim added. "It's kinda messy."

At the end of the meal, we tried the duck-bone soup. Although that name was not appealing, the broth had a flavor and temperature that probably would aid digestion.

Jim turned to Naomi. "Did your father carve a roasted duck up into small pieces as fast as this guy did?"

With her gentle voice, Naomi answered. "I don't know. I cannot remember ever having roast duck in our house."

Jim accepted her answer and made a guess of his own

that put us all on the spot. "Is that because duck is expensive?" He looked from Naomi around at the rest of us.

The bill arrived, and it was given to Jerry. This interruption allowed the mood to lighten. We all had a laugh that they assumed the man at the table would pay. Jim leaned in toward his mom and asked, "Was this dinner really expensive? Did we use too much of our tourist money?"

"It was expensive, but we'll be fine," Danielle answered.

Naomi looked briefly at all of us and then directly at Jim. "This meal cost as much as one month's rent for the room I live in here in Bejing. Jerry was right when he told you that you are richer than most of the people in the world. But today we shared meals as special friends. Even here I will remember that I shared it with all of you because of friendship that came when God let me meet Virginia two years ago. I could never have come here except for you including me. Thank you."

We were quiet and not just from being full as we stepped along the sidewalk. The day was fading. Maybe it would be sundown before we returned to the guest house. I saw Jim looking back at the restaurant entrance after Danielle took pictures of him beside the bright yellow duck. Then he glanced ahead at Naomi. He hurried to walk beside her as we walked to the bus stop.

Chapter 9

Who takes a child into the back of beyond?

Our flight left from Beijing's domestic airport to travel to Nanjing domestic airport early Monday morning. I had double-checked to make sure everyone had clearly printed tags on the checked bags and kept track of their carry-on bags. Jim had a window seat. Danielle had the middle seat and Trudy sat next to the aisle. I sat across the aisle from Trudy. Jerry had the middle seat on our side, and a Chinese passenger had the window seat.

We were tired from walking and sightseeing in Beijing, but the energy of looking forward to more that was new felt like electric excitement empowering us. Nanjing would be the place we would live with all the other SEP volunteers and learn about living, teaching, and learning in our assigned host towns and cities.

Jim leaned toward all of us and said. "It was sad saying goodbye to Naomi."

"It was," we agreed.

We were silent but not sad. I thought we must feel the responsibility ahead in an area unlike any we had known.

Did Jim feel that too?

"You will meet other wonderful people, young people like Naomi. I'm sure." Danielle sounded positive. Jim's nose almost touched the window. He did not turn toward his mother, but we could tell he listened while we discussed the past full days in Beijing

"I learned a lot about China, and we saw so many famous sites," Trudy said.

"Naomi isn't a professional tour guide, but she sure knew plenty, and she's so sweet. I hope she will have a good career and life. Will you be able to keep up with her, Virginia?" Danielle asked me.

"I'll try. It's worked well so far with her qq email. Naomi and some of my former students use my college edu address. I want to get my own qq address so it is easier to communicate with friends in China."

"I have Hotmail," Trudy announced.

"I have that too," Danielle said

"I have Comcast and will use that, but not much while we are here." Jerry added.

"Amity training is helpful, especially if we all participate. Even Jim can choose what to go to this week. The options will start tomorrow. People are arriving today, mostly from overseas. They'll be feeling jet lag that we worked through on our day trip to the Great Wall."

"Are other Americans coming?" Jim asked with perked up interest.

"Yes. Most of the volunteers will be from America, but Amity will have some people from Canada, England, and even some from countries in Europe as long as they speak English clearly. They want native speakers of English, but they take people who are fluent in English even if they are not native speakers. There are always more requests for an SEP team than Amity can meet."

"Will people come from New Zealand and Australia?" Trudy asked. Jim turned to look toward me at the mention of those famous and distant lands.

"I don't know for sure, but one of my team members in 2004 told me that the accents of the New Zealanders and Australians are too unusual, too strong. China has had English studies based on England's vocabulary and expressions since the 1990s. In the 2000s they've been using and studying American English, but New Zealand and Australian accents and expressions are different and difficult for the Chinese to understand."

"Is the training in a really big hotel?" Jim asked.

"Yes. Amity tries to find conference centers and hotels that can host large groups easily. They have assistants, college students or recent graduates who are available to help volunteers. The location will make it easy to get into sections of Nanjing by walking or buses or taxis."

"No buses or taxis for me without Naomi or someone like her." Trudy announced.

* * *

That evening in the hotel we gathered to look at our training packets. Nanjing was only the beginning. Each meeting, new face and different name tag invited us to learn more about Amity staff and the other volunteers.

On Tuesday, July 4, we went to the main floor for Amity training. *Happy Independence Day!* We Americans greeted one another, but everyone seemed in a celebratory mood.

We spent a lot of time with a team from Leeds,

England. They expressed the same surprise we had felt at the sight of so much construction and high-rise buildings on the ride from the airport to this conference hotel. The hotel, sleek and modern, seemed incongruous on its historic grounds. On this acreage, negotiations had taken place between the Kuomintang led by Chiang Kai-Shek and the Communist Party in 1946.

"Anyone want to go for a walk?" Jerry asked at the start of our afternoon break. Blocks from the hotel we saw a hospital, a public library, a lake, more buildings under construction, and then a small pedestrian shopping mall. Trudy and Danielle wanted to explore the mall.

Jerry and Jim said they'd walk around the small lake, then back to the hotel. I wanted to go back to the hotel, see if I could find MeiLi, a wonderful Amity staff person I'd met in 2004. I also wanted to study the packet of information for the week.

After a couple of hours, Jerry, Jim, and I waited in the lobby for Danielle and Trudy, We talked to other Amity volunteers but kept watching the main door. Finally, we saw Trudy among several people who entered the hotel. We needed a careful second look to see Danielle.

"Mom!" Jim shouted as he recognized her. Trudy laughed at our expressions.

"My long hair was just too hot," Danielle said. She ran her hand around her ears and neck, both easy to see as she had opted for a pixie haircut. Her shoulder length honey colored hair was gone. Even her bangs were short and spaced to a light fringe.

"She gave the beauty parlor people a first-time experience," Trudy told us. "We didn't speak Chinese, and they didn't speak English. They had hairstyle books they showed Danielle after she used her fingers like scissors to tell them she wanted a haircut. They felt her hair and mine and talked a-mile-a-minute.

"A woman came in, I think a regular customer of theirs, and she knew some English. She said they had never cut a westerner's hair before. They were very nervous. It was a young man hairdresser who finally sat Danielle in his chair."

"It feels great and will be easy to wash and dry and live with in this heat. I love it. They seemed very happy that I liked the cut and asked if they could take pictures."

"Your mom will be a model in their window pictures, Jim. Pretty cool, huh?"

Jim still studied his mother's new look. "Your hair is as short as mine now." He walked all the way around his mother. "Do you think Dad will like it? He says he liked your long hair."

"It will grow back," Danielle replied. Her joy in the short cut dimmed. She took Jim's hand, and said, "Let's go have dinner. Are we eating in the hotel?"

"Yes, it's convenient." I answered. "The official Amity training welcome is tonight. Starting tomorrow, Amity will take care of all the meals unless we choose to go out on our own. Tomorrow, plan to sit in on as many cultural trainings as you can." I looked around for our young man. "Including you, Jim."

* * *

A breakfast buffet awaited us. We had seen this before in our hutong hotel, the typical food choices for western breakfasts and for Chinese breakfasts. Everyone on my team had a little of each except for Jerry. He had preferences based on habit and texture. This concerned me because cereals were one of his favorite breakfast meals. Jerry also liked milk on his cereal and during the day. I told him he was like a kid with the way he drank cold milk. He might have to go weeks without traditional American foods.

Trudy cared most about having coffee and simple foods. Danielle seemed open to trying new foods but would stick with favorites. She was very happy with baozi. Jim seemed to follow his mom or Jerry in choosing food. How would they do with a month of non-western choices?

We had large group meetings every morning for an hour, then choices of cultural options 'til lunchtime. Ninety minutes to rest and then special tours in Nanjing, seeing and learning about that city's culture and history by immersion. Once Nanjing had been the capital city of China. It had also been devastated by the Japanese in 1937.

We visited graduate schools and the Nanjing Seminary. One of the people on our bus was a team member I had worked with in 2004, Doug, from Boston, and he had as many facts to tell about the Nanjing Seminary and any other place we visited as a tour guide would share. Though he spouted facts in a know-it-all tone, he had been a responsible well-prepared teacher on my 2004 team. Only his philosophy toward short term volunteer programs conflicted with mine. He advised me not to get attached to any of my students.

"Keep a personal distance. Do your work well. Then go home and forget about it. That's what I do and I have done short-term work in several countries." Doug advised. I doubted any of my team this year would agree with Doug on his outlook for our program.

We went to an Amity Art Center. Crafts, paintings, and sculptures for sale were made by students in a variety of Amity programs. We saw fancy malls and poor streets.

Many streets made our hutong in Beijing look like a million-aire's road. One tour took us to Sun Yat Sen's tomb and the National Archives.

The great and historical places impressed us, but not as much as the migrant camp. Amity has a ministry outreach to the Chinese migrants who line up every day in a Labor Market hoping for employment. They live under plastic and usually have nothing but the clothes they wear. Amity helps to supply basic needs and has a school for the migrant children and any of the locally impoverished who live near the school. They have no money to buy a pencil, paper, book, school uniform, or shoes.

We visited a bakery where Amity trained young people who had Down's syndrome. Amity taught teens skills that would allow them to earn a living. They could work in a bakery or restaurant that baked pastries and breads. These Amity efforts clenched our hearts in a way that the palaces and museums could not.

Even more amazing was the Amity building that had a school for the blind and deaf. A parent could stay with their child to learn best ways to communicate and to help the child move to success in independent life skills. The blind and deaf children learned to read, a skill their parents often did not have.

Friday morning, all the teams went to the Amity Printing Company where Christian materials, especially Bibles, hymnals, and Scripture calendars were printed. The Nanjing Amity Printing Company created materials to serve varied needs and communities. Back in our rooms we discussed the irony of the world's largest Bible printing company existing in a country run by atheistic leaders. Just as my 2004 team did, we each purchased a well-constructed leather covered Bible, even Jim chose one. He picked out a New Testament in Mandarin and English.

Friday evening, Jerry and I left our other team members to go spend a few hours with MeiLi. I had been happy to keep in touch with her since 2004, and in 2005 she had studied for a year at a University in the United States. MeiLi stayed with us on holidays and long weekends. Now she worked for a University in Nanjing in their English program, and she was married.

Her husband also worked in a leadership role in another school's English program. MeiLi still hoped to earn an advanced degree in the United States, but for now she had found happiness with her husband. They enjoyed their shared passion to help students reach high goals and international understanding. Their work went in both directions. They helped students from English speaking countries to settle into life and study in Nanjing while helping students of Nanjing to prepare to study in an English speaking country.

"I shall pray for you and your team," MeiLi said as she walked us to the taxi stand after a relaxed long evening of discussion.

"Thank you."

"I talked with Jessie. I know you are going to another place that has never had an Amity team, a much smaller town than the city of Wuhai."

"We will be glad for your prayers. I am hopeful for a better team experience this time. We are friends. We met and discussed service, teaching, and we have gathered special materials that will help us. My team knows there will be surprises. We even brought a surprise with us."

"You did?"

"A ten-year-old boy. His mother could not come for this

SEP unless her son came along. He has blonde hair and blue eyes and has already caused a stir wherever we have been." Jerry said.

"A ten-year-old boy? He must be an unusual child to come to China for this time. I am surprised the government gave him a visa. What will he do while you are teaching?"

"He is well-behaved. His mother brought different kinds of games for him, but we thought we would have him sit in any class he chooses. I don't think the teachers will mind. He is an unusual sight, and he enjoys talking with people. I think the teachers will enjoy having opportunities to talk with him. He likes learning Chinese and we have books where he can practice writing characters."

"I am still surprised."

"We were too," I said.

"Have you seen any of your 2004 team members back this year?"

"Only Doug. The others did not come back."

"Doug, I remember him. He was tall, over six feet. He talked like a walking encyclopedia, but he had a great voice."

"Yes, that's the man. He did a good job with a team that had such different outlooks on teaching and purposes for volunteering. I'm thankful this year to have my husband and people who are my friends. We share faith and goals. My team is friendly, considerate, even the ten-year-old, and they trust God to help us each day. I needed them for the many times when I look to solve my own problems instead of waiting for God's timing. I feel very hopeful about working with this team."

"Amity is thankful for people like you who will go to new areas. I believe your efforts will be blessed. None of you go alone because God goes with you."

* * *

On our flight from Nanjing to Ningxia, Jessie, an Amity location coordinator, traveled with us. I explained her role to my team. When an area had never hosted an SEP, Jessie came with the team, met the hosts, checked the facilities, and helped us with her fluent Chinese to start well by communicating for us with the host administrators.

Danielle, Trudy, and Jerry felt relief with Jessie traveling with us. It showed in how they talked with Jessie. Jim sat next to the window to my right.

"Jessie checked out your other teaching place in 2004?" Jim asked.

"Yes."

"That's her job for Amity?'

"Only one of them, she has a full-time job teaching at a University in Nanjing."

"She's a really pale American. I already have a better tan than she does."

"You do. You're like Jerry. Something about your Dutch heritage lets you tan."

"What color will the people be where we are going?"

"Different shades because this town has a mix of Chinese and Mongolians, plus some other groups. You know China has over fifty ethnic groups."

'I learned that. I went to two Chinese classes in the training time. My mom went to one."

"I think you say the Chinese words you've already learned very well."

"I've been watching cartoons, and the weather report every morning. I can understand them. They use the picture weather charts and have lots of other pictures."

"That's fantastic, Jim. Maybe you'll be a person who learns languages quickly."

"But Mom says you're not supposed to speak Chinese?"

"Not with the teachers or their students. We are supposed to immerse them in English, but we can talk to other people with some Chinese. People in this little town who are older than teenagers will probably not know any English. And you're not a teacher so go ahead and learn. Use Chinese when you can."

"Mom said, you really liked the first place you went."

"It was one of the best summers of my life, though days had situations I never expected."

"And you don't know about this new place, the Left Banner town?"

"No, it is new to Amity and to me. That's why Jessie will go with us. She checks out new places to make sure they have everything we are supposed to have for our work."

"Is it right in the Gobi Desert?'

"Gobi Desert, hmmm, I should tell you, Jim. Gobi means desert, a waterless place, so when you say Gobi Desert, that's like saying desert desert."

Jim laughed, and everyone else looked at him.

"Don't say Gobi Desert, Mom. Gobi means desert. It's like saying desert desert."

Jessie said, "In Chinese, Gobi is enough because that refers to the actual Gobi."

Smiling, Jim leaned back and looked out the window. He saw how the land changed from the verdant southern land around Nanjing to plains, mountains, and desert.

Now the plane was descending into Yinchuan International Airport in Ningxia Province. I closed my eyes and reviewed all we had crammed into our week in Nanjing. My stomach fluttered, and not with motion sickness. Had I overestimated how we would work together? Were we all expecting too much from Jim?

This start would be entirely different from my first day in my 2004 location. This time our hosts had to travel two and a half hours southeast crossing into another province to meet us at Yinchuan Airport. Then there would be the two-and-a-half-hour ride back to their town in the Left Banner. Hopefully their translator would help us get acquainted.

"We flew over a big city. Is this our spot?" Jim asked with excitement.

"This is Yinchuan. It is in a different province from where we will be working, but it is the airport closest to the Left Banner. Yinchuan is the capital city of this province, Ningxia."

"Everything looks brown and tan."

"But there's some green. Look! I see green on the mountains. People in the desert areas work to grow as many trees as they can."

Jim nodded and continued looking out the window. "It's like we flew to Mars," he whispered on our smooth landing in the capital of Ningxia Province.

"We will only be in Ningxia a short time before we will cross over into Inner Mongolia," Jessie reminded all of us.

Jim turned to me. "It's gonna be awesome."

Virginia Heslinga

Map of Provinces, Autonomous Regions, Municipalities, and
Administrative Regions

China has twenty-three provinces, five
autonomous regions (Inner Mongolia, Xinjiang,
Guangxi, Ningxia, Tibet) 4 municipalities (Beijing, Tianjin, Shanghai, Chongqing) and two
special administrative regions (Hong Kong and
Macau). Ningxia is the smallest province that
connects with Inner Mongolia.

Chapter 10

Arrival Gifts

After staying awake until almost dawn on our first Sunday in the left banner, I fell asleep as I heard Jerry leave the little hotel suite to go out for his usual walk. What soothed me to sleep was remembering the ride from the Yinchuan Airport with our host administrators, a head English teacher, and her twelve-year-old daughter.

When we had arrived, we had been greeted by unexpected rain falling on the drought-dry land. We'd left the airport and the built-up area of Yinchuan behind us and entered farmland. Even before the clouds disappeared glimmers of green appeared where everything had been so recently been only shades of brown. Topping that with a rainbow seemed like an exclamation point reminder to trust God. So why was I still nervous?

I slept soundly for a couple of hours and had to rush to meet the team in the lobby of the hotel. Jessie was there talking with everyone in her reassuring tone. Principal Chimeg, our main host administrator, had arranged for us to eat our meals in a restaurant just a block from the hotel.

The plan had us only in the hotel for today and Monday. On Tuesday we would move to rooms in the school dormitory that were usually filled by students and teachers who lived far away in places where schools were small or nonexistent.

"The town square was lively this morning," Jerry said as he walked with us. "People were doing Tai chi, Qigong, even some dancing. I didn't understand anything except 'Nihao,' but people waved at me inviting me to join them."

"Did you?" Jim asked.

"For about ten minutes. I tried to do what people around me were doing. I made most of them smile and a couple covered their mouths as they laughed at my efforts, but they were kind."

"We could all try to join in once we are settled in our accommodations and know our schedule," Danielle suggested.

Jessie told us Principal Chimeg had called and explained she wanted us to visit the only registered church in town. She did not want us to worry about seeing our assigned classrooms until Monday. I felt anxious to see the classrooms we would have, but it would be rude to push for what I wanted. Calmness and patience stood as essential elements for leadership in China.

"Did Principal Chimeg seem nervous to you, Jessie?" I asked.

"Tense, though that started to disappear when she saw how delighted you all were to get out and look at the remains of the Great Wall where it separates Ningxia from Nei Menggu. She expressed amazement at your excitement over going up to that ruined wall and taking pictures there. The sandstorms and people taking stones for their own building projects certainly makes the wall barely recognizable here compared to how people see the wall in Beijing."

"If more sand covered it, no one would even know it was the wall." Jim added. "It doesn't look like the Great Wall out here."

"I didn't even know it ran between Ningxia and Inner Mongolia," Danielle added.

"Mr. Guo looked like we made him laugh." Trudy recalled, and we agreed. Mr. Guo, the vice principal, was more round than tall, not stern, or dignified in appearance as Principal Chimeg. He smiled much more easily than she did.

"It was thoughtful of Principal Chimeg to bring the person who will be your main translator for the time you are here. She knew I was traveling with you and could be the translator, but she wanted you to meet Gladys." Jessie said.

The principal and vice-principal had brought Gladys to the airport to meet us. Gladys had brought her daughter, Sally, because she knew a child of one of the teachers would also be with the team. Jim said, "Sally is nice. She speaks good English. I told her I was learning Chinese. She pointed out the Huáng Hé when we crossed it and told me to say it until I got it right."

"You said, Huáng Hé, Yellow River, well, Jim." Jessie complimented. "Do you know why it is called the Yellow River?"

"Sally told me silt makes it look brownish yellow. Silt is mud, right?" He looked from Jessie to his mom. They both nodded.

Danielle said, "The Great Wall...who knew we would drive right through an opening in it to go from Ningxia into Inner Mongolia. The Great Wall doesn't look so great out here."

"It's a good thing Jim asked, 'What's that?' as we approached the opening that has been cut into the wall for the highway. None of us would have guessed what it was." Jerry said. "Hard to believe they would just cut a chunk out of the Great Wall for a highway to go through."

"And remember walking on top of it? That section of the wall was just wide enough on top for two of us to walk side by side, and we had to do that carefully with all the holes," Trudy added.

"I wonder if people we will meet have ever seen the Great Wall where it is still in excellent condition. It sure has been sandblasted and taken apart to nothing impressive out here." I said. "In 2004, the young man, Ye, told me everyone he knew hoped to visit the Great Wall to feel fulfilled as a citizen of China, but no one he knew had been to the Great Wall near Beijing."

"Our hosts didn't want to walk on the lumpy eroded wall with us," Danielle said.

"Maybe they did," Jessie commented. "Part of being a host in China is to make sure your guests have the best experience. They must take care to watch for your safety. I think Principal Chimeg is feeling that responsibility heavy on her. Plus, there is the whole matter of face."

"Faces?" Jim asked.

"'Face,' not faces, is a person's reputation, the respect they earn and the respect they are shown by others. To lose face means to be embarrassed, to feel shame, like you've made a mistake that might never be forgotten by anyone who knows you," Jessie explained. "The Chinese value their reputation for being the best at accomplishing their responsibilities. Being a host is an important responsibility. To host foreign guests who will live under one's care, that is a huge responsibility for the person, their family, and the community."

Jim's expression showed he had grasped the concept and responsibilities. "So we need to help make sure their face is good."

"Just try to think about people's feelings while you are here, Jim. Very little children won't worry about 'face,' but I'm sure Sally is old enough to feel concerned about being respected, about having a good reputation for doing her best."

"Do I have to worry about face?" Jim asked Jessie.

"You have a great face and spirit, Jim. Be yourself; kind, generous. You'll do fine through this whole visit, and I think you will be a popular young man."

Somehow with all the conversation, memories, and questions, we managed to enjoy a big breakfast. While we were finishing, I said, "It wasn't long after the stop for us to explore the remains of the Great Wall, that we heard the typical question of greeting when we got back on the van."

"Did you eat?" Jessie said with a smile.

"When Gladys asked, 'Did you eat?' I never expected she would pull out the variety of snacks, hot and cold for us to have. It was like a magic food box." I said.

Jerry smiled as he said, "Only Sally took one of the bags of pickled spicy chicken feet."

"But Jim tried them." I laughed and said, "He sure hollered when those spices hit his mouth. The crunchy bits of the chicken feet didn't bother him, but I don't think he ever had anything that spicy hot. Danielle said it must be flaming because Jim even eats wasabi."

"*Bù là.*" Jerry answered. We laughed and I felt thankful again to have a team that could spend time together, confront cautions about cultural expectations, share a meal, and laugh.

Trudy said, "I thought the wheat strips were spicy. It was good there were those spring rolls too. They tasted great, mild but flavorful, and those bottles of jasmine and red tea were as good as you described."

"What did you think when Gladys offered White Rabbit Candy?" Jessie asked.

"I thought of *Alice in Wonderland* and said no thanks," Jim answered as he finished the last *baozi* on his plate.

We shared another laugh, but as that faded, Jessie said, "I think on this Sunday morning, in our review of arriving here yesterday, we should discuss the special way God indicated your arrival as a blessing. After we were back in the van and driving into Nei Menggu, didn't you notice how dry the province looked?"

"More brown and dusty than in Yinchuan and along the area where we could see the Yellow River," Danielle said. "It would be tough to live where everything seems so dry and colorless."

Trudy said, "The land looked parched. Everything looked miserably dry."

"I'm glad you didn't say that on our ride," Jessie said. "People know when their land is in poor condition. They wish to show it in a way that helps them feel proud of it."

"And then it started. I leaned forward and stared through the front windows, then out the side windows, then at everyone else to see if I was imagining it," Trudy whispered.

"It was so light at first, barely a mist, like a cloud had dissolved over us." Danielle said.

I remembered the mist, like the thinnest veil of a light rain falling on the windshield that showed it was not a hallucination. It fell steadily. The driver pulled over and stopped, and he turned on the windshield wipers.

"Principal Chimeg said. '*A blessing! You have brought rain.*'" Jessie recalled.

"It was never heavy, but the rain fell for almost ten minutes." Jerry said.

I thought back to the driver smiling. His eyebrows raised high in delighted amazement. We all looked out the front window. The few dark clouds that had come into the desert blue sky faded. A rainbow that might have had one end in the Yellow River spread in a huge arc over the road in front of us.

We could see the rainbow no matter where we were sitting. Sally and Jim went to their moms. Their excitement talking in English about rain and rainbows touched my heart. The driver opened the van door. Sally and Jim stood staring just a moment at the rainbow, but then they moved to leave the van through the open doors.

Gladys and VP Guo, Trudy and Danielle took pictures of the rainbow. They seemed as excited as Sally and Jim.

The van driver stayed parked on the road until the rain stopped, and the rainbow faded. His smile looked as if he had felt the blessing of the rain. He waited patiently for all of us to take our seats again and resumed driving to the Left Banner.

Jerry and I exchanged glances and smiles as everyone returned to their seats. The van doors closed. Jerry had whispered to me, "It was a God-incidence. For sure. There was no better way to start out our time here. The administrators, Gladys and Sally, they will tell everyone about the needed rain and rainbow that appeared after we crossed the border into Inner Mongolia."

Chapter 11

Sunday, Spittoons, Settling, and Surprises

Trying to be like the Chinese who tried to be on time as a mark of respect, we arrived early at the spot where the van would come for us. The air had scents of dry dust, livestock, fried dough, and the sun-dried bricks heated long hours each day by the powerful sun. No breeze, just stillness. The van arrived and stirred the air.

This school van, smaller than the van that had brought us to the Left Banner, took us to the one registered church in town. Jessie chatted cheerfully with the driver. I saw the usual amazement at her adroit use of Chinese.

Inside the church, scents were different, old mineral smells, and near the seats we had down front, unpleasant sharp scents of menthol, herbs, and tobacco from the spittoons. Jim paid close attention when people in the church used the spittoons. I had told my friends that lots more spitting happened in China than we heard or saw in the US, but I had not told them that even in churches spittoons were placed near doors. The spittoons were made of porcelain or metal.

"Spitting in church?" he whispered first to his mom who looked as surprised as he was. Then he leaned toward me, frowning, and repeated the comment.

"It's a health thing for many people here, Jim." He still had a frown, but it faded.

The choir director was a young man who also led the singing for the whole congregation. Jim liked to sing, so when we sang the songs we recognized in English, Jim sang along with us in English. We sang *Sunshine in My Soul, This is the Day*, and we hummed along when the church sang a song we heard in the Amity training.

I took the same notepad and pen to church for Jim to practice writing Chinese characters during the service. In China I found preaching went longer than an hour. He did pay attention and listen when the choir sang.

A young woman gave the sermon, and an older woman read Scripture. Both had strong voices but little animation. Delivery style did not seem to matter as much as content. People listened, nodded, and some said Amen in agreement with a point.

After the service people clustered around us and welcomed us. Any young person who knew English was pushed forward by elders and encouraged to talk with us. We stayed talking for almost an hour. Individuals especially wanted to practice English with Jim. He handled all the attention that came his way with a smile and sincere interest. We did not see any other children in the church service. Only a few looked like they might be teens.

As we walked toward the van after church for a ride back to the hotel, Trudy asked, "Don't people bring their children to church?"

Jessie explained, "In 2005, China passed regulations reining in participation for religious activities that included children. The regulations have been explained as a safe-guard to protect young people from getting involved in cults. The restrictions extended to religious literature and church activity groups for children and teens."

Before we boarded the van, the choir director caught up with us and invited us to see the tiny store next to the church building. It looked freshly swept, clean, but had the scent of a small space shut up for hours. The choir director showed us some thin paperbacks.

Jessie translated titles about following Jesus and studying the Bible. They had New Testaments, hymnbooks, plaques with Bible verses, and scrolls with verses done in beautiful calligraphy. A few posters of scripture verses written in calligraphy decorated the walls of the tiny store. These posters caught light from the windows and literally shone with their messages.

Gladys waited outside of the store. When we joined her, she asked, "Will you need me to come to church with you every Sunday?" Her voice sounded like a wish we would answer, "No."

Jessie talked with Gladys in smooth Chinese and told us later that she had explained we would find volunteers from our students who had an interest and a willingness to attend Sunday morning services with us. They would help us to find the scripture passages and translate by sitting near us and whispering to us.

On the ride back to our hotel, Gladys's cell phone rang. None of us had brought a cell phone to China. Not all of us owned one. Over our time in China, many young adults seemed shocked we had not brought our cell phones.

When Jessie concluded the call, she turned to us and said, "That was Principal Chimeg. You will not move to school dormitories. They have discovered two problems that will need major work, construction. You will stay at the hotel for your time here. Principal Chimeg and Vice-principal Guo will meet you for lunch today. They will explain plans for the welcome dinner this evening."

As we neared the restaurant, Gladys spoke to the van driver. He stopped so she could leave. In the doorway she turned back and said, "I am sorry I cannot have lunch with you. I have some family matters to take care of today. It is good Jessie does not have to leave until tomorrow. Tonight, there will be a special dinner for you in an upstairs room in this restaurant. The mayor and other leaders will be there with Principal Chimeg and Vice Principal Guo. Jessie will help you as much as I could. I will meet you tomorrow at school, at eight o'clock as Principal Chimeg suggests. It is good to start days at the school before the sun is high in the sky."

Then she left us. We stood near the park center. The town had a swimming pool with a slide, but the pool was empty. There was an old plane in the park. Jessie said it was a Russian model from World War II. Jim wanted to explore it. Danielle said, "Some other day, Jim."

"We'd better have a light lunch if the ceremonial welcome dinner will take place this evening," Jessie advised. We agreed and my team asked her again to explain the expectations for polite participation in the dinner.

I told them about my first dinner in 2004, and how the only male on the team surprised everyone by refusing any liquor. With gracious tact, Jessie quickly explained he had taken a vow to avoid liquor. The Chinese and Mongolians took vows seriously but found it amazing that a man would vow never to drink liquor.

"What about you, Jerry?" Jessie asked.

"I come from a family that does not drink alcoholic

beverages, but in time with Virginia's Italian family, I have experienced a variety of drinks before, during, and after a dinner. I don't choose alcoholic beverages when we are out on our own for dinner, but in a situation where the hosting includes presentations, toasts, and drinks, I'll accept and sip. Virginia tells me you did so well at sipping no one could tell how much you took during the toasting."

"It's an important skill to master here," Jessie said with a smile.

Trudy and Danielle both had experience with mild light beers to heavier alcohol, but I warned them about the strength of baijiu. "Remember if you can, what they call wine, the baijiu is like vodka, but about 60% stronger than you would be likely to have tasted."

"I sip to avoid offending and to get through all the toasts." Jessie added. "But it is in our favor that women are not expected to drink anywhere near as much as men."

"Do I get some *baijiu*?" Jim asked when we arrived at the restaurant.

A chorus of adults saying 'No,' answered him.

"Let's have a meeting in Virginia and Jerry's little living room after lunch. The textbook will help all of you to meet the needs of teachers who participate in the program, but I know you are not all full-time teachers like Virginia. Still, you have all taught. All the teachers of English who have come to the Left Banner's SEP to be your students know that you have come as volunteers. China has a variety of beliefs on fate and going through cycles of life that do not encourage volunteerism. Your students will be curious and watching to see if you are here because you are bored rich Americans or if you truly care to help them gain skill in English."

"But you're right that we don't know about teaching like

Virginia. She's been teaching for thirty years, pre-school to graduate school. I am nervous," Trudy said with her usual honesty.

"Use the text. The Amity text has been created by someone who knows the culture and language. There are more topics and activities in the text than you can use here in a month; topics like why language teachers should be language learners, why English is so hard, what is the most important role of a teacher, and why learning about a culture should help the language learner—to which you all can relate. And the activities in the text work well. We look at them and revise them and add to them as needed each year.

"As a team, I am sure you have realized you need to have regular times of gathering, reviewing, discussing, and especially praying," Jessie reminded us. "You have already seen how plans can change quickly. Keeping in close communication and praying together is essential. This hotel will be nicer accommodation than many teams have. Use the afternoon break not just for lunch but talk over questions students ask and come to some consensus on a response."

"I don't mind staying in this hotel," Danielle said. "But won't it be expensive for the school? We take up three rooms, four while you're here, Jessie."

"It is unusual to have this kind of comfort in one of the remote locations, but you will have the walk back and forth to school each day. I doubt they will use the van for all the back and forth. It won't be uncomfortable in the early morning, but by your lunch break it will be in the 90s or higher." Jessie reminded us. "That's 32 to 40 here. Often, if it goes above 40, which is 100 in Fahrenheit, schools will not have classes in buildings of brick or cement.

Trudy said, "The school is closer than the church, so that's fine. Good exercise."

"Jessie, do you think it will be okay if I go to the internet café across the street after we have our team meeting?" I asked.

"You know how to sign in at an internet café?"

"Yes. I learned that in Beijing in 2004 with my young friend, Naomi."

"Everyone in town knows the foreigners have arrived. Do what you need to at the internet cafe but leave yourself some time to rest before dinner tonight. You know how important these ceremonial dinners are to our hosts and this culture. Now, we'd better go to the restaurant since Gladys said Principal Chimeg and VP Guo will be there for lunch with us. Remember it is always important to be on time because it is a mark of respect."

We did not have a table on the main floor which, like restaurants in the US, was open in order to seat many diners. We had a dining room to ourselves with the principal and vice-principal. It was on the second floor in a lovely room decorated with wallpaper in flocked gold designs on a flat silver background. Jim had never seen flocked paper so he went over to touch it.

"Like thin velvet." he announced. Jessie translated and the principal and vice principal smiled. I thought they were pleased to have introduced something new and high quality to an American child. We had a round table for eight.

When the dishes arrived the room filled with the aromas of garlic, food cooked in sizzling oil, scallions, pickled vegetables, ginger, anise, and braised lamb. The milk tea, a favorite of Jim and mine, had the blended scent of tea and steaming goat milk.

"This is a feast," Jim announced, and his wide eyes expressed what we all felt. The principal and vice-principal were even more delighted with Jim's pronouncement. More than a dozen dishes, but the element of casualness showed up in no liquor. Whether because they knew none of us enjoyed drinking liquor or the fact that we had a child with us, we just had flavored teas and milk tea.

"Milk tea is fun," Jim announced as he added the full variety of available ingredients to the bowl of tan tea made with goat milk and dark tea. Choices to add to the bowl of milk tea included yogurt, toasted millet, tiny dumplings filled with meat, and salt.

"Isn't it salty enough?" Danielle asked him.

"You know, when they make milk tea with water, milk, and tea leaves, they also add salt," Jessie supplied. She then translated for the two administrators. This lunch time was extra work for Jessie since Gladys could not attend. Graciously, Jessie translated conversation, questions, and answers.

Later, when we gathered in the living room of our little suite for a team meeting, it was four thirty. While reviewing plans for the next day and the process of interviewing the teachers who would be our students, we also made plans for Jim to have toys available. Danielle had packed some travel games that she had not yet shared with him. I thought she was wise to gradually reveal them.

We decided that on Monday afternoon and on Tuesday, when we interviewed the SEP applicants, Jim would be visible at a table outside the classrooms. He said he would work on filling in the special workbooks guiding practice of writing Chinese characters.

"I think it will show them I want to learn their language too," he said with his childish sincerity.

We knew our students would want to talk with him while they waited for their interview or after they had completed the interview. We hoped the distraction of Jim would help those waiting for interviews to relax.

"I need to see the school tomorrow with all of you since I have to leave in the afternoon," Jessie said. "Based on how this experience goes, we will decide if this area can ever host another team. We don't have the final say. We can only make our recommendations to the government. They make the final decisions.

"Principal Chimeg wanted to have a van pick us up and take us there in the morning, early. Should that work?" Jerry asked.

Jessie chose her words carefully, "Sometimes administrators do not see the needs in a classroom that will affect the teacher and the students. It depends on how much time a principal has had in a classroom. I do not know if Principal Chimeg did any teaching before she took on the role of principal.

"We already know that they have some major problems at the school's dorm buildings with pipes. We may find some in classrooms too. Classes stopped because the school year concluded while you had your training time in Nanjing. I don't know what you will find in classrooms. Let's pray. Then you can have a rest. We can walk together to the restaurant about ten minutes before seven."

* * *

Just two blocks beyond the restaurant, I had noticed an internet café. We were supposed to have a chance each day at school to use computers, but I wanted to check messages today. Having a ninety-minute lunchtime with the principal and vice principal was a surprise. Then came the team meeting. Now I wanted to see and send email.

"Do you want me to come with you?" Jerry asked.

"I think if I go myself it will be less attention grabbing. I am not a tall skinny Dutchman like you."

He was glad to take a nap, and I hoped the chance to rest would help him through the evening. Jerry does not like ostentatious shows, piles of food the attendees could not possibly eat, or elaborate ceremonies. The welcome dinner would have all three elements.

When I got to the door of the internet café, it was covered with advertisements and stickers. I opened the door and found a flight of narrow stairs in a dark hall. It smelled like cigarette smoke, yesterday's fried food, and old air. I went up the steps as quickly as I could. A young man sitting at a small table at the top of the stairs had a computer in front of him.

The walls had posters advertising video games. Beside him was a filing cabinet. The room was small and on this second level the air seemed suffocatingly stale. I looked to the right. There was a room about five times the size of the entry room with long tables holding computers on each table.

I pointed to that room and showed the young man my passport. I did not have to ask the price as the hourly cost appeared on a sign right next to him. I took out the required yuan. Internet cafes require prepaying. He took the yuan and passed me a notebook, a three-ring notebook with a page for each computer in the larger room.

Every computer open to the public had a number. He pointed to a page with number three at the top. I nodded and printed my name on the first blank line, US, and then my passport number. Chinese citizens gave the number on their identity card. The young man pointed to the room with all the computers. Each computer had the number centered above the monitor. Others in the café were absorbed in playing video games.

I used the email I had set up for China and checked for messages from home.

Only two short messages appeared but in the middle of them, was an email not from anyone in the United States. It was the email address that I had used over the past two years to communicate with a person who had been a high school senior and incredible help to my team in 2004, Ye.

Ye had wonderful abilities in English, but unfortunately, he did not get the score he needed in English to go to college. Though his family had low income, his parents and some other relatives had scraped together enough money for him to have another year at a special English school in a larger city. This course advertised student success in passing the college entrance tests. He would have a chance to take the college entry exam again because he had completed the special English intensive course.

Now, Ye had finished the program. Instead of resting, he had taken a bus across hours of the rugged province to arrive at the Left Banner. His message appeared in light green letters on the dark screen.

> *Miss Virginia, I heard you were in the Left Banner, and I have a break. I completed the exam and took a bus to the Left Banner. I am in the city. Have you arrived? Where are you? I am going to check with hotels. If you see this, tell me where you are staying. Your friend, Ye*

I stared, blank for a moment on how to respond to such news. He had remembered the weeks of 2004 so vividly he had come to meet me and this new team.

My response.

Dear Ye, It is great to know you are in this town!

We are in a hotel behind a tall restaurant. I can't read the signs to tell you the street. As we came into town on the main street, we turned right at the corner near a restaurant. The restaurant sign has jasmine flowers on it. The street beside and behind the hotel is as narrow as an alley, and it leads to a parking lot with a fence, but one portion of the fence is open. That leads to our hotel. It is not easy to see the hotel. I will go back to the hotel now. We have a welcome dinner in a restaurant at 7. Then we will go right back to the hotel. Tomorrow morning we will see the school for the first time.

Ni de laoshi, (your teacher)
Virginia

I was frustrated that I had not brought a hotel card with me! That at least would have a phone number on it. There wasn't more time now. I had to take steps to remove the history, close the browser, log out, and hurry back to the hotel to get ready for dinner.

Could Ye possibly find me from the haphazard description I had given? The town was less than a tenth of the size of his hometown. Few hotels in this town would host westerners. It was overwhelming to think of the long bus ride Ye had taken to meet again. I told myself that if any stranger to the Left Banner could find us, it would be Ye.

Chapter 12

Feasting then Found

The welcome dinner left us full and aware of the hope and appreciation among leaders for the Left Banner schools. Their graciousness made the celebratory dinner seem like an important beginning. We were escorted to a dining room with a spring theme and a round table for twelve on the second floor of the restaurant that would host almost all our meals.

Though Amity had done its best to prepare volunteers for the ostentatious and ceremonial aspects of formal dinners, we still felt wide-eyed at the attentive service and multiple dishes. The difference here compared to my first experiences with ceremonial dinners was less toasting with baijiu. I assumed this occurred because of Jim's presence.

"Good thing the plates are saucer size," Jim whispered to me. "Jessie told me I don't have to eat what I don't want to eat, but you are team leader and have to try everything. Some of it smells weird and looks lumpy."

I whispered a warning back. "Remember as soon as you empty one plate, they will give you another,"

This night the appetizers included Mongolian beef tongue served with cucumbers and tomatoes. We also had a sweet and sour pork dish, and a slightly spicy crabmeat and tofu dish. Eating crabmeat in this region seemed weird to me, but it was polite to try at least a little of each of the special dishes. Jim's favorite were the light spring rolls with chicken filling.

The main dish, Principal Chimeg explained, was *tsuvian*, stir fried meat and vegetures with hand cut noodles. We had the national dish, *buuz*, the large, steamed dumplings filled with mutton and flavored with onions and garlic. Mongolian barbecue, called *khorkhog*, was tender as butter. In restaurants *khorkhog* is cooked in a large pot. Traditionally it is a common barbecue meal of nomads who cook whole animals over hot stones in a container. Our *khorkhog* was goat.

The drinking of *baijiu* was limited to one toast from each administrator to our team. Jessie explained that only two people of our team drank alcohol, so we could return toasts with fruit juices at our places or with tea. Even Jim received a welcome toast from the vice principal.

To our surprise, Jim stood as soon as Vice-principal Guo addressed him. Jim couldn't have returned a toast better if he had memorized a script.

"Thank you," he said to Vice Principal Guo. "I am very happy to visit your town and see your country. You have lots of good food." The hosts smiled at his words.

We also had *huushuur*, small moon shaped fried pastries filled with lamb, spices, and onions. *Chanasan makh* was boiled fatty goat salted and served on platters with potatoes, carrots, and cabbage. Soup in this dinner was served as a side dish. Jim picked up his bowl of *lavsha*, a noodle soup. Ever since that first bowl of breakfast in

Beijing, he showed delight at picking up bowls to drink out of them.

"I like soup at the end of the meal," he said softly to me. "It helps melt the other stuff."

When dessert arrived, Jim only had a bite of the first desert. It was *Aaruul,* made from strained yogurt that had been pressed and dried. I thought it had a sweet-sour flavor. Jim did have a handful of little Mongolian butter cookies, *boortsog.* They had a crunchy outside but a soft dough with fluffy inside.

I did not have a seat near enough to Principal Chimeg to ask anything about Gladys. Her absence concerned me. Gladys had seemed disturbed by the phone call she received. That seemed so long ago. Emotionally and physically this Sunday was full.

Only when we stood to leave did Principal Chimeg mention Gladys. Principal Chimeg apologized for Gladys missing the dinner but expressed concern. Gladys's mother-in-law was very ill. The responsibility to care for the older woman would fall on Gladys. I knew that in China, after marriage the wife had first loyalty and responsibility to the husband's family.

Back at the hotel, the usual two young women receptionists greeted us with a cheerful, "Welcome." Their broad smiles dissolved into giggles.

We had entered the hotel, responded to their greeting and walked toward the elevator. It had room only for four people. Jerry and I let Jessie, Trudy, Danielle, and Jim go up first. The young girls who greeted us still giggled. As the elevator door slid shut, I turned and saw a young man I hadn't noticed before. Recognition hit me like a gust of fresh air.

"Ye!" I shouted in surprise and delight.

His smile widened. "Ms. Virginia, you were difficult to find. I asked at hotels, but none gave me a clear answer. Then, these reception girls giggled so much when I asked if the American teachers were staying here, I stayed. They did not hide the truth well."

"Jerry, this is Ye." I loved seeing the two of them meet. They shook hands.

"I've heard a lot about you, Ye," Jerry said warmly.

"Welcome to China, Mr. Jerry."

"Virginia said you helped her team in 2004 more than anyone, and you were not even one of her students."

"I was honored to sit in classes with Ms. Virginia and the other teachers."

"I've heard you had more English vocabulary than the teachers who were her students and you can sing many English songs. And Virginia told me you were a great help with supplies and activities."

"I could have done more," Ye said with the common Chinese habit of not simply accepting compliments.

"Ye, where are you staying? I can get a room for you here."

"No, no, Ms. Virginia. I have a place. I have a break now while I wait for my test results. I was in Wuhai with my parents when I saw your email about arriving in Nei Menggu. The Left Banner is only a few hours away from Wuhai."

"What are the test results you are waiting for?" Jerry asked.

"In the required national exams at the end of my senior high school, I missed the necessary score in English by three points. My other scores were high in Mandarin and Math. The only way to take the test again is to go for a year to a special English program. I had to live in another city to take the course. The course has finished. I took the test for university acceptance again."

I knew the course had to be incredibly expensive for Ye's family. "We will be very happy to have you spend time with us, Ye. We have the son of one of our teachers with us. He is ten, smart, and friendly. I think he will be glad to have someone as young as you with us."

"I will try to be like a big brother. You know I have no younger siblings."

"Come tomorrow morning at seven. We will meet then on the fourth floor in room eight. I will introduce you to the team, we can have breakfast together, and then we will have our first visit to the school."

"This is a poor area, Ms. Virginia, not like my city."

I turned to Jerry, "Wuhai has wealth from mining and industry, plus they have plans to create major changes by creating a dam on the Yellow River."

To Ye I said, "We had a student guide in Beijing, a friend, but we paid her for being our guide. You'll be a wonderful assistant, but we insist on paying you for your work with us."

His resistance to accepting payment gave way to my position and insistence as team leader. He nodded his acceptance, and we walked with him to the hotel entrance. I was struck by how much this reunion with Ye settled qualms in me.

We did not know what we would find tomorrow. What we encountered at the school would show us the shape of the work ahead. Jessie would not even be with us for the full day. We didn't know what would happen with Gladys. But Ye had found us. I trusted this was not simply a lucky time of reunion.

Lu saw the carry-on case. Naomi revealed lessons about

life in China we would not have known with such personalized emotion. Amity reinforced team spirit. A rain shower and rainbow soothed the land and the Principal's worries about hosting an SEP team. The administrators and leaders shared generous hospitality and their hopes. Jessie had the experience and tact to help us get started. Ye, twenty now, had skills in English and finding necessary materials. He had journeyed to meet us and found us.

God was in each day with us. I recognized that, but sometimes it seemed God's care came to prepare us for something more that would test us. My ongoing struggle with trust caused me to wonder if Ye's arrival boded something more difficult ahead.

Chapter 13

Embracing Changes

F ace took a big hit when we arrived at the school. There was nothing we Amity people or Ye could have done to prevent the loss of face for the administrators. We had no idea what we might have to do on the first day at the school. Jessie said sometimes teams had to clear and clean rooms when a school did not have students who cleared out their desks on the last day and no custodians had cleaned thoroughly over the five weeks of summer vacation.

I suggested that we dress in our most casual clothes. We could change our clothes during the lunch break to look clean and fresh during the first afternoon of the required interviews with the teachers who would be our students. In this part of China, the lunch break gave everyone three hours because of the heat. Local people went home for food and rest in the lunch break.

Jerry went down to the hotel lobby at 6:50 because we did not want Ye to face any problems coming upstairs. Jerry and Ye arrived at our room along with Jessie, Trudy, Danielle, and Jim.

"Come in, come in everyone. This is Ye. He was the most advanced high school student in English that I met in my first summer as an Amity volunteer. Ye was a tremendous help in finding any materials we needed and in getting good deals."

"How old are you?" Jim asked Ye.

"I'm nineteen. How old are you?

"I'm ten. How do you spell your name. It sounds like Yea."

"Y-e."

"Let's have a seat and make more complete introductions." I said and suddenly the little living room of our suite was full. "Why don't you each tell Ye something about yourselves and this time in China."

Jim spoke right up. "If I was home, I'd be alone. My dad travels a lot. We have a farm too. I do farm chores. I am raising turkeys. I came with my mom, and I'm learning Chinese."

Danielle said, "Jim is right about being alone if he was home. I said I would love to be an Amity volunteer, but Jim had to come with me. We both like to travel and meet new people. China has been overwhelming in differences, but we like it so far."

"I'm Trudy. I'm a newly retired nurse. Like everyone else, I will use Amity teaching materials, but I will also have enrichment lessons on health issues. My brain and senses were overloaded in Beijing and Nanjing, but it is quieter here, life seems slower, and people know one another. They seem friendly, although I feel like a walking item of curiosity."

Ye said, "I have not been to Beijing or Nanjing. They are much larger than any city I have visited. This Left Banner town is small and quiet. It is much smaller than my city where I met Ms. Virginia and Amity people in 2004."

"Isn't Beijing your capital?" Jim asked.

"Yes, it is the nation's capital, but we also have capital cities for each province."

"We have capitals for states." Jim added.

"The capital for Nei Menggu, Inner Mongolia, is Hohhot."

"Have you been to Hohhot?"

"Not yet. I might go there to a university."

"When will you choose?" Jim persisted.

"We do not choose on our own. The government looks at a student's test scores and tells the student where to go to university. Sometimes two universities are named. Then the student can choose one of those."

Jim looked thoughtful but didn't ask anything else.

Ye added, "It is an honor to meet all of you. China has not such a strong spirit for volunteering, but I think my generation is considering the value of volunteer work."

I said, "Let's start our meeting. We'll review the plans for the morning. We know this afternoon we will start interviewing teachers to find their English level. Try to remember not to use contractions when you speak. They are harder for English learners to understand, and most people here probably are familiar with British English more than American English. They will have to get used to our accents. In 2004, it seemed to take a week before our American accents were understood. Ye will be with us, and I am sure he will see and hear things we might miss. Jerry, would you start our time of preparation with prayer?"

Jerry prayed. He asked God to guide us, to let His love show in our words and deeds, for health and safety for everyone joining the Amity SEP. We automatically bowed our heads when Jerry prayed. Upon lifting my head, I saw Ye sat with head up and looked at all of us. I realized he might have been offended to be a part of a circle of people praying. Before I could think of how to tactfully ask about his feelings, he spoke.

"I have heard about people praying, but I have never heard anyone pray."

Jim looked like he was about to comment but Danielle gave a quick touch of her elbow to his arm. He stayed quiet.

Jessie spoke to Ye, "You probably remember from 2004 that Amity volunteers are Christians. Prayer is a part of each day for Christians, individually and with others."

"If you are ever uncomfortable with the praying, you can step into the other room." I said and the others nodded.

"It's fine. I am glad for new experiences."

"Let's review our plans for today," Jessie said. "I will try to look at all the school facilities before I leave this afternoon. Every school has to give a list of equipment, spaces, facilities, and procedures they follow. Sometimes they forget something or list something incorrectly. We want you to be safe and happy in your work here. Remember, flexibility in the work is crucial. I know you brought a lot of good materials to decorate the classrooms and to create a lending library for your students. Hopefully, we can have a clear idea of all the arrangements before I leave."

* * *

Vice Principal Guo met us in the large rectangle of dirt surrounded by a single-story set of classroom buildings creating a U around the rectangle. Outside the classrooms long overhangs made of some synthetic material to repel heat were connected to posts and offered shelter from the sun. Cement walkways under the shaded overhangs existed as a border between the classroom buildings and the bare central area.

VP Guo spoke, and Jessie translated. "When the students are here, we have ping pong tables in one part of this open area. They like to play ping pong when they have a break."

We followed the vice-principal to the row of classrooms on the east wing the ground level classrooms. He unlocked and opened the door. Then he stepped back with a motion that indicated we should enter.

"You will have four classrooms," he said as he followed us into the room. Jessie translated again, but everyone fell silent. Jumbled furniture, crumpled papers, overturned metal trashcan, and empty snack wrappers were on desks and on the floor. The classroom had been shut since the last day of school. Sand and dust still had accumulated even though windows and doors were shut. I saw no windows or doors fit the frames tightly.

"This is a dirty messed up room," Jim announced, his blue eyes wide as he turned in different directions looking at the classroom.

I didn't know how much English VP Guo understood, but Jim's tone of voice and expression seemed clear. VP Guo spoke to Jessie. Then he left.

"He is going to unlock three other rooms in this wing of the school." Jessie said.

"It is a surprise these rooms were not cleaned for you," Ye frowned. He spoke softly, and he had not spoken in front of VP Guo. Ye moved farther into the rooms than any of us. He went to the farthest corner, then looked back at our group. Like me, I knew he could remember the clean organized classrooms the Amity team had encountered in his home city in 2004. The head teacher had opened those doors to those well-aired rooms with pride.

Jessie said, "The rooms need to be swept, furniture straightened up and everything wiped down before this afternoon. We can do some of it, but the school must have someone to tend to the buildings." Jessie left us like she'd turned into a power generator.

We stood in silence. We had no cleaning supplies with us.

"They should give us some buckets and rags, and we can at least clean the desks, chairs, and bookcase tops." I hoped my tone sounded positive.

"The hotel has laundry service. I think we can work all morning. We'll get dirty, but we can use the laundry back at the hotel. With teachers arriving this afternoon, we don't want them to come into rooms like this." Jerry said.

"I will help." Ye announced. "I will find cleaning supplies."

"I'll help too." Jim said just before Jessie returned.

Her face did not have any sign of good news on it. "VP Guo went to talk to Principal Chimeg. He said their caretaker had to leave on the last day of classes. The caretaker was sick and old enough to retire. He left quickly, and everyone had too much to do to find a new custodian. They locked the doors and did not check on the rooms.

"The school hired someone else last week. He has been working in the big building where they have offices, science classes, a computer lab, and the auditorium you will use once a week. It's large enough for all the students in the SEP to gather for the joint weekly meeting. Usually teams hold those on a Wednesday. VP Guo will get the new man to come right away and help clean these rooms."

"Let's divide up the work for straightening and cleaning," Trudy said.

"As soon as we have some cleaning supplies, we can each go to a room. We have to interview the teachers in different rooms so we can have multiple interviews taking place in each time period." Jerry reminded us.

* * *

The custodian, new to the school, helped us by giving us buckets of water, rags, and large boxes to fill with trash. He apologized for not having the rooms cleaned. I felt sorry for his loss of 'face.' Jessie spoke with him to encourage him and told us no one had told him the classrooms were left in such a messy condition. He worked with us, providing fresh buckets of water from an inconvenient spigot, and told us he would mop all the floors while we had lunch and rest.

Principal Chimeg and Vice Principal Guo arrived at 10:30 with cool bottles of tea for all of us. They insisted we rest and apologized for the conditions of the rooms. Principal Chimeg brought two more people she had hired for the morning and up until the interviews started at three. These day workers would wash windows, wipe down doors and walls, and help with mopping of the rooms in this school made of cement blocks and clay tile roof. Every community in China had people looking for employment, even if it was just half a day.

I felt they studied us while we took a break and enjoyed the cool drinks. Chinese tradition prefers hot drinks in hot weather. They believe a hot beverage makes a person feel cooler. We could not drink from general water sources in China and were thankful for the tall thermoses of hot water delivered to our rooms each day. We knew not to ask for ice.

In rural areas having a freezer to make and keep ice was rare, and ice cubes would be from tap water or outdoor spigots.

Jessie translated the principal's apology and instructions. "We had many changes at the end of our school year. I am sorry you have done this cleaning work. Please return to the hotel to rest. The rooms will be ready for interviewing teachers when you come back at two-thirty. The van will arrive at 11 to take you back to the hotel.

After Principal Chimeg left, Jessie told us, "The toilets are in a low building beyond all the classrooms. You'll see a walkway opening in the long section on the south side of this U design. One side of the bathroom building is for males, one for females. No separate facilities for teachers. They have the slanted trough style. This is common at many rural schools."

"What's a trough toilet?" Jim asked.

"Let's go look," Ye said to him.

When we arrived at the hotel, I asked Ye if he had everything he needed. I was concerned about him having enough clothes and accommodation where he could shower. I knew that people could wash clothes more easily if they had a shower because they could wash the clothes in the shower. Ye was twelve years younger than my son, but we had worked together for enough weeks in 2004, that I felt as if he was a son in China. Through email we had stayed in touch.

Ye assured me I need not worry about him. I knew he would do that with his independence and pride in pursuing his goal for entering a university. He was so thin. I was sure he must have worked very hard and not had sufficient food in his year studying English in a city far from his home. I doubted that his mother and father together earned much above China's poverty level.

Before she left, Jessie told us that a van would arrive again to take us to school in the morning. We just had to wait in front of the restaurant. I could tell I wasn't the only one feeling nervous as Jessie gave us final instructions.

Ye met us in the restaurant at noon in different casual clothes. He saw Jessie off with the rest of us. When Jessie was about to get into the car that would take her back to Yinchuan airport, she gave the advice I had heard from her in 2004. "Each of you, remember, every day will have surprises while you are in China. Embrace them and remember the Lord is always with you. I will be praying for you and so will other people here and in your families, hometowns, and churches. You are good friends and that will help through challenges that come your way."

Just minutes after Jessie left, while we lingered talking about Jessie's words, Gladys arrived. She got out of the van that would take all of us to the school. Gladys said, "I am sorry to have missed saying goodbye to Ms. Jessie. I wanted to be here earlier. I had to talk with Principal Chimeg at her office. It is a pity. I can only help you today as a translator. I explained to Principal Chimeg that my mother-in-law is very ill. Taking care of her is my first responsibility. I will be leaving this evening to go to her town, Bayannur. It is far from here and I don't know when I'll be back."

Chapter 14

If God Hears and Answers

"Ms. Virginia, Principal Chimeg and I feel concern because we do not have others here fluent in English. Principal Chimeg will want to talk with you this afternoon when the interviews have ended for the day. I can help with that conversation, but this evening I will have to take a bus to my mother-in-law's home."

Change, unplanned or planned made me feel off balance, like I might have missed a step. We expressed concern for Gladys and her family. Sally would go with Gladys, so that young friend would no longer be available to keep Jim company. With Jessie gone too, I felt like this SEP could unravel. We told Gladys sincerely that we would pray for her journey, the care she would give, her mother-in-law's health, and for the time she and Sally would have with this grandparent.

The rest of the ride to the school was quiet, and we needed to put on our welcoming smiles even if we were worried. We'd meet our students, hardworking teachers of

English from this desert region. These teachers of English we would interview to find out their comprehension level for spoken English and to hear their level to speak English. They milled about outside the classrooms.

Gladys stepped out of the van briskly saying, "I will go tell the teachers who will be your SEP students that the interviews will start soon."

Jim followed Gladys. He dashed out of the van at a jog with Ye close behind him. I could see Jim smiling at the teachers gathered in different spots. He said hello to them, plus "Hi, my name is Jim," but he hurried to look in the classrooms. Ye waited outside the building watching Jim run from classroom to classroom. After looking into classroom four, Jim came out smiling and gave the thumbs-up sign.

Before we left the van, I spoke to the team. "Embracing change means trusting we will find the way through the challenges of the unexpected. The teachers have come from many small towns, far smaller than this town. They have already made a commitment that requires their sacrifice of time and money. They are eager to learn. The Lord will help us. Remember all the help we've had so far, amazing help. This will be a month of encouraging and helping our students." Everyone nodded and moved quickly from the van toward the people who would be our students.

We had interview questions printed. Every year in each SEP location, the teachers of English had to be interviewed so classes could be grouped according to the different ability levels. Some of the participants had such poor comprehension skills of spoken English they could only answer the most basic questions. What is your name? Where is your home? Sometimes they answered yes to every question.

We worked until six-thirty, taking ten to fifteen minutes per interview. In the evening, we would compare student ability levels and decide how to group the classrooms. Tuesday we would have interviews again, all day, with a shorter lunch break.

When I walked my final interviewee to the doorway, I spotted Jim and Ye talking with a group of teachers. Jim seemed happy to be Ye's shadow. I expected he would continue to learn Chinese from the friendly way people approached him. Ye, as I remembered from 2004, had skills in starting conversations, vocabulary, guiding, and finding solutions to problems. The changes presented to us looked difficult, but with the assistance of Ye, we had found what we needed. I hoped Principal Chimeg would agree.

Could the principal see that Ye, technically a student in transition, could step into a role substituting for her school staff member? Would the fact of Ye coming from a city far different than her town work against accepting him? Were citizens of China allowed to share an apartment with foreigners? I had no idea.

Our suite had that spare bedroom. No additional housing cost would be needed because Jerry and I would gladly share the space with Ye. Could I help Principal Chimeg and whoever else she might have to consult to break out of their set expectations for an acceptable translator?

I heard Danielle, Trudy, and Jerry approach. Gladys was with them. "We can take the van back to the hotel." She turned and called to Ye and Jim. "Time to go now."

While I watched Jim and Ye come to the van, I remembered Ye said he would have at least ten days, maybe two weeks before he knew his next steps. This could only be another God-incidence. But would the administrator accept a person as young as Ye for our translator?

When Principal Chimeg came to talk with us, Gladys would do her last bit of translating for us, and I would propose that Ye become our translator. He had stronger English than even Gladys, though I would not say that. Ye got along well with everyone on my team, especially Jim, and Ye never shirked any work. He looked for ways to be helpful.

We had the room for Ye. Another God-incidence because Ye could live in the small bedroom of this suite. It would be no extra housing cost for the hosts, and I would pay for his meals if the principal would allow Ye to be our translator. No one could have foreseen Gladys having to rush away after Jessie left, and we could guess this town would not have another person fluent in English to be our daily translator and constant assistant.

When we got out of the van, I told everyone to go on except for Jerry. He stayed while I explained my idea to Ye.

And Ye's quiet response was quick, "I would be honored to help you."

Before the principal arrived Ye agreed to our ideas about paying him for his work as an assistant. The only extra cost to the school would be meals Ye would take with us. I did not think we should offer to pay for those as it might cause embarrassment, loss of face, to the principal.

Gladys, Principal Chimeg, and VP Guo arrived.

"*Huanying, Huanying*," I greeted them, trying not to show nervousness of what I was about to suggest. After formalities we took seats. We five adults filled all the chairs and the little couch. Ye squatted comfortably by the wall, such an easy position for him but foreign to us. Jim had tried that position once and ended up falling over. Even though he was young, Western practices did not train the muscles for that pose.

Principal Chimeg spoke to me. Gladys translated. "We are at a loss. There is no one in this region to do my work. Principal Chimeg has contacted other towns who have sent teachers to this program, but no one with advanced skills is available immediately for these four weeks."

"I am thankful for Principal Chimeg's efforts. I think we may have a solution. Jessie always reminded us to be flexible, to trust that answers would come. I think we have an answer." I gestured toward Ye. He stood up.

"This young man, Ye, worked helping our team in 2004. His English and Chinese are strong, and he even speaks one Mongolian dialect. He's waiting for his university placement, and he is here and willing to be our daily companion translator and assistant."

The room was so quiet that I felt like we were holding our breath.

"He needs a place to stay," VP Guo said. Gladys continued translating for us.

"You have given us so much space in this suite that he could stay here. We have a bedroom we are not using. No additional housing costs are needed, and Jim already sees Ye as a big brother. Jerry and I would be glad to have Ye stay here. We have two grown children and are used to sharing living space."

Principal Chimeg turned to look directly at Ye. She began speaking Mongolian. I recognized it from words and sounds we had heard in the Left Banner. Ye responded calmly, also in Mongolian.

She switched to Chinese and said more to Ye. He

119

replied without hesitation. Back and forth, she spoke in one language, the other, and Ye answered. We watched this verbal exam layered with quick calculations.

Finally, the two administrators spoke to one another in Chinese, then stood, nodding and smiling. Gladys stood too and said, "They find the presence of Ye a lucky solution. Principal Chimeg wants to know if you are completely comfortable having Ye share this suite with you."

"Yes," Jerry and I said together.

Both administrators spoke to Ye. VP Guo spoke in Chinese. Principal Chimeg in Mongolian. Ye gave responses that sounded very respectful, and we saw them out. Gladys lingered a moment in the doorway.

I took her hand and said, "Gladys, you have been a great help, and Jim will miss Sally. We will pray for you and for your mother-in-law's recovery."

Gladys gave me a slight smile and said, "If God hears and answers your prayers, I'll return before you leave." I stepped out into the hall and watched Gladys until she disappeared in the elevator.

When I returned to the living room, Jerry had a hand on Ye's shoulder and was saying, "We're a team of three in this little suite. I hope you know how thankful we are to have you join us as a translator. I agree with Virginia that you seem more like a Chinese son. We have a son at home who is only a few years older than you."

I was glad to see Ye did not step away from Jerry's casual affection. I did not know if his father casually placed a hand on his shoulder.

When they saw me, Ye stepped toward me. "I'll come in the morning, early. I've already paid for the room I have for tonight."

I hugged him a quick goodbye. When he stepped into

the hallway, Danielle, Jim, and Trudy appeared in the doorways of their rooms.

"Are you our new translator?" Jim asked.

"Yes. I will see you in the morning, and I will move in with Mr. Jerry and Ms. Virginia."

Jim dashed over and gave Ye a quick hug. "I'll be your helper."

"I will be happy to have you assist me, Jim."

Goodbyes echoed around him as he took the stairs down. He preferred stairs to the elevator. "I hope we won't be a huge burden to him," I told my team. When I was back in the living room with just Jerry, "It does seem like this was meant to be, doesn't it."

"It sure does," he answered me and wrapped me in his arms.

* * *

Morning arrived with the jolt of awareness as powerful as espresso, and my team had fresh energy. They were focused though. Ye seemed a quiet stabilizer. Jim followed him like a shadow. Jim's admiration was obvious as he mimicked words he heard Ye speak as greetings.

Teachers awaiting their interviews relaxed and smiled at this blonde, blue eyed American speaking their language. We stopped interviews at 11:45 to take the afternoon break. Since it was already almost 38 Celsius, we enjoyed having the van drive us to the restaurant. Most dishes were still unfamiliar, but rarely did we ask what was in the food. We ate slowly, looking at what we were given, glad for anything familiar. Then a small glass bowl with something orange, icy, and cold enough to frost the dish was put in front of each of us.

Jim tasted it right away. "Sweet tarts!"

Jerry tasted it next. "I see why Jim was reminded of sweet tarts. It's sour but smooth and sweet." We all took a spoonful. The taste and texture, cold, sour yet sweet, refreshed us.

Ye said, "It's *shagaa* in Mongolian. I think in English it is Sea Buckthorn. Alone, it tastes sour when you bite it. I bit the raw berry when I was small. It pulled my mouth together and almost choked me. This is sweetened probably mixed with milk and whipped, not too sweet. It's good so cold, like ice cream."

We enjoyed this dessert. Jim finished first. I almost laughed out loud at the way he sat back like a little old man who had eaten a big meal.

Jim asked. "Do you have a girlfriend, Ye?"

Danielle laughed. "Jim the matchmaker?"

"What's a matchmaker?" Jim asked.

"It's a person who tries to match people with someone they could marry." Trudy said.

"Oh," Jim frowned in thought, but just for a moment. His smile returned. "Naomi could be a good wife."

Ye answered, "I have been too busy studying and working to pay for my rent and food while I studied. No time or money enough to think about marriage."

With enthusiasm, Jim said, "Naomi. You could marry her. She's pretty and has a good job. She knows English as well as you."

We all laughed, even Ye. The emotion shared felt light and real.

At that moment, I felt something start to shift in me. We had come here nervous, encountering so much new, facing literally messy challenges, mental, physical, spiritual and emotional challenges. Changes that felt like growing pains. They affected our mindsets and the shape of our days.

Were we all changing? Had overcoming the unexpected difficulties and a positive start in the hours of interviews infused us with courage? Had we turned a corner on worry as a team? Or was it something else, not in them, but transforming in me?

Chapter 15

Helping and Hindering, Tact and No Tact

B y the end of the afternoon on Tuesday, we could see there would be 95 teachers in the one month-long Summer English Program (SEP). The top group would be thirty, the next two levels would have twenty-three in the homeroom classes, and those with the least English ability in speaking and listening comprehension would be a group of nineteen. Smaller classes allowed for more interaction.

Because the temperature was still high, the van appeared again at six-thirty to take us back to the corner where we could enter the restaurant or walk to the hotel. When we exited the van, it was six-forty-five, so everyone agreed to have supper and then to go to the hotel. We would all try to have a quiet evening reviewing of the Amity text and plans for the next day, Wednesday.

We would have a full morning schedule for everyone. The school administrators had planned an opening day welcome assembly for the afternoon. All we had been told was that we would walk to the newest building that had a large auditorium.

So far, my team arrived everywhere early, to team meetings, to the school, and to meals. They genuinely enjoyed preparing to work with the teachers of this remote desert region. It was a relief and boost fulfilling my hopes to have a team of people who wanted to show respect to their students and work hard with them.

"I am looking forward to getting to know my homeroom class," Trudy said as we walked to the hotel after dinner. We felt united in the desire for students to enjoy the weeks with us while they worked to improve listening comprehension, clear fluent speaking, and teaching skills. Each evening, we said goodnight in the hallway where we had our rooms. We hadn't seen anyone else on this floor of the hotel.

I mentioned this to Ye. He looked thoughtful for a moment, then said the hotel probably wanted us to have the privacy and security of the floor to ourselves.

Jim yawned. He was an amazing ten-year-old, but I still wondered if that would last through the weeks ahead in China. So far, the unique experiences and having television, his games, and someone like Ye, had helped Jim to avoid missing his dad and everything he had at home.

One obvious disappointment was that we did not have all the supplies we had hoped to use with starting activities. Supplies like markers and sturdy cardstock paper could be used to make name tags that would help us to learn and remember names. Making name placards on the first day of class, an opening day activity, had worked well for my team in 2004. I thought we could use this practice in The Left Banner.

Students enjoyed creating their name cards. They wrote their name boldly on the front of the card and some simple facts about themselves on the back of the cards.

Standing the placards on each desk allowed us to use names easily during class time. They could be carried from one classroom to the next. And at the end of the day, one student from each class would take all the placards back to the homeroom.

We wanted a relaxed activity to start our time with the students. Amity had explained the high level of tension in China's education system. Only our students who were teachers working with the youngest elementary classes would have time for fun and relaxed activities. We did not want to add stress to this first day. Listening to our American accents would require enough stressful concentration. Hearing and understanding a foreign language required different skills than reading it.

At the door of our suite, Ye told me and Jerry, "I am going out now. I think I saw two stores that open early and will have the supplies you wanted."

"Shall I give you some yuan?"

"Let me search first. If I find the supplies, I can give the vendor the money in the morning on the way to school."

"We're leaving for school by 7:30," Jerry said.

"Business owners are in their shops by that time. Sometimes earlier. Mr. Jerry will you go for a walk at 5:30 again?"

"I plan to do that each day."

"May I walk with you?"

"Sure, if you would enjoy that."

"Walking is healthy. I walked often with my father when I was a child before he went to work. Walking is good here and for open conversation." After this comment, Ye turned and left the hotel.

"Jerry," I asked as we entered the suite, "you will be careful what you say to Ye about China, won't you?"

126

"He expects open conversation and says it is safe to speak freely in wide open places. I will be honest in response to any questions he asks."

* * *

Even with one bathroom, no difficulties arose by having a third person in our little suite. Ye preferred to shower at night right before bed. That was a common practice in China.

Jerry liked to shower in the morning when he got back from his morning walk, and I preferred morning or during the long afternoon break. We rarely had to use the little kitchen, and between the table and chairs there, the living room area, and having our own bedrooms, we did not get in one another's way. With Ye, it did feel like having a son sharing a family apartment.

Ye and Jerry were out on their walk when I got up. They arrived looking happy and talking. While Jerry went to shower and dress, I asked Ye about their walk and conversation.

"Mr. Jerry notices details of life in this town and asks me about them. We will walk in different places each day to learn the whole city."

"You ask him questions too?"

"Many. I think on our walks we will learn much from each other. This is an honor and help to me."

"You are making the days here much more enjoyable for Jim and Jerry, and you are a help to all of us by doing that."

"Ms. Virginia, I did find a place to get the supplies you want for the name tags and class activities. The owner gave me a sales slip." He showed it to me. "If you give me the yuan, I will go to his store and get the supplies before classes start. Jim can help me sort them. We will deliver them to the classrooms." He turned to go to his room, but I was still nervous about how blunt Jerry could be.

"Ye, do you know the word tact and understand the meaning of speaking with tact?"

"Yes. I know tact. I have seen you use tact, Ms. Virginia."

"And Jerry?"

With a big smile, Ye told me, "Mr. Jerry does not worry about tact in early morning."

* * *

Not until we were outside on the cool seventy-eight-degree morning walking to the school, did I ask Jerry, "Do you think the morning walks with Ye will be good for both of you? He seemed to like the time with you today."

"Yes, we both ask one another questions."

"Did he ask you anything this morning that seemed political? I think that he wants to be outside, away from buildings in case you two discuss anything that could be a problem for anyone to overhear."

"He did ask me why I chose to be a pastor. He has met a Daoist priest and a Buddhist priest, but never a Christian pastor."

"A conversation like that could definitely be a problem in front of some people. Anything else that stood out to you?"

"He asked me what I thought of Mao."

"That's logical for him to wonder about. Ye is a young man who loves his country and has only known the China that Mao created. What did you say?"

"I told him I thought Mao was brutal, triggered mass starvation for millions by his ideas for the Great Leap forward, and that Mao was probably mentally unbalanced."

I grabbed Jerry's arm and pulled him to stop. Trudy and Danielle were so far ahead of us they were already at the park. Ye and Jim had not returned from planned errands. I faced Jerry. "You didn't really say that to Ye?!"

"Yes, I did. I also said I saw Mao as a megalomaniac mastermind. Ye knew the word *mastermind*, but not *megalomaniac*, so we talked more about the meaning and evidence of it in a person."

"Jerry! You wouldn't say anything like that to a class where someone asked you that question, would you? Every class will have at least one person who reports any negative things we might say about China. In our hotel, the restaurant, or any buildings, we have to assume other people who know English can hear us. We need to be careful of what we say."

"I told Ye, I would be honest and wanted him to be honest with me too. Don't worry. I can control and speak carefully to our students or inside any building. I know what I need to do. I understand tact."

"Yes? Ye told me you don't worry about using tact."

Jerry laughed. He took my hand, and we followed Trudy and Danielle to the school. They had turned around to look at us, smiling, when they heard Jerry laugh so loudly. I wondered if they'd be smiling if they knew what Jerry had said to Ye about Mao.

Jim had gone with Ye to the store to pick up the classroom supplies we wanted. Would Jim be someone who did not worry about using tact? At least he was a child and didn't know the history of China the way Jerry did. Jerry had been a history major for his undergraduate degree.

What in the world would he share with Ye in their early morning conversations?

* * *

The first morning of our classes whirled by with careful enunciation while talking, instructions, questions, short get acquainted sharing, laughter, and singing. In all our classrooms we introduced the Amity textbook and gave one to each student. We gave a plan for how we would complete the chapters, a schedule for how the classes would change during the morning, the enrichment classes in the afternoon, and for anyone interested, we would teach baseball two times a week.

"How will we do baseball?" a young man from a family that owned a camel ranch asked. He had chosen the English name Solomon because he heard Solomon, a famous king, had wisdom recognized around the world. He shook his head as if to say, impossible, when Jerry told him the Bible's Solomon had 700 wives.

How and where would we teach baseball? "Solomon," I said, "I brought a wiffle ball and bat. It lets people practice baseball, but the ball will not go too far away. We can play in the school courtyard."

"What's wiffle?" a beautiful petite Mongolian woman, Anu asked. Not everyone in our classes had chosen an English name, and we would not insist that they do. Anu's name was easy to say, Ah nuh.

When we had been through the plans and procedures, students had put their names on their textbooks, and the questions had slowed, Ye and Jim showed up in our classroom's doorway.

"We have all the fun stuff," Jim announced. Ye smiled

and carried a large box to my desk. Jim brought a ream of multicolor cardstock to the desk.

"We have delivered these supplies to all the other classes," Ye told me. "Sorry to interrupt, but I know you want to do the name cards at the start of classes."

"Thank you, so much, Ye and Jim. Yes, we will work on these right now."

"That's what they said in the other classroom," Ye told me.

"Do you two want to stay here?"

"Ye is going to take me to the park in the center of town." Jim sounded happy even though his blonde hair showed sweat along the airline and his face was pink. They left quickly as we said an enthusiastic thank you.

In the package and boxes they delivered, I found enough colorful markers in the box so that every set of three people in the class could share one package. Anu got up quickly to give out the markers. Another woman, Amelia, gave everyone a piece of cardstock. I explained that the fold should be made horizontally. When I taught elementary classes, the children in our country called that horizontal fold a hot dog fold. If we folded paper vertically, they called it a hamburger fold. Everyone in my class knew the difference. They folded the cardstock carefully.

For a while, I could just rest and watch these teachers put their names on one side of the name card and five adjectives that described them on the other side. They looked relaxed while they worked and talked in three extremely different languages, Mandarin, Mongolian, and English. I circled the room, chatting with students, then went up and down the center section. We had arranged each room so that activities could be done with a partner, or with a group of three or four. Chinese students can work intently on their own but excel at collaborative work.

"Let me hear more English in your conversations," I said when I walked around the classroom watching them work. My presence drew English from them, but once I passed by, the English would fade. Their national language of Mandarin dominated. I knew how hard it was to listen and work for hours in another language, so today, only encouragement was needed. I hoped this name card activity went well in the other classes.

Amity supplied dozens of activities to fill our weeks and give students a chance to develop listening and speaking skills. We would all use discussion, role-play, small group tasks, talks like informal lectures, listing, graphing, word families, idioms, songs, sentence building, paragraph building, skimming, and surveys. While working in English, our students would have opportunities to work on skills their own students needed in determining the purpose, communicating main ideas, identifying and supplying details, recognizing the gist of a heavy reference description and the concept of paraphrasing.

I thought about the difficulty of working in another language and felt thankful that most of my team had experience as language learners. Jerry had studied French, Hebrew, and Greek, though only French for conversation. Danielle had learned Spanish to use in her work when she lived in Nevada. Trudy had basic Spanish but when she trained young nurses she had worked with English Language Learners from many countries. I had some Italian, French, and Spanish before 2004, but since returning home had tried to learn more Mandarin.

The responsibility we all felt working with these motivated adults rested like a heavy backpack on us because we knew this might be the only opportunity our students would have to work with native English speakers. Every hour was precious. As I worked with my students, I remembered how quickly Jim had picked up Chinese words and phrases. Immersion worked well, but we only had the hours of our class time to immerse our students in English.

Chapter 16

Soldiers at the Internet Café

fter lunch on this first day, I had so much adrenalin that I did not want to go back to having the traditional nap time. I wouldn't. Instead, I would go to the internet café and check my email. Everyone else went back to the hotel, except Ye.

"I will go with you Ms. Virginia. You have been to the internet café here before?"

"Yes, but I will be glad to have your company."

Ye did not show any surprise or disapproval of the internet café. Even when we walked up the stairs in the narrow hall, this did not seem odd to him. Internet cafes in China that I had seen frequently seemed dingy with dark environments.

"You may as well use a computer too, Ye. I will pay for two."

We were assigned computers right next to one another. We both checked email and interacted with senders. Then I still had some time left on the hour I had paid for, so I browsed topics about the region. Last, I remembered a friend had told me to learn about Ha Jin, a

Chinese writer. Many Chinese writers lived in the Shanghai area.

We would go to Shanghai after the SEP because Amity would hold the debriefing for the experience in a hotel in Shanghai. When the Amity time concluded, I planned to stay in the country a little longer. I had been invited to work for a week with an experimental school that specialized in languages in Shanghai.

I told the team I would do this and Trudy said she would stay with me. "I figure this is a once in a lifetime trip, so I may as well stay a bit longer, see more, learn more."

Jerry had to get back, and Danielle and Jim would be on the flight back with him. I didn't expect to have a chance to meet any famous Chinese writers, but perhaps I could see the area where Ha Jin lived. Maybe he lived near one of the universities, museums, or parks I would try to visit in that huge city.

I typed Ha Jin into the search bar.

My computer flickered, then went dark. I turned to Ye to ask him to help with the computer, but at the moment I turned, his computer went dark. Down our row and the other rows in front of us, we saw the computers all go dark.

People started standing up and talking softly. We were in the row nearest the sign-in office. They looked at us and beyond toward the office.

"We should go, Ms. Virginia." Ye said. He took my arm and led me out of the room with rows of computers. We went to the narrow dim stairway, down the stairs, and to the street. Ye took my arm with his hand at my elbow and hurried us across the street.

"What happened, Ye?" Other people also had exited the internet café, all younger men, not one female.

"What did you search after email?" Ye asked.

"The name of a Chinese writer. Ha Jin."

Ye had kept hold of my arm and was guiding us both back toward the hotel.

"What do you know about the writer?"

"I don't know anything but his name. A friend told me he's a great writer. I thought learning about him while I was in China since he is Chinese would be a good idea. Do you think that is the problem?"

"It depends on what he writes. What does he write about?"

"I don't know. That's why I did a search for him. If my search shut down the internet café, what will happen?" I felt a deep chill thinking of getting into trouble in China. Surely no Amity leader had been arrested or deported!!

Back at the hotel, Jerry was reading. One glance up at our faces and he could tell from the expressions something disturbing had happened. I told him.

He asked Ye, "What will happen if Virginia's search shut everything down?"

"The authorities will check who worked at every computer. If they see it was a Western visitor who typed in an illegal search..."

"An illegal search?"

"Something not allowed to be read or studied."

"Every computer can be checked for searches?"

"Yes."

"But how is that possible when this country is so huge and they probably don't even visit every internet café."

"Our government is very efficient." Ye answered with calmness showing he felt this was a normal expectation for government supervision of internet usage.

Jerry continued, "And if they find it was a western visitor who did the illegal search?"

"Probably nothing, unless the same search or another problem search occurs."

"Let's not tell the others about this." My heart fluttered and my mind jumped to worse case possibilities with the local authorities. "Our team will worry unnecessarily instead of enjoying the welcome ceremony and reception afterwards. I want them to go to the ceremony without any extra stress."

Jerry and Ye agreed. We would talk about it this evening, possibly in the park before we were all back in the hotel. There was a twelve-hour difference in time between our location and the east coast of the USA. Danielle and Trudy had talked about going to the internet café during tomorrow's long afternoon break. I would have to warn them about doing any random or wide searches.

A van came at 2:50 to take us to the school's main building. As we passed the side street that had the internet café, both Ye and I looked out the window toward it. Soldiers in the field uniform of fatigues, a camouflage pattern, stood outside. One soldier stood on each side of the door. They held rifles.

A deep breath and prayer helped me calm down a little. Jerry was holding my hand, but I didn't say anything to him about the soldiers. That could wait until later. Would those guards be gone by this evening? How long did it take for the government to check everything searched on all the computers? Was Ye correct that when they figured out it was a Westerner they would not proceed with any other actions?

* * *

The welcome ceremony had a full auditorium with stadium spaced seating. The chairs had a comfort level rare in China. The auditorium entrance for attendees was on the fourth floor of the school's main and new building. That meant eight flights of stairs. Ascend one, make a turn. Ascend part two between each floor. The second floor had the entrance for the main stage, but we did not find out about that during the first week.

All the teachers in the program were present. School and town administrators from the Left Banner sat on the platform. Our host principal was waiting at the bottom of the steps to the platform. She motioned to Ye, I guessed what was coming, that she would ask him to be the translator. Talk about being put on the spot!

He agreed. God bless Ye! I thanked God again for sending him to see us. How would we have managed without a daily helper proficient in languages? The program here in the Left Banner might have lost a week while the school looked for a fluent translator. It might even have been cancelled if Amity couldn't send someone to be the translator. Principal Chimeg handed Ye a portable microphone.

"Do you have to get up on the stage with that?" I asked as he sat down next to me.

"Not while they are speaking. I can just translate here, with all of you, without the microphone. When you speak, I will stand up by the platform and use this microphone so the administrators and teachers will all know what you are saying."

The principal introduced the superintendent, a local

Communist leader, who gave us an official formal welcome. Then the head city administrator welcomed us. Third, Principal Chimeg, expressed her hope for us and the teachers who had come from such a wide area to build their English skills in this Summer English Program. Ye did well keeping up a flow of language telling us what the administrators said.

Then it was my turn. The head of every SEP team needs to give a speech at the welcome ceremony, at ceremonial dinners, and at the closing program. They include thanking hosts and affirming the work the students would do. More formal language, not like a lecture, but suited to a special occasion, needed to be used. I had written a short speech of two paragraphs. Having worked with translators before, though none as young as Ye, I enunciated clearly and stopped after each sentence.

Polite applause followed each of the speeches. Nearly seventy minutes had gone by in the auditorium. No one minded because this building had air-conditioning. I had no idea where our teachers stayed. I had not been in the dormitory building this school had, but since it had major problems, I doubted many of our students stayed there.

Now Principal Chimeg went to the podium to announce that on the first-floor refreshments awaited everyone to celebrate the welcome. She wished everyone success in reaching the goals of successfully passing the course evaluation.

I felt sorry she ended with that reminder. Test taking is so stressful in China. Ye was an example of how test scores could decrease or improve one's options. There are not multiple opportunities to retake tests in China. For these teachers, passing an evaluation, or not, would affect their jobs and pay. Knowing this and still wondering about repercussions for my search at the internet café, my appetite was nil.

We walked downstairs to the first floor for the refreshments. No reluctance appeared among anyone else on the team or in the teachers and administrators who mixed. The local Communist leader who acted as a superintendent for the school and some other organizations found out that Danielle had been a tennis instructor at a resort in Arizona. He asked Ye to stand with him and Danielle and to arrange a time to play tennis. When he found out Jerry also played tennis, he said he had a coworker who could join, and they could play doubles. I felt surprised to find they had tennis courts in the Left Banner, but Jerry and Danielle did not show astonishment at this fact.

A date for their tennis was set for Friday afternoon. This worked well because every Friday classes would end at noon. Teachers could leave to go home for the weekend if they wanted to and had enough money to travel back and forth. None of them had a car. They took buses to commute. There was no train station in this town.

I stood back to watch how the teachers interacted and was impressed to see the administrators socialize with the teachers. I had not seen this in my first experience working with Amity farther north in Inner Mongolia. Administrators there maintained an authoritative distance. I wondered if this difference connected to having a female principal. Around the world, female leadership styles had more connective elements.

Everyone enjoyed the refreshments. Labels had been put in front of the various dishes. The labels certainly helped me and my team. Jim explored all of it and soon happily found the buffet had three kinds of dumplings.

Aloo gobi, aaruul, baozi, boortsog, buuz, huushuur,

wheat noodles, rice noodles, small, sweet tomatoes, bowls of what we identified as watermelon, cantaloupe, and honeydew melon appeared. Bottles of water were available. Looking at the slim build of our students, I thought this buffet might be a feast for them. In my first year working with Amity, I hadn't heard from any other teams of a school having a welcome buffet time of socializing for everyone connected to the program.

I had one of the small saucer size plates like everyone else and wooden *kuaizi* like fast food Chinese restaurants at home gave to customers. But I only took a few bites of *baozi*. Though Ye did not look worried, I watched the doorway and imagined soldiers coming to the school looking for me.

The first time I had been to the internet café they had recorded my passport number and had me sign my name. The government always knew where foreign teachers lived while working in China.

"I won't need any supper," Trudy said as she came up to stand with me and Jerry.

"I won't either," Jerry agreed.

Ye had been watching Jim. "I don't think Jim will need anything else either."

"What's that about Jim?" Danielle asked as she joined us.

"We were commenting that Jim seems to like all the food at this buffet."

"Yes," She agreed. "I think we should walk back to the hotel, slowly. Maybe we should even walk around the entire park once."

"That is a great idea, Danielle." I thought I would much rather tell the team about what happened at the internet café while we walked outside rather than back in the hotel. Naomi, Gladys, and Ye had implied people had more privacy for conversations outdoors than inside places like hotels, restaurants, schools, and other buildings.

When we walked back to the hotel, I would ask Ye to walk far ahead with Jim. Maybe Ye could even make it fun by turning it into a racing game. As people began to leave the buffet reception, I made my way over to Ye.

"Please come with me so I can speak to Principal Chimeg." He nodded and followed me to the principal.

"Principal Chimeg, thank you for this wonderful welcome reception. Everyone has enjoyed this time of socializing. It was thoughtful and generous. Everyone feels it is a special start." I hoped whatever loss of face she had felt Monday would totally dissipate.

Ye translated her response. "We want your time with us to go well for your team and all the teachers. It is lucky that your young friend Ye came to visit. We have seen the signs fate has sent for your work here. We wanted the teachers who are your students to feel welcomed too."

"It is very generous. Thank you. My team and I enjoyed the delicious refreshments so much that we would like to walk back to the hotel at a leisurely pace. We appreciate the van rides at the hottest times of the day, but we will be fine walking back now, and we will walk here in the morning."

The other administrators present had come up along-side Principal Chimeg. It was an appropriate time for them to depart. The superintendent commented how pleased he was that he could play doubles tennis with Americans, and one of them a tennis teacher.

"It will be a unique honor for them," I told him.

Principal Chimeg said, "But we will continue to have the van for you at noon and to return at 2:45."

"Thank you. Thanks to all of you again. This welcome set a good tone for the Summer English Program." Nods and goodbyes were offered. When the administrators had walked in a group to the exit, I turned to Ye.

"I want to tell the team about the internet café incident on the way back to the hotel. Jim does not need to hear what we discuss."

"Yes, Ms. Virginia. I will lead Jim far ahead."

"Thank you for understanding and your constant help."

"It is my privilege and honor. To have people like you come and work for weeks for no pay helping teachers in China is a gift to my country." He smiled and went to Jim.

I gathered Jerry, Danielle, and Trudy. After I told them Ye would walk back to the hotel with Jim so that we could walk farther behind and talk, the relaxation in their body language disappeared. They could tell some unusual information would be shared. I hoped they would accept it calmly.

About a block away from the school, Ye said to Jim, "Let's race walk to the park. We can use some of the equipment there." And off they went.

Danielle turned to me and said, "What's up? You know I am as competitive as Jerry is in playing any games. I am really thrilled we get to play tennis out here in the back of beyond with administrators. I never would have dreamed of such an opportunity. Tennis courts at the edge of the Gobi. Are you now going to tell me and Jerry that we have to lose the matches we play with the Superintendent and whoever he brings along with him?"

Chapter 17

School on Saturdays?

"I didn't get that far in my thinking, Danielle, but that's something to consider. If you and Jerry are much better players, I would suggest not winning every game. However, meeting an administrator and Communist official who is excited about playing tennis in whatever courts they have here makes me guess he learned tennis somewhere else. Maybe he has practiced over years. He could be excellent at tennis."

Trudy asked, "In this environment, it has to be an indoor court, doesn't it? We didn't see any tennis courts in arriving in town, and it's a small town."

"Look," I stopped and pulled us together as a group. Everyone looked toward the park, still a couple of blocks ahead of us. We could see Jim on the equipment. Ye stood near him.

"Not at the park, look to the right. Look at the corner and street behind me where the internet café is...but don't stare."

They looked and saw what I had already spotted.

Soldiers still stood on guard on each side of the door to the internet café.

"What's going on?" Trudy asked.

I told them as briefly as I could about what had happened. I also explained the reaction Ye had and his explanation about what probably would happen.

"Well, I'm not going there anytime soon," Trudy announced. "We can ask Principal Chimeg to let us use the school computer room at the end of our teaching day. Even a half hour will allow me to check email. I do not want to go to jail OR get kicked out of China. Who was the guy you looked up?"

"If I knew I wouldn't have been looking him up."

"I expect he has been in trouble with the government," Jerry added.

"I think we should keep walking," Danielle said softly. "God has done great things for us so far, providing Naomi as a guide. She was wonderful with Jim, and the communion service in Beijing was a unique special experience. Trudy got her carry-on case back in no way that could be coincidence. We visited the Great Wall on a non-busy day. Trudy didn't have a heart attack hearing Jerry belt out 'How Great Thou Art' from the top of the wall, and think of the rain while driving here, then the rainbow. Because of the pipe problems or whatever, we get to stay in a comfortable hotel."

Trudy chimed in, "And Ye showing up when we had no fluent interpreter. Jim is so happy to have a young person like Ye here. Principal Chimeg allowing Ye to be our translator. Ye finds items we need for our lessons at low cost. I believe God will help this internet café situation to fade away to a nothing."

We nodded and agreed. Jerry put his arm around me as

we continued walking. Once again, I felt chagrined. I had not been the one to call to memory all the amazing events that showed God was working through this whole experience for us. As the leader, I felt grateful almost to tears for learning from this set of teammates. I'd been so set on trying to manage everything, that I had missed how much God worked through them to guide me. I needed my listening skills to match my attempts at steering.

* * *

We arrived back at the hotel with no one stopping us. No one came to the hotel to speak to the person who had looked up Ha Jin. We discussed how attentive the students seemed in our classes and their willingness to try the activities.

"I was nervous about being asked about controversial topics," Danielle said.

"Why?" Trudy asked.

"Hasn't Virginia told you about some of the questions she had from her classes in 2004?"

"Oh, yes. I guess I haven't thought about that. Everyone seems focused on advancing in English speaking and comprehension to listening. I think we'll be fine."

Another unusual day, and morning arrived fast. Before breakfast at our host restaurant, we met as planned at 6:30 for a review of the day's plans, words of encouragement from the Bible, and prayer.

Jerry and Ye had already gone out for the 5:30 am walk and talk. They were ready for the day when the team gathered. Though we never told Ye he needed to attend these team meetings he did. I knew his attitude came from growing up in a communal rather than individualistic culture, but he also had a heart to help with excellence in all he did. His humility and tact provided a model for me.

Every day, when we passed the front desk in the hotel, the young ladies said, "Good morning," in clear English. They smiled at us but batted their eyes at Ye and giggled. He smiled back. I expected that as a handsome young man he had faced flirtations in the two years since I had first met him.

The morning had a refreshing coolness by comparison to midday. Though our glance toward the internet café was brief, all of us, except for Jim, looked toward it. Soldiers still stood in guard poses outside the entryway.

Walking to school helped relieve some of the tension that came with seeing soldiers still guarding the door to the internet café. Street sweepers were out at work, stores were opening, and people exercised in the park. The air had a mixed scent of sand, dust, and spices.

Before we got to the school grounds, Jerry asked Jim to help him set up some classroom displays. Looking from Jerry to Ye, I realized Ye had probably arranged with Jerry to take Jim away from all of us. Ye watched Jim leave, then approached Danielle.

"I saw a scooter at a store near the park. It is a reasonable price. I can barter the price down even more. Do you think Jim would like it? He could use it going back and forth to the school. Some other young people ride scooters in the park. He could make some friends."

"He has a scooter at home so we would not need to take it home, even if we could. We can't. It would be way too awkward. Could we leave it here when we leave?"

"I know you bring prizes for the party at the end of the summer training. Maybe some teacher would select it because they have a child."

"That sounds like a good idea, Ye. Yes. I would do that." Danielle reached in her purse to give him some money. "Do not let Jim get the best most expensive scooter. He stands out enough. Tell him to find a scooter like the ones the other children are riding."

"Yes, Ms. Danielle."

* * *

In my life experience in other countries, a day going totally smoothly makes me nervous. While the rest of the team felt buoyant because of how well the classes had gone, I felt on edge. Often, I thought God gave us a lull or a bit of smooth sailing so we could get some rest before a major challenge.

Music often helped lift my spirits, and in all my years of teaching I had found ways to use music in classes. My team in 2004 had found that a successful boost to the enjoyment of learning and practicing English came through teaching our classes songs.

Each day we started the class with our homeroom song. We had each chosen a different simple song and changed some words to make it about English. Learning a language and memorizing words came more easily when set to music. This 2006 team agreed music would be a good addition and enjoyed choosing familiar short choruses that allowed for easy changes.

Just as I had seen and heard in 2004, the people of Inner Mongolia took delight in singing and were not shy. A few of the male Mongolian students sang out so enthusiastically that we could hear them in the other classrooms. And each class had people who had ability to harmonize. I loved hearing the classes sing to start the day.

Our students liked the Amity textbook and the experience of changing classes that allowed them to move around for a few minutes. Frequently in China, students did not change classes. The teachers were the ones who moved from classroom to classroom. This made sense since class sizes were double or triple the size of a large class in the USA.

Each of us saw all four groups in the morning, though we had the most time with our homeroom classes. Engaging them in casual conversation before moving to the textbook established a calming environment.

When we exited our classrooms at noon time, the van waited to take us to the restaurant, Jim circled the school courtyard on his new scooter. A deep brick red, it seemed to make this blonde-haired, blue eyed, peaches and cream skin toned child stand out even more. At home children wore protective gear like helmet or knee and elbow pads, but not here. Having a scooter in the Left Banner seemed to require only the skill to avoid bumping into anyone.

"I'll race you to the restaurant," Jim called and set off pushing off on the flat hard packed dirt, leaning forward sightly and gripping the handlebars, one knee slightly bent on the scooter's deck and the other foot on the ground. Ye waved at us and with an easy jog followed Jim.

In the van we glanced toward the internet café and breathed more easily. The soldiers were finally gone. We saw people going in and coming out of the doorway. I thought I might even use it again, but I would do no more unknown searches.

Lunch, nap time, and the ride back to the school continued to feel easy. This differed from my 2004 experience in the first week of the Summer English Program. At the concluding days of that year working in China, in the debriefing days, I had not heard any other team say they had easy days in their first week. Because of the frustrations of the lack of shared goals with my 2004 team, it was the hard-working hosts and students who made that time wonderful. I wanted to return to see what I'd learn with a unified team.

Each night in my journal I tried to list something I learned or was learning in that day. Even with the team I had this year, easy made me nervous. Even with the ease we had, I felt on guard for difficult times ahead. I needed to keep praying for a more trusting spirit. I should accept it as grace and stop building a guard wall against the next test.

I didn't mention my concerns to anyone else. Ye knew from our early morning team gathering that we had expected to use the computer room in the administration building. So far, that opportunity had been offered only once.

While Jim sat in the back of Danielle's classroom drawing and reading, Ye left the classroom area. We found out later he had talked to Principal Chimeg and arranged that at the end of each teaching day, we could have an hour to use the school's computers. He told us this as our team gathered at six pm.

We thanked Ye for settling a time for us to use the computers, but he did not have the kind of happy smile that was on all our faces. Ye told us, "Principal Chimeg would like you to teach on Saturday. In China, students have classes on Saturday."

"Ye, is this like a bargain? Did the principal agree to let us use the computers if we agreed to have classes on Saturday?" I asked.

"No. You may use the computers. I will walk to the computer classroom with you. Principal Chimeg said she wants the teachers who are your students to have more time to learn. These teachers have classes Monday through Saturday at their schools."

"But they came here thinking it would be Monday through Friday." I didn't mention that was what Amity expected too. Ye said nothing. He waited calmly. I looked at my team. "What do you think?" I asked.

Trudy said, "You're the one who has done the SEP before. What do you think?"

"Amity does not expect the SEP teachers to work on Saturday unless you count English corners as work, but I explained those are relaxed, even fun. We weren't going to have English corners, those spontaneous gatherings of any local people who wanted to practice English, until next week. We could see that any time we are at the park people would come to join us with friendly curiosity to speak with us."

"Didn't you say host schools take the SEP teams on field trips on Saturdays?"

"Often, they do, but that is not a requirement. That is not part of what they have to provide for Amity teams."

"Would it add a positive note for Amity if we teach on Saturdays?" Jerry asked.

Jim had come out of his mother's classroom and heard the mention of school on Saturday. He said, "I wouldn't want to go to school on Saturdays!"

Chapter 18

Teaching, Talking, and Trusting

Principal Chimeg stood in the entry way of the building where we all went to use the computer room. My team stopped behind me. Ye came up alongside me.

"Principal Chimeg, thank you for agreeing to our use of the computers after our teaching day. Ye also told me that you think we should have classes on Saturday." Ye smoothly translated.

"Yes. Many teachers have come from far away and probably will not ever have an opportunity again to have time with native speakers of English as their teachers."

"Amity does not usually plan for including Saturdays, but if you think this will help the teachers, we will have Saturday classes."

"Good. We will continue to have the van provide transportation in the heat of the day."

Principal Chimeg nodded to us and left. I turned to look at the team. "I guess she'll make the announcement in some way tomorrow."

"Vice Principal Guo will visit the classes to make the announcement." Ye told us.

I didn't say anything but felt a connection to the issue of 'Face.' The role of principal might be too dignified to go to each classroom making announcements, especially about changes that might not be appreciated. I hoped my words to her and agreement had been suitable.

Sighs and silence, then Danielle said, "It is good to show we will go along with the principal's desires for more learning."

"Mom, I don't think your students will want Saturday classes."

Danielle laughed lightly and pushed Jim forward into the computer room. "You don't know that, Jim." He looked from her to Ye, as if to say, you should tell her I'm right. Ye did not say anything to Danielle.

Jim also did not use the computers. I thought again what a unique young man he was, sensitive to helping others but cautious. I had warned the team to stick to email when using the school computers and to be careful with any messages they sent.

I tried to explain, when we were outside, that no school computers had privacy features. "Censors in China, as I had learned the scary way, could hone in on any messages unless a person used a VPN."

"What's a VPN?" Trudy asked in the parking lot near our hotel when I delivered the warning later.

"VPN stands for Virtual Private Network. It encrypts the data so no one else can read your search or messages. China has a super firewall. Think of it as the Great Wall of the internet. It blocks access to loads of sites, apps, and other services. A VPN can go around these blocks by using a server outside of China. So, VPNs give a layer of privacy from the censors and firewall."

"Oh my gosh, why does China allow VPNs?" she asked.

"Their use is restricted, but for now they are allowed. There probably is a way the censors could determine if someone was using it in a subversive way, but I couldn't explain all the processes China uses to watch and guard internet connections. Plus, just like a person could get scammed by buying a phone card that doesn't work, people can buy VPNs that don't go through the great firewall. I'm sure that eventually VPNs will be made illegal, but for now, they work."

I didn't remember having any such conversations with my team members in 2004. We hadn't known one another before Amity put us together, and we all had reasons for joining the SEP program that were not oriented to simply serving. This team in 2006, my own team of close friends, conversed freely and had a united goal in the SEP for service.

Jerry put his hand on my back. "You made a generous decision. We'll all do fine."

"I agree with Danielle and Jerry," Trudy said, "But I also agree with Jim. What do you think about the decision, Ye?"

"I think I am just a student and translator, so I will follow Ms. Virginia's decision."

* * *

No one had any bad news in the emails they received, so we felt good leaving the school grounds. Frequently if we left later than six-thirty or seven we walked back to the restaurant and the hotel. Jim did loops past us and around us on his scooter. Pausing by the park, we enjoyed the refreshing green of grass and flowering plants. In the evenings, the sight of different ages of people talking together, unhurried, also refreshed us.

Trudy and Danielle were fascinated by the split pants solution over diapers for babies and toddlers. They often wanted to stand near family groups and watch how the babies who could barely walk and sure-footed older toddlers just squatted and did what they needed to through their split pants. No need for diapers here. Although sometimes we saw children with a disposable diaper inside their split pants.

Babies and toddlers wear split pants, kaidangku, which leads to early toilet training.

One evening, with Ye nearby to translate, a mother and grandmother told us, the *kaidangku* is practical. A child does not have to remove clothing to eliminate. Often, with easy and timely elimination potty training can happen fully by age two. Parents and grandparents see cues in the child and can whistle or shush in a way to help the child avoid having an accident.

Some parents and grandparents carried something to

pick up after the child as people in the United States pick up after their dogs. Other people just ignored whatever appeared on the sidewalk or in the grass. No one seemed bothered by any of the common split pants behavior. Out of our team, Trudy appeared most concerned and walked carefully when many little toddlers were out on the sidewalk near the park. The Left Banner residents, like other people I had met in China, were glad to supply answers to our questions. Because my team was composed of parents and Trudy was a grandparent, common concerns made for friendly exchanges about teaching and training children.

Whenever Jim stood with us, or parked his scooter near us, children of different heights and ages approached us on their scooters or walked over to us. "They're my friends," Jim said happily. The young people seemed to understand, and they nodded. Most of them tried talking to us with at least one sentence or question. How exciting it must have been for them to practice their required study of English with native speakers of the language.

Ye told us, "They study English in school and feel happy if you understand them."

"Sure," I responded for all of us. None of them looked much older than Jim, and most looked younger. Their questions were simple, but we were impressed. Each of us knew high school students who took a foreign language but would not try to speak it to native speakers of that language.

The questions rolled out more smoothly in English than we had heard from some of the teachers we had interviewed. Perhaps it was childish lack of inhibitions, or the excitement of talking to people from the United States that let them call out their questions. Maybe it was the fact that Jim and Ye had already spent time with them. Jim was learning more Chinese every day. He had learned greetings, nouns, verbs, and even some words in the Mongolian language.

Then by early evening, as quickly as they had arrived, the children suddenly lifted their faces as if scenting something in the air. Delicious smells wafted to the square from nearby open street stall vendors. Reminded of supper, the boys and girls with scooters said goodbye and scattered like pool balls.

The air didn't seem to have a dust smell at this hour as we left our spontaneous English corner and walked toward the restaurant. The Amity suggestion of holding an open session of speaking with people in English had caught on quickly. I expected Ye had helped in explaining all the foreign teachers wanted to talk with local citizens who wanted to practice English.

When we finally left to go to the restaurant, Jim zoomed off fast on his scooter. He had time to turn around, ride back to us, tease us about being slow, and then go back toward the restaurant. Ye was never far behind Jim.

After Jim parked the scooter at the bottom of the three steps we used to enter the restaurant, Danielle asked, "He can leave the scooter there, Ye?"

"Yes, Ms. Danielle."

She turned toward the rest of us as we walked up the steps to join Jim and Ye.

"Why do I believe that so easily?"

Trudy answered, "I remember Naomi telling us that if a foreign visitor was robbed, the thief would be in worse trouble than if he had stolen from a Chinese person."

Jim stood very still and looked sad. "Naomi's dad was robbed and killed."

"That is very sad, Jim. I know Naomi felt your sympathy for her."

"Maybe I asked her too many questions."

"Naomi didn't mind. She liked you a lot, just as Ye does."

"We can ask Ye if he agrees with Naomi about how criminals try not to rob or hurt foreigners here." Danielle added.

"Yes. Ye is inside waiting beside our table. We can ask him what he thinks about Naomi's opinion of who is safer in China." Jerry commented.

In our bedroom that night Jerry and I quietly discussed our day. With the delight in the dishes served, we almost forgot to ask Ye about theft and other crime in places like his city and the Left Banner, but Danielle remembered and asked. He assured us Naomi's ideas were correct. The reputation of the nation depended on China's citizens treating foreign visitors well unless people who were drunk wandered foolishly into dark dangerous sections of cities.

I didn't tell him that I knew of people who had been misled or ripped off while visiting some of the provinces in China. Robbery even could happen in banks if a foreigner did not have the exchange rate and trusted the teller without having a Chinese friend like Naomi along.

Ye was proud of his country and believed the best about it even though my tactless husband talked bluntly on their morning walks. Between Jerry and Jim, Ye had two avenues to learning honest opinions and insights into Americans and their views. Would this help him or hinder him in his hopes of a career in serving his country? I wondered how he had done on his exams and where he would go to college. Surely he had passed the test this second time.

Though the soldiers were gone from the internet café, we knew people watched us. When we talked to each other, our students and the host administrators listened to us. Because China had required English language education since the start of the 21st century, younger people anywhere in the country had their attention caught by the sound of people speaking English. How much did older people know? Highly educated adults who had studied in major cities knew some English, like I knew some Chinese, but at a low level unless they had studied more on their own.

We had learned enough to feel inhibited in our conversations inside buildings. Did anyone listen to our meetings in our little suite? We met at a similar time each day. If anyone was listening, they would hear us discuss how our classes responded to different activities, pray and talk about service, and encourage one another in trusting God to help us with challenges in any day. It is possible they listened to us in our casual conversations too, but we couldn't know that. We didn't dwell on this concern.

In our classrooms anyone who worked for a Left Banner school might be a person who had the responsibility of reporting anything objectionable that a foreign teacher stated. I needed to remind my team in morning meetings about word choices and tact. This team cared about one another and shared encouraging comments and ideas.

Ye sat in each meeting with us and no one minded. I stopped worrying about Ye taking offense from Jerry's blunt comments. Why? I don't know. I certainly didn't worry about Ye saying anything negative about us to any authorities. Why would he? My normally suspicious mindset had slipped that thought into my consciousness, but I dismissed it.

Chapter 19

Changes, Competition, and Camels

O ur first Friday in the Left Banner should have made us feel relieved and ready for a rest on Saturday and Sunday. No field trips had been mentioned by any of the administrators here compared to having the 2004 hosts explain their plan for field trips each weekend. Some schools had empty miles and poor roads, and no tourist sites to visit. Some schools could not afford any extras, so no Amity teams counted on field trips.

Now that we had agreed to teach on Saturdays, we discussed this again at our morning meeting. We prayed for grace, wisdom, strength, and that God's love would be evident in all we said and did with and for our students. We discussed how much effort it took to avoid using contractions, trying to enunciate clearly, varying the voice volume, and interjecting emotion for emphasis. We reviewed the supplies we had and plans for the unexpected additional day.

Ye stayed with us. Usually his attentive listening did not affect his calm expression. He answered questions when asked. Often, he talked with teachers who were our

160

students and without giving us names, he shared what they liked and what they found most difficult. Ye told us our classes would like to learn more songs they could use with their students, songs that told stories or had lots of vocabulary. Ye also said the teachers wanted to know more about our own stories, our life at home, our work, teaching stories, and the answer to how we chose to come and participate in Amity's SEP.

Jim and Ye arrived earlier than we did at school. They spent time with some of the teachers who had arrived early. During the lessons, Jim alternately enjoyed time outdoors with his scooter and Ye, or he sat in the back of his mother's class working on puzzles or *Learn Chinese* workbooks. When Jim was in the classroom, Ye visited one of the other classes. In constant concern to help, Ye sat near the door in case something was needed by one of us.

By late morning, our last class before the lunch and rest break, VP Guo showed up in the doorway with Ye beside him. VP Guo had not ever been full of smiles, except when the rainbow and rain showered our arrival ride into the Left Banner. Now he looked more serious than ever. He spoke rapidly to Ye. Then VP Guo left.

The class sat up alert. I expect many of them heard what VP Guo had to say, but they did not whisper to one another. They watched and listened.

Ye said, "VP Guo visited the other classes. He started down at the end of the row with Mr. Jerry's class to announce we would have Saturday classes. People had not planned for Saturdays. The students objected. Many could not participate in the changed plan including Friday afternoons and Saturdays. Now, there will be no Saturday classes. The original Amity suggestion for schedules will be used. With no Friday afternoon classes, students can travel home if they want or need to."

"Thank you, Ye. Do all the classes know this?

"Yes, this is the last class Vice Principal Guo visited. The decision is to not have Saturday classes. Vice-Principal Guo has made the announcement in Chinese and Mongolian."

"Thank you," I said conscious of the full attention of my students on this exchange. I turned and asked the class if they had any questions. I wondered if VP Guo starting by giving an announcement first with the only male teacher, affected my level of 'Face' with the students. I certainly could not know that and doubted I would ask Ye.

Ye went outside. I saw Jim walk to join him. They both walked to the parked red scooter.

Refocus on the class, I told myself. Amity wants to promote opportunities for classes to engage in authentic and valuable discussions in English. We had a surprisingly rapid flow of conversation now about change, plans, priorities, and purposes. The class was animated and expressive. Their seriousness and passion emerged in even their uneven spoken English. Listening was different. The students brought up the importance of flexibility. Most had followed family and community rules for all their days.

It seemed too personal to ask them if they would travel home or if they planned to stay in the Left Banner for the weekend. Whatever their plans, the classes surprised me by objecting to Saturday classes. When the authorities made a plan, underlings did not usually object. Following the rules of higher ups without complaint had been connected to cultural expectations since Confucius. Jim had guessed right. We gathered to walk back to the restaurant or hotel, Ye returned with VP Guo.

"Vice Principal Guo asked me what you did on week-ends when you were in my city. I told him the school took you on field trips on Saturday, sometimes for a few hours, sometimes for a long day."

"Yes," I agreed. "But schools do not have to arrange field trips. That is not an Amity SEP requirement."

"He has some ideas for a big day, but that would be for next weekend. The Helan mountains are not too far and very beautiful with ancient temples and a staircase of marble to the top of one of the high mountains. They want to take you on that trip next weekend. You can see ancient carvings in rocks. The school would take a bus so some of the students from every class will also be able to go along on the trip with you."

"That sounds wonderful and very interesting. Those carvings, petrographs, are very special. We would enjoy seeing any of that." I responded and the team agreed.

Ye translated and VP Guo looked relieved. His smile appeared for the first time this day. Then VP Guo frowned again. He said more and Ye also frowned.

"Vice Principal Guo has no idea what we can do on short notice for tomorrow."

"I know what we can do!" Jim announced.

VP Guo and all of us looked at him. Jim realized we were waiting to hear his idea. He continued. "We can ride camels. We can go out in the desert and ride camels. Some of the teachers in the classes have camels at their homes. Solomon's family raises camels. Someone will know where we can ride camels. Will anyone at school believe me if I tell them I rode a camel in the Gobi? Can we get pictures?"

None of us said anything. Jim certainly had presented an idea that suited this region, but it wasn't like we were at an amusement park or a tourist center that offered camel rides. Maybe the teachers would have an idea of where this could be done in one of the deserts that bordered the Left Banner. The Principal and Vice Principal would have extra work to arrange this, and what would such an outing cost for their budget?

Once again, I worried about putting them in a position where they would be in danger of some embarrassment. While we stood there silently, the man who now had the job of school caretaker came rushing up behind our conversational cluster. He spoke quickly to VP Guo. Ye listened. VP Guo nodded and seemed to dismiss the young man, then spoke to Ye.

"Vice Principal Guo has just learned the Superintendent and his assistant would like to play tennis later this afternoon, at five, with Mr. Jerry and Ms. Danielle."

We looked at Jerry and Danielle and waited. Jerry spoke first, "I'd be glad to do that. I guess it would be doubles?"

Ye spoke with VP Guo, then turned back to us. "Yes, it would be doubles, probably for two hours of play. Then they would like to take you all to dinner at a family restaurant the superintendent enjoys."

Jerry and Danielle agreed. "Can I go and watch you play?" Jim asked.

Before Ye had translated, VP Guo answered, "Yes." Jim looked very happy.

I glanced at my team to see if they noticed that VP Guo had understood Jim's question and answered directly and clearly in English.

Amity in the training reminded us that many people could understand some English since China had made learning English a priority. We always needed to be careful in what we said in public to one another and to citizens of China who talked with us.

VP Guo said something to Ye, then a quick *Zai jian*, goodbye, to all of us. He hurried away. Jim looked at Ye and asked, "Did he say he had to hurry to see if we could ride camels tomorrow in the desert?"

Ye said, "I think you are learning Chinese well, Jim. That is almost exactly what Vice-Principal Guo said."

* * *

We arrived at the restaurant long past our usual lunch time. Since we would have dinner later, we didn't mind this mid-afternoon lunch. We rarely ordered. Instead we let the restaurant serve us a few different dishes. We did not want to seem demanding or as if we felt entitled.

Everything they had served us had been delicious so far except for one dish that smelled horrendous. They set this odd smelly dish down beside me, the team leader. Jim looked from the dish to me, eyebrows up, eyes wide.

"That stinks and it looks bad. Are you going to eat it?"

"As team leader, to avoid being rude, I have to take at least a taste, Jim."

"It looks like guts."

I took a taste and passed it on. No one else took any, and Jim's guess was correct. I found out the smelly dish was pork intestines chopped into segments and cooked in heavy spices.

Today, the other dishes we recognized and enjoyed. *Aloo gobi*, was a fragrant and delicious potato curry, and *lavsha*, which was a thinly sliced beef with onions, carrots, cabbage, and garlic, and larger than usual vegetable dumplings. In our first week the restaurant served a wider variety of spiced dishes, but as they cleared the dishes they could see not much of the spicy food had disappeared. Danielle tried them and so did Jim and I, but they felt flaming on our tongues.

The unexpected change in our schedule let us all have extra time to rest this Friday. I asked Ye if he would go to the Internet Café with me. In my teens I rode many frisky ponies and poorly trained horses. When I was thrown, I always got back on the horse to show it I was not afraid. I felt fearful about returning to the internet café, and I wanted to change that by returning to use the computers there.

Ye raised his eyebrows slightly at my request, but said, "Yes, Ms Virginia."

"We'll come back quickly. You will still have time to rest before you go with Danielle, Jerry, and Jim to the tennis match."

"I am looking forward to seeing that tennis. Will they win, Mr. Jerry and Ms. Danielle?"

"I don't know. I think the superintendent looks very athletic. Since he invited them, he probably feels he has a good game to offer."

Ye frowned slightly and asked, "If they could defeat the superintendent and his assistant in every game, would they?"

"Jerry and Danielle are competitive, Ye, but they also know they are guests. This is a special opportunity. They also know the superintendent has invited us to go out later to dinner."

A sliver of a smile appeared on his face. Ye said, "Tact again, Ms. Virginia."

We went to the internet café. The young man handling the sign-in looked concerned, but Ye said something to him, and I was given the sign-in book. After I signed in, I passed the pen and book to Ye, and he signed too. I paid for both of us.

I checked email, sent some email, and looked up nothing extra. Ye sat beside me and also seemed to do email. We signed out, said thank you, and I let out a soft sigh of relief as we left the building. I wondered if Ye felt the same. He showed the most expression when talking with Jim. Otherwise he showed the control of a stoic.

Back at the apartment, Ye went to his room. I sat in our little living room and enjoyed a quiet time sitting and reading, reviewing, and praying. I hoped the tennis experience would be good for everyone, and that the odd on-again-off-again teaching time for Fridays and Saturdays was truly settled.

Jerry and Danielle had shorts and T-shirts with them that were suitable for tennis, and the right kind of gym shoes. The superintendent would provide the rackets. Danielle came to our door. She had an energetic sparkle I had not seen for a while. Not only would she be able to play a game she enjoyed, but the opportunity was an unexpected treat.

Jim, at her side, looked just as happy. "Trudy is going to take a nap but said she would pray for Mom and Pastor Jerry to have good games."

"I'm sure they will," I said, but inside I did not feel sure.

Then Jim added with a puzzled expression, "Trudy said Mom looked like Billy Jean King. Who's that?"

Ye had entered the room in time to hear Jim's comment. Now he looked like he wanted to know the answer too.

167

Jerry answered, "Billy Jean King is a famous tennis player. She won 39 Grand Slam titles, and some people think she is one of the greatest tennis players in history."

"How come I never heard of her?" Jim asked.

"Do you watch a lot of tennis or news about tennis?"

"No. I like baseball and basketball."

"Billy Jean King retired in the 1980s."

"Wow, I wasn't even born, and she was already done with tennis."

Jerry continued, "Not totally. She went on to be a coach, the first woman commissioner with the World Team Tennis League, and then a commentator on tennis for some television stations. She is still a league coach now, and she is featured in the Tennis Hall of Fame."

"Big compliment for you, Mom." Jim grinned at his mother.

As they left, I caught hold of Jerry, gave him a hug and a kiss. I went to the door and watched them go down the stairs to the lobby. The superintendent would have his car and driver pick them up and bring them back.

* * *

Hours, I had more than two hours to wait. I tried to take a nap. Sleep did not come. I had plenty to read, lessons to work on, and I could pray. Sometimes prayer felt like work, not restful meditation. I reached for my journal. Maybe I could untangle more knots that blocked insight.

I listened to music too. My small CD player and the music I brought calmed me and reminded me of the solid rock in my life. My favorite for this trip, and one Jerry had listened to with me, was Amy Grant's *Rock of Ages...Hymns & Faith*. It had come out in 2005, but Jerry and I could both sing one of the songs, "Anywhere with Jesus." Places this summer sure fit into the 'anywhere' category for us. I felt like it was my anthem even when I didn't feel I belonged in the places we visited.

Near 6:30, I heard their voices in the hall. I leapt up and went to open the door.

"Mom and Pastor Jerry won the first set, but not the second," Jim announced like a line judge who had finally been allowed to talk.

"It was a great indoor court." Jerry said.

Danielle laughed, "But it almost killed me."

"What?" Trudy and I asked in unison.

"A chunk of cement fell from the edge of the roof. It almost hit Mom." Jim said.

Danielle said. "We did not let it bother us, and the games were good. We didn't need too much translation. The superintendent looked serious, almost angry over the cement, but he stayed calm. Jerry and I stayed casual, and the superintendent and his partner relaxed. The superintendent even said the scores in English. Ye watched and kept Jim company."

"The building had air-conditioning, not on high but comfortable. I need to get a quick shower. The car is coming back for us at 7:30." Jerry left us, but Jim continued describing more about their afternoon.

"The car is a big black car, kind of like a short limo. It can fit six people in the back. You can sit three people on a seat, and the seats face each other." Jim was still talking as Danielle escorted him out of the room. Ye shut the door behind them.

"Did you enjoy watching the games, Ye?"

"Yes. I didn't have to say anything at the start. They nodded to each other. The superintendent pointed to their side of the court. Jim told me they would warm up. I didn't know what that would include, but I watched.

"I could tell when the games started. They all looked more serious, and they concentrated. They called out the scores. Numbers in English and also Love."

"Yes. Love is a funny word to call out in a competition. In tennis, it means zero."

"How does love mean zero?" His face showed more confusion than I'd seen this summer.

"I've heard different versions, and none of them say love is a zero. Love is always important." I hoped he would smile, but he stood waiting for more explanation. "One story says using love in scoring comes from French. The word in French is, l'oeuf, and that means egg."

"I think I see. The egg resembles the shape of a zero?"

"But there is another theory. People who play a sport do it for the love of the game. Even if they get zero points, they love playing. Can you understand how this could lead to calling out love when someone has zero points?"

"I think so. It reminds them and people watching that they love the sport even if they don't win points."

"You are very good at figuring out meanings and explaining them in English, Ye. I hope your test scores will arrive soon for you and show your excellence in English. You were kind and extra helpful to go along and watch the match. Did you understand how they were doing and enjoy watching?"

"Ms. Virginia, when Ms. Danielle and Mr. Jerry kept winning in the first set of games, I felt nervous. The superintendent and his assistant came close to winning some of those games but did not. The score was 7-5 in Mr. Jerry and Ms. Danielle's favor. The administrators congratulated Ms. Danielle and Mr. Jerry on winning.

"They took a break and had bottled water, but right away they started another set of games. Jim was happy. He told me he thought his mom and Mr. Jerry would win this set too.

"But they didn't."

"No. The first games were very close, but the superintendent and his assistant seemed much stronger in each additional game in the second set. They won the set 6-4."

"Some people, Ye, even tennis pros, take a while to warm up. They play a bunch of games before they do their best. Tell me, did they seem evenly matched in skill and athletic ability to you?"

Ye looked pensive, as if he was thinking about how much to say.

He said, "I studied them carefully, faces, body language. I think each side understands hospitality and tact. In these tennis games, I am sure each side used tact. I cannot decide which side used the most tact. What do you think?" Ye asked me with a smile.

"I think I will ask Jerry about his tennis tact."

Chapter 20

Who gets the naughty camel?

O ur team meeting on Saturday morning started later and went longer than our weekday meetings. We relaxed in the circle in our tiny living room. I thought we all still felt the fullness of dinner the previous evening.

"That dinner felt very special even though it wasn't formal." Trudy said.

"I was glad for the lack of formality," Jerry said.

"If we were royalty, then royalty was very into dumplings." We laughed at Danielle's comment. "Jim is watching a special cartoon. He probably will watch it for an hour. He said it helps him learn Chinese and is funny."

How surprised we had been to see a different section of the little restaurant where we had our meals. We had not known about the splendid rooms for private dining upstairs. We followed the superintendent and Principal Chimeg into a room with wallpaper showing cranes in flight near a river, mountains in layered majesty, and calligraphy.

"What does it say?" Danielle asked pointing to a few rows of the gorgeous writing.

"They're poems," Ye answered.

The room had one oversized table; one of the largest tables I'd seen. We sat alternated among our hosts. Ye sat between me and Principal Chimeg so he could easily translate for anyone at the table.

The superintendent said, "One of my childhood friends opened this restaurant eight years ago. It might look expensive in these private rooms, but it is priced for families to enjoy these rooms. Often the rooms upstairs are busier that the open main floor."

"Did you and your friend both grow up here?" Jerry asked.

"No. We started out here, but after primary years, my parents sent me to live with my grandparents in Yinchuan. Then I went to University in Beijing. My friend developed his business skills. He owns a few businesses in this town."

Waiters, some of those we recognized who served us down on the main floor, brought in trays and served us sliced duck, the ingredients to create duck pancakes as we had in Beijing, jiaozi filled with pork, boiled mutton, noodle and vegetable dishes, and they placed beautifully arranged salads in tiny dishes precisely beside each person's main plate.

One of the town leaders started the toasting, but again it seemed light and informal. I looked at Jim regarding everything happening and was thankful again that he was on my team. Jim put together a duck pancake because of what he had learned in Beijing and after taking a big bite, chewing it with obvious delight, he said, "This is better than the duck in Beijing."

Our hosts beamed. A man who might be equal to the mayor stood to toast Jim. Our smart youngest team member stood at once. They walked around the table until the stood side by side. Because Jim only came to the height of this man's chest, it was easy for him to follow the instruction of politely keeping his glass lower than the older more important man. Jim was toasted for his bravery and behavior, and Jim toasted this gentleman for having a wonderful town and for giving us a delicious meal.

Even Ye looked surprised at the aplomb of Jim's posture and toast. I did not get to see if Ye had a chance to eat much. He was busy translating through the entire meal.

Just when this post-tennis match feast seemed about to end, the waiters returned with bowls, like parfait glasses. We could tell from the condensation on the glass the contents were cold. Inside, we did not find the buckthorn treat, but mango and strawberry sorbet.

Our lively dinner time concluded with best thankfulness and good wishes. I could not keep careful track, but it seemed everyone had participated in toasts and conversation. It was good to see people toast Principal Chimeg and VP Guo. They certainly had coped with a week of changes and frustrations. The responsibility for all of us must weigh heavily on them each day.

When we left the restaurant, we didn't talk until we reached the parking lot between the restaurant and hotel. Trudy broke the silence. "Okay, Danielle, Jerry, tell us. Did you let the superintendent win the second set of tennis?"

Danielle answered, "I did not travel halfway around the world to throw a match."

We stood still and looked at Jerry who was holding my hand. Ye walked on the other side of Jerry. Looking from me to each member of our team, Jerry said, "I've been having reminders and lessons in using tact."

* * *

I opened the door to our suite each morning when Ye, Jerry, and I were up, dressed, and ready to welcome the team. Jim arrived first this Saturday. He seemed energized from a good night's rest and excitement about the day.

"Camels today! What time did Principal Chimeg say the van would pick us up and take us to ride the camels?" Jim's excitement seemed almost tangible as we waited for the van that would arrive at 9:00 a.m.

Our team loaded into the comfortable but seatbelt-less van. Sitting in the air-conditioned van gave a different view of the stark environment of the Left Banner. Because it stood so close to the Gobi to the west and other deserts to the north and south, I thought it seemed like an outpost of a town. The buildings were low and sturdy with the exception of a few buildings in the center of town that had four or five stories.

Leaving town we passed traditional small homes, plain in color and design but with windows trimmed in bold colors. We were early so the dust that usually seemed to drift in the air had not yet appeared. We had clear blue sky and bright sunshine. We passed a small temple with prayer flags lining its walkway and the edges of the roof.

"Harsh but also homey," Trudy commented while staring out the window.

"What?" Jerry asked.

"The Left Banner, it has the harshness of vast desert stretches, but a homey look in the sudden little stores with their red flags and advertisements. Yet modernity is approaching."

"I can't read the writing on the store signs," Jim sighed. "I've learned some Chinese characters for food, but Mongolian letters are just squiggles."

We agreed, and I saw the principal and VP smile. They

did not seem offended. I knew they also appreciated Jim's interest in Chinese and what he had learned.

Looking out the window I saw that trees were fuller and growing closely together around the park and at street corners. They thinned as we came to the outskirts of the town. Danielle must have noticed the same change because she said, "I wonder how they are doing with desertification."

Ye had translated, and now Principal Chimeg turned to speak to us at a fast pace, but Ye kept up. "We have the same program Ms. Virginia encountered in Ye's city. Citizens are responsible for planting trees each year and for caring for the trees they plant."

Green growth became sparser. Golden ridges of dunes almost shone reflecting the powerful sun in the blue desert sky. The road had more long curves and around each hill of sand appeared multiple ridges in a palette from white to ochre, earthy tones all.

"How do any plants survive out here?" Jim asked. "I do see some bushes, but not many."

"Those are common in deserts," Ye supplied. "I don't know their English name. They have deep roots and can reach underground water. See how they are near rocks? That gives them some shade and moisture."

While Jim continued staring out, Ye translated to the non-English speakers in the van.

"Still no camels," Jim said with some concern.

VP Guo spoke to Ye who then turned and told us, "Camels eat plants. The government does not want them to roam freely anymore. When wandering camels are found, they are taken to special areas. Once many more bushes and grasses grew here, but camels destroy vegetation."

"Were there ever lots of plants, even grass?" Jim asked.

"Long ago, yes, even trees, but people cut them for firewood. They cut too many."

A bit of sadness had come into our silence. Then we rounded a bend, and gasped. A cluster of camels appeared standing in a loose group.

"Camels!" Jim shouted. The flock was composed of various sizes and colors; tall, woolly, tan, and brown. One was completely white.

Our hosts smiled. It was a child's words that lifted the mood of everyone in the vehicle.

"There's a white camel, just one. Is he special?" Jim asked. "Are there albino camels?"

We saw a flock of camels: beige, tan, brown, and one white.

"White camels are not common," Ye said. Then VP Guo spoke and Ye translated, "White camels are often naughty camels."

"Naughty?" We all asked.

"Not docile. Not always good for carrying riders."

"You mean they might buck, like broncos?" Jim sounded thrilled.

"Buck?" Ye asked about this word he apparently had never encountered.

"Jump up and down," Jim added. "Have you ever seen a rodeo? Cowboys ride bucking horses, called broncos. They have a contest to see who can stay on the longest while the horse or the bull is bucking."

"No prizes for riding bucking camels here," Ye said.

"Maybe they will be easy to ride. Look. They have two humps. We could lean back on one and hold on to the one in front."

"Do you know the difference between these camels and a dromedary, Jim?" Jerry asked. I noticed Ye seemed eager to hear the answer, but he stayed active in translating for our hosts.

"No. What is it?"

"A dromedary is a camel with one hump. Virginia and I rode them in Egypt. It feels very wobbly, even with a saddle because you are seated on top of that one hump."

"I've never been on any camel. Have you Mom?"

"No. Horses, plenty. A mule, a donkey, and a burrow, but no camels."

"I rode a pony at the fair that came to our town every summer," Trudy added.

The van slowed to a stop. Five Mongolian men stood around the camels. Their clothing had faded colors from time in the sun, but they wore hats that caused Jim to ask, "Are those Mongolian cowboys?"

Ye said, "They are workers from the camel farm nearby. Just beyond those dunes."

Jim nodded but quickly slid out the van door that VP Guo had opened. The inward rush of hot desert air rushed over us. When we stepped out, it was onto hard gritty earth.

"I thought the Gobi would have soft sand," Trudy murmured.

"In some weeks the wind blows loose sand away." Ye responded.

Jim took several steps toward the camels. He turned to us and said, "*Hao le ma?*" Are you ready? "I am ready to ride a camel, a *luòtuó*."

The white camel let out a loud rumbling grunt, and we all laughed.

"Do you think the camel was impressed that you know how to say camel in Chinese?" Danielle asked Jim.

The Mongolian cowboys smiled at him and the oldest looking one came over to greet us. All the camel handlers stepped forward but the one with the lead rope on the white camel gave a tug on its lead rope. We saw the animal yank back then stand tall. Heavy-lidded eyes and drooping lower lip had curves that seemed to say, Are you ready for me?

"They brought nine camels," Ye said. "Enough for all of us and one for the lead guide."

Jim walked closer to the camels. The men smiled and motioned for Jim to continue. The camel near Jim was tapped with a walking stick at the knees. It bent its front legs and rested leaning down and forward. A man lifted Jim onto the saddle between the humps. A tap on the camel's side caused it to rise to its full height. Jim laughed with delight.

"This is the best!"

"*Luòtuó*." Jim said again and grinned at us from his high and secure seat.

"Say that again please, the word for camel," Trudy asked.

Ye spoke more slowly. "First syllable, low, say it

abruptly, downturn in the voice. *Twah*, for the second syllable sounded like it was rising. *Low twah. Luòtuó.*"

One of the Mongolian cowboys brought a camel for Danielle. Another man brought a free-standing set of wooden steps. Danielle easily used the steps placed on the left side of the camel. From the highest step she easily took a seat on the padded leather saddle.

Now the man who had helped Jim get on the camel connected the rope leads of the two animals. Apparently, we would all have ropes connecting our camels for a ride out into the Gobi. We could also see that the men only had four saddles. Some of us would ride with thick blankets instead of saddles.

Beyond all the camels, a man rode up on a horse. He looked like a cowboy from his boots, jeans, long sleeved shirt, and wide-brimmed hat. The horse he rode, dun in color, was stocky and muscular. It had a summer coat. To survive winters in this region, animals would have extremely heavy winter coats but shed those for the summer. The dun horse looked like horses I had seen in pictures of horseback-riding events at Mongolian festivals. The rider and horse looked well-suited to one another, strong, and ready to move in a moment.

An odd noise drew our attention. One of the nine camels made a complaint in a rumbling noise, then a sudden deep bellow. Which one made the sound? The white one.

Ye explained, "They brought enough camels for the number of people in our group, including the administrators, and for one of the men from the camel farm. That man will ride a lead camel for our trek farther into the desert today."

I touched the side of a camel near me. The camel's tight wool also felt like a light summer coat. More noises came from the camel with the white wool. Some were high pitched.

Jim asked, "Ye, how do you say, naughty?"

"*Táoqì.*"

"Say that clearly and slowly again for me," Trudy asked.

Ye said it with breaks between the sounds for us. "*tou chee lowtwah.*"

"Naughty camel is *táoqì luòtuó?*"

"Yes."

Jim turned and with a big smile called to me, "Ms. Virginia, who gets to ride *the táoqì luòtuó?*"

Chapter 21

Camel Riding, Town Exploring, and Surprising Information

I didn't answer Jim immediately because the white camel continued to pull against the rope the handler held. Its bellow sounded like a mix between warning and fear. Another man attached a second rope to the white camel. They laughed more than they frowned at the white camel's resistant behavior.

A man placed the same wooden steps Danielle had used in front of me. I stepped quickly to get into place on a heavy blanket the man had placed between the two humps on the tan camel's back.

Trudy followed what I had done as the steps were moved to another one of the tan camels. Principal Chimeg was next. Trudy and Principal Chimeg had saddles. Then VP Guo settled onto a thick blanket between the humps of the camel he would ride.

Virginia on a Bactrian camel in the Gobi.

Only I wore a skirt. It was a long skirt of light comfortable fabric. My first summer working for Amity convinced me that skirts provided practical advantages. They were cool and did not have to touch the ground or floor when I used a toilet.

Everyone else today wore trousers or shorts. The camel handlers ran out of blankets. Not that one would have stayed on the white camel that moved erratically, pulling the handlers one way, then the other. And one person had waited for everyone else to get settled on a camel. Now that person would indeed get to ride the naughty camel.

Jim shouted, "Mister Jerry! You get the naughty camel!"

Jerry on the naughty camel, on, off, and on again.

After Jerry was seated, the camel lurched up so suddenly I feared he'd be launched onto the solid packed sand. The camel dropped forward fast, hindquarters in the air. Jerry gave one startled yell as he held on tight to the front hump. "Whoa!" he shouted. I had no clue if even camels owned by English speakers knew that command.

The Mongolian men holding ropes on the camel signaled Jerry to slide off. He did. The rest of us watched. One man held the nose ring rope tight. He turned the camel around in a tight circle twice. Then motioned for Jerry to climb back onto the animal.

Jerry had only been on a couple of horses over the years since we had met. I like riding horses, so sometimes he went on a trail ride with me when we were on vacation. He didn't find horseback riding comfortable. Now here he was with the least docile camel and no saddle. He would just have to hold tight to the front hump, lean firmly against the back hump, and trust the man who still held tightly to the rope.

I glanced quickly around our group. Trudy looked most

concerned. Danielle's expression seemed to ask, *Is this really happening?*

Ye frowned. So did our hosts. Jim looked like he didn't know whether to shout encouragement or laugh.

The camel tried once more to rid itself of the rider by jumping straight up. Jerry gave a short shout, but he stayed on. No one else shouted anything because we didn't want to upset any other animals. Jim's eyes were wide. The short Mongolian man pulled the rope in an abrupt motion. He talked to the camel in a scolding burst of words. The white camel stood still. The other man closest to the white camel said something.

Ye translated, "He said you have the youngest camel, Mr. Jerry."

Somehow with talking, scolding, and rope pulls, the white camel stayed settled. Jerry stayed seated between the humps, and the camel was securely attached to the end of our line. Jerry would be last in our caravan.

That older man who had supervised Jerry stayed closest to the white camel, walked along beside it for a part of the journey out. I glanced back often, thankful for my calm camel, but soon felt more relaxed into the rhythm of the ride.

We went around the hill that had prevented us from seeing the camel farm. The man who had walked along beside the white camel left us when the camel farm was in sight. He waved at us as he disappeared over a dune, but we saw him eventually on the flat ground near the farm buildings and pens. We didn't see any other camels at the farm, but pens held plenty of goats and some sheep.

The man on the lead camel occasionally looked back at the rest of us. He seemed at ease with how we rode. The Mongolian cowboy rode alongside our line of camels.

Whether his nearness was as a guide or a threat to the camels, they walked docilely along.

Farther out, dunes varied in height as if the wind had shaped them playfully with no intent of any set pattern. Sometimes we saw stretches of rock ridges. Once we crested a dune and saw a small lake. I thought it must be an oasis but none of the animals seemed interested.

"That water is no good," Ye told us.

Soon we made a wide turn and started the return journey. The temperature rose as we rode along. I leaned back against the hump behind me. This seat seemed secure enough to relax my grip on the hump in front of me. I knew camel's humps were made of fat, their energy source in case they had to go a long time without food. Their coats and faces looked healthy too. I especially liked studying their eyes with heavy lids and long thick lashes.

Even the naughty camel continued to behave on the return trip. I wondered if the man on the horse continued moving up and down the line with a purpose of affecting that young camel's behavior. He rode beside our line until we came to the place where our van was parked. He waved at us and said something we learned later was goodbye and good luck in the Mongolian language. When we watched him ride away, I thought of how people watched the Lone Ranger ride away.

Jim stayed close to the two remaining handlers who would take the camels back to the ranch. "Mom, can we get one of these? A real Bactrian camel?"

Danielle laughed. "I'll check zoning laws when we get home."

The camel handlers gave Jim a pat on his back and gently touched his sun-bleached hair. Jim's hair seemed brighter blonde now from all the days he had been spending out in the sunshine at the park and at the school. His skin was a sun-kissed golden tan, and his eyes looked a brighter blue. Chinese and Mongolian people always stared at him, but Jim just stared back, smiled, and sometimes spoke to them in Chinese. That always made people smile.

Then the men spoke to Principal Chimeg. Ye said, "They say Jim is a good boy. They touched his hair hoping its gold will bring them good luck."

Their action made me think of how much I wished to settle whatever the unfinished longing was in me. We humans could willingly reach out for something that might help us. Even when our longings were different, we had hope in common.

On the way back to the town, Ye explained that rules for the autonomous region prescribed specific areas where people could go as tourists when there were no paved roads. It didn't matter if people went in vehicles, on horses, donkeys, camels, or walking. Even the farms, like the one we had seen, had government rules to follow about where they could put a building, how big the pens could be, what kind of animals they could have, how many animals they could have, and activities they could do.

Perhaps we felt tired from the heat, from the long empty road on the way back to town, from camel riding. It seemed like we were nearly napping when Jim spoke up.

"You know something we didn't see in the Gobi?"

"What?' Danielle asked.

"Poisonous snakes and scorpions."

"Does the Gobi have those?" Trudy asked Ye.

"Yes. Gobi Pit Vipers are venomous, and Chinese scorpions exist in the sand and under rocks."

We stared at him, and I said, "You didn't think to tell us this before we went out there with no boots? I saw all the men who assisted on the camel ride had some kind of boots."

"It is my tact," he said.

Our laughter sounded nervous and was stirred by the challenges of trust and communication on this Saturday field trip. What a variety of experiences we'd had from tastes to tennis to the *táoqì luòtuó* in this first full week.

* * *

Yawns emerged from all of us during lunch. In the walk back to the hotel, naps and plans for later in the day emerged. The trip into the desert and camel riding had been super, but it tired us more than we expected. Even Jim said he liked naps here, but he never took naps at home.

"That's true," Danielle said. "He even gave up naps early as a baby. Once he could walk there was no more napping unless he played so hard that he just fell down somewhere and slept for a few minutes. He'd get up and be active again until bedtime."

Jim and Ye made plans to meet after an hour's rest. They would go to the park or explore another section of the city. Jim, on his scooter, and Ye walking near him. I often wondered what our experience would have been like if Gladys had stayed as our translator. Jim would have had Sally as a companion, but would he have had the chance to spend so much time at the town square and with other children?

Jerry and I slept longer than an hour this afternoon. When we got up, we made tea in our little kitchen. We'd share some with Trudy and Danielle. While we enjoyed relaxing with the tea, I mentioned, "I really want to visit Wuhai, the city where I was in 2004. I told my hosts and students that if I ever came back to China, I would bring my husband to meet them. Since no weekend field trips were planned here, I think Jerry and I could take a bus to Wuhai for a weekend. Do you want to go with us?"

"Truthfully, I wouldn't mind a totally lazy weekend. Jim and I would stay here. I have never enjoyed bus rides."

"I'll stay with Danielle and Jim. You two should be free to just think about time with your Wuhai friends."

"I'll ask Ye to talk to Principal Chimeg then about Jerry and me going to Wuhai for a weekend. It would be on our third weekend here since they have planned the Helan Mountain trip for next weekend. The fourth weekend we leave Saturday morning to go to Shanghai for the debriefing days. I will let Principal Chimeg know you three will be happy to have a weekend on your own. You'll go to the little church on Sunday?"

"Sure. They are sweet people, very welcoming," Danielle said.

Trudy added, "I have some students who have said they could go and be translators tomorrow. I think they're curious."

"That's great Trudy." I was happy to hear that some students might go along as translators.

Jerry said, "Let's finish reviewing plans for this coming week, and go out and explore everything that surrounds the town square."

* * *

While we walked on the sidewalk across from the town square, we saw Jim and Ye having fun and conversation with local young people. The Left Banner did not have any kind of shopping mall in this year of 2006. The stores surrounding the town square were small but in the evening people of all ages took walks around and through the square.

Some tiny food shops specialized in Mongolian snacks: *khuushuur, boortsog, aaruul, buzz, huushuur,* and chocolates. In some places, tiny shops had just a couple of specialties such as pine nuts and fried dough. We saw stores that sold only bottled beverages or milk products. There were everyday retail shops, a pharmacy, a couple of banks, home goods, souvenirs, electronics, a video store, small grocery stores, and a tobacco shop. But no place sold items tourists would buy as souvenirs. Tourists had not yet visited this Left Banner.

We went into a hole-in-the-wall video store that shocked Trudy and Danielle. I had told Jerry what kinds of videos appeared in China, all the worst. If something special like *Titanic* was offered, it was pirated and poor quality. Famous films would run for a short time and then show portions of another movie not advertised on the box.

The gross horror movies, C and D movies from our country embarrassed us. Did the people here really like such bloody gore? B, C, and D television crime shows gave such awful impressions of people, life, and entertainment in the United States.

"Ick, I am glad to get out of that store," Trudy said as we stepped back into the sundown light over the park.

"I saw the same awful selection in 2004 in video stores, and not just in rural places. If you go in the video stores in the cities, you see the same selection."

We walked to the park and spread out so people would feel free to approach us to practice English. The park proved to be the best place for casual English corners any time we were willing to go and spend time there. Since people of different ages gathered so quickly, we decided to keep the English corners spontaneous and public.

This time of casual conversation bridged cultures well and helped us connect to Left Banner residents as friends. When some of our students came, conversation had more depth in English and even people who knew little English stayed to watch and listen. Parents of the young people who talked to us evidenced pride that their children could have conversations in English with the first Americans to visit their town.

We thanked the people for talking with us and told them we hoped we would meet and talk again. Any time they saw us we would welcome conversation with them. People dispersed slowly going toward another activity or their homes in the comfortable evening air. The temperature was already below eighty Fahrenheit, twenty-six Celsius. Jim rode his scooter next to us rather than ahead as we walked back to the hotel.

* * *

That night, back in our suite, I thanked Ye again for the help he gave us each day.

"We should be paying you double the translator fee. You are constantly working with us and for us. We appreciate you, and your companionship for Jim is invaluable. We laughed about you deciding to tactfully not tell us about scary dangerous desert creatures, but we know you look out for us in many ways."

"Ms. Virginia, I think about your safety, but you believe it is God who protects you?"

"Yes, Jerry and I both think God protects us."

Ye was quiet, as if he could not understand my appreci-

Virginia Heslinga

ation and compliment to him if it was God who was making sure we were safe. What could I say?

"Ye, we believe that on this earth, people can live as the hands and feet of God, that God uses people to accomplish his plans. Ask anyone on this team, and they will tell you that we think God sent you here to help us."

"Even if I do not believe in your God?"

"Even then."

Ye nodded but said nothing except, "We should rest. Mr. Jerry and I will still get up early to take our walk."

Chapter 22

Within Silk Threads

Jerry can fall asleep in two minutes. I stay awake thinking over the day, the next day, wondering, reflecting, and praying. This Saturday night I stayed awake wondering if our openness with Ye was too comprehensive. Had we allowed too much responsibility to fall on him? Did it come from believing God provided this outstanding young person as a help, that Ye in our lives was a God-incidence rather than a coincidence? Did it add tension to the choices Ye had before him?

Over my decades of teaching, I had found some students stood out in a way that attached to my heart and prayers. Ye was one of those people. Ye still checked email each day for news of his test scores. No news yet, just silence and suspense. I do not like real life suspense. In books and movies I enjoyed suspense, but not when it came to events or actions that could affect my life or that of someone I loved. Had we entangled Ye too much with our project and purposes?

If God brought Ye into our lives to help us through the SEP, had God brought us into Ye's life to help him through what was his unknown future? Ye and Jerry, my dear husband with little tact, would definitely have serious conversation on their Sunday morning walk.

* * *

I made sure to be up when I thought Jerry and Ye would arrive back from their walk. The door opened, and it was just Jerry.

"Where's Ye?"

"He went to the Internet Café to look for test score information again."

"Did you continue last night's conversation?"

"Yes, and it was good to talk. Maybe later, when you and I take a walk, I can tell you more. Ye is a smart thoughtful young man."

Jerry went to shower and get ready for the day. I knew we would be with all the team now until after church, but hopefully we could take a walk on our own and talk sometime in the afternoon. My team was still thinking about snakes and scorpions when we went to breakfast.

"I thought I might dream about vipers," Trudy said with a smile. "But I didn't."

"I didn't either," Jim said, "but I had a dream about riding a camel to school, my school back in Massachusetts."

Danielle laughed, "I can tell we're going to be discussing camels for a long time."

Our usual breakfast in this restaurant had a few choices each day. We enjoyed the steamed *baozi*, dim sum, and a drink made of soybean milk. Some mornings the restaurant served fried dough sticks, *youtiao*. Jerry thought these were as delicious as donuts, but he missed regular milk.

We walked to the little church. Ye sat between Jim and

Jerry and translated for them. A young teacher from my homeroom class, Anu, appeared at the church. She was staying in town because her home and school were farthest away of anyone in the program. She lived near the spot where the country of Mongolia, the China province of Gansu, and the province of Inner Mongolia touched one another.

Anu, petite and cheerful, caused me to wonder how growing up in a land of extreme climate changes, in a small village, low in population, and with hardly any modern development had contributed to her happy nature. In our class, she asked the most questions. She also arrived at least twenty minutes early for each of our sessions. Though her spoken English had grammar errors, she adjusted quickly. I thought she was smart and brave. I wondered if she might be a person with whom I could stay in contact over the miles and months. Anu had a positive energy and a voracious desire to learn about the cultures of English-speaking countries.

"Ms. Virginia, I wanted to help translating for you today."

"Anu, that's wonderful. Thank you. Yes. We would be happy to have your help. Sit between Danielle and Trudy. You can help them find the text in their Bibles, and I will be able to listen to you, too."

Trudy also had a student show up, Liza. She sat between Trudy and Danielle. Anu sat between Danielle and me. Having three translators made it easy for us to follow along through announcements, Scripture reading, and the female pastor's sermon. For the Scripture reading, since few people even had a portion of the Bible, a young adult read loudly and clearly a line from a verse, and the people repeated that line.

"I could learn more Chinese with this repetition," Danielle whispered, "though not as fast as Jim is learning it. He has actual short conversations with people in town."

Our translators were surprised when we sang along with two of the hymns. We sang in English while everyone around us sang in Mandarin. We had long known most of the words to "What a Friend We Have in Jesus," and "Trust and Obey."

As I had seen in my first trip to China after the purchase of a Bible printed in Nanjing, people were fascinated by the leather covered Bible. The Bibles we each purchased were in Chinese and English, a revised English, not the old King James version. It had two attached satin bookmarks, labeled thumb guides marking each book of the Bible, and maps and diagrams in the back pages.

Places where anyone could purchase a Bible were just as rare in 2006 as they had been in 2004. Books like a Bible were extra expensive to discourage their purchase. In 2004, when we had the class parties at the end of the SEP, the Bible was placed with the items the teachers could choose as prizes. Giving students an option to choose a Bible at the conclusion of our time was a good idea because many of them were curious about this book of the Christian faith.

I invited Anu and Liza to join us for lunch. How much she understood of our chatter as we walked along, I didn't know. We talked faster when we were on our own than when in front of our classes.

We did not have to pay for Anu or Liza to have lunch with us. Principal Chimeg had given the restaurant instructions to serve our party whether there were two of us or ten of us. She wanted to make sure we felt at ease inviting someone to join us.

Over lunch we discussed how much government guidelines influenced what schools taught. Anu and Liza said we should have these discussions in our classes too. They wanted to know how our classes were supervised in the United States. Who studied our lesson plans? Who chose textbooks? Who supervised classrooms?

I'd been told every school in China had a person who supervised content of the classes for how it aligned with what the government wanted in its schools. Whether they had attended college or not, and in rural locations some teachers of English had not gone to college, everyone knew that government approval guided curricula and practices. Amity wanted us to respect national and local expectations.

After lunch we said goodbye to Anu and Liza. Ye and Jim set off for the town square. Danielle and Trudy wanted to go to their rooms to work on lessons for the week. Jerry and I realized now we could take our walk. We held hands while we talked.

I learned that Ye had many questions about how an intelligent person could choose to believe in God. He wanted to know if Christians respected science. He wanted to hear when and how Jerry chose to believe in God. Ye had asked how Jerry let the belief in the Christian God affect his daily thoughts and actions. He asked about the attributes of the Christian God and Jerry talked with him about the attributes of Jesus.

"I am glad you already had the habit of taking walks before this came up." I said.

"Ye asks questions very freely when we are out walking. We probably will never know what he thinks of everything we discussed. We both ask questions of each other's ideas and beliefs. I learned more about what he knows of Buddhism and Daoism. He thinks maybe his father's parents were Daoist but doesn't know. His mother's mother was Buddhist."

"Does he have curiosity about faith in God?"

"Near the end of our walk, I did ask if he would like to know how a person could become a Christian. He said he was interested to learn how that happened for me, so I told him my personal story. I also told him some people describe their faith as being a follower of Jesus instead of using Christian as a label. He seemed surprised when I told him a person could become a believer even with doubts. I hope I communicated that we learn and mature in faith just like we do in other areas. God knows our needs, accepts doubts, and will respond."

Jerry and I had made a loop that went back to the hotel. Outside the hotel, Jerry told me, "Ye stopped and stood facing me. He thanked me for telling him my personal beliefs, for the instruction and discussion. That was the way our faith conversation ended. He said he was going to go to the internet café to check his email before we met for breakfast."

* * *

Our late afternoon meeting on Sunday had a relaxed companionship. Now, we began with prayer, then started reviewing the pluses and minuses of class activities in our first full week. The small victories of the week helped encourage us as we made detailed plans for week two.

We still would start the day with music. Our students would know all four simple theme songs soon. Using the Amity textbook every morning gave solid content and activities for advancing English skills. In the afternoons, we would continue giving our special area presentations.

Mine included holidays, special events through the year, famous educators, plus songs and games that would include American Sign Language. Danielle's talked about sports and hobbies, and since she also was active in the Parent Teacher Association, she could also talk to them about what the schools in our community offered and required of students, parents, and teachers. Our students had constant curiosity about comparing details of our culture to theirs.

Trudy talked about health practices and expectations from the birth of a baby to taking care of elders who had no family or friends to take care of them. Jerry led the classes in conversations about sports, geography, current events, and travel. He would also teach them the game, Password. That game provided super practice with vocabulary, and he started with simple words. The class enjoyed listening to the clues a participant used in the back and forth choices of words, and each round caused some laughter.

For the weekly gathering of all the classes in the auditorium, we had movies. *Eight Below* would take everyone to Antarctica and focus on amazing dogs. The people of Inner Mongolia valued their dogs as companions, protectors, and guides.

We also had the movie, *Christmas with the Kranks*. That too sparked conversations about family traditions, relationships, and holidays in both cultures. Our students wanted to hear how we decorated our houses at Christmas time, what we ate, what we gave as gifts, and how we celebrated with family. Any holiday stirred many questions; usually to know how we personally celebrated the holiday.

For the last week, we had decided to include role play presentations around acting out a traditional western wedding ceremony and a Thanksgiving dinner. We'd involve our students as much as we could in the roles and have as many props as possible. Most of our students seemed to enjoy role play as much as singing.

"Some days I still get nervous, but our students are wonderful. I am really glad to do this work," Trudy said. Each of us shared something encouraging from our first week.

Danielle said, "Even though the first day, seeing the classrooms in poor condition, losing our translator, was upsetting, I feel like I'm in a good rhythm now with each group. I really like my homeroom class. I'm glad to start each day with them, plus they have been asking if we are going to teach them baseball. They saw Jim and Ye practicing with the wiffle ball and bat."

"I think you can introduce baseball this week. Aren't you planning to do a lesson on baseball idioms, Jerry?"

"Yes. The Amity notes remind us that idioms are a major part of English study."

"Jerry, you should teach them to sing, "Take Me Out to the Ball Game." You have a great voice, and so do our students," Trudy added. "We should share song ideas that come up because the students do relax when they sing in English. I have a bunch of health sayings and children's songs I'll be using."

"I'm going to use "There Was an Old Woman Who Swallowed a Fly." I said, "The lines are repetitive and have humor. Students will see that each creature she swallows gets larger, and they can use that concept with their students to build comprehension and vocabulary choices. They can substitute other creatures as long as each one is larger, plus it has a surprise ending. My students, like students in our country, say learning stopped being fun when they got to middle school. I'm glad if we can give them something enjoyable every day.

"Speaking of enjoyable," Danielle said, "Do you think we might be asked to play tennis again?" Danielle asked.

"Sure, it's possible. Would you want to?"

"I would. When I'm on a tennis court playing singles or doubles, I feel comfortable and focused. Sports have always relaxed me."

A sharp knock on the door broke the relaxation of our review. Who could it be? Jim and Ye would just have entered. We sat still except for Jerry rising to go to the door. He opened it, and we saw VP Guo. He looked around the room and did not see Ye. His concern was obvious.

"Ye is out with Jim." I said. I hoped he could understand that simple sentence.

"*Duìbùqǐ,*" he said. I knew that meant sorry. He started to turn to leave. Behind him we heard Jim and Ye coming from the staircase. VP Guo turned and walked back into our living room. Jim and Ye entered right behind him. They both smiled at the vice principal.

VP Guo greeted them but immediately talked rapidly to Ye. I saw seriousness become obvious on Ye's face.

Dear Lord, now what? Just when I thought we had settled into a good plan and pace, something had disturbed VP Guo. I couldn't think of a good reason why the vice principal's rush of words and tone would so quickly move our translator from a happy young man to a concerned adult. Had we entrusted too much to Ye?

Chapter 23

Waterlines, Shifting Ground, and Mountains Ahead

The news Sunday evening was that the Middle School where we held classes would have some major work on pipes and structure done this week. Administrators expected the work would be finished in two days, but VP Guo's words on the timing lacked conviction. The SEP classes would continue, but tomorrow morning we would go to another building at a local college building. A few blocks from the junior middle school where we held classes, a university had one building as a branch in the Left Banner.

"Your students will find out in the morning when they arrive." VP Guo added.

"When should we move our materials?" I asked.

"The university rooms are locked," VP Guo added. "You will meet in one large room, like our auditorium and share your teaching time. Take turns. Perhaps you can have some rest more than on other days." After a nod and quick, "*zai jian*," VP Guo left.

While we stood like dumbstruck clods, Ye added, "VP

Guo told me to escort you in the morning. Students will find you, but some may be late."

We shared new ideas for our collaborative teaching and were about to part for the night when another knock came on our door. Ye opened it and saw one of our usually cheerful desk girls standing there, unsmiling. Another problem right here where we lived.

Repairs in town she said, repairs created problems in many sections of the town, and in the hotel. We would not have water from faucets or shower heads for two or three days. The hotel would deliver double the amount of thermoses filled with boiled water. The restaurant was not on the same water system. It would be safe to have meals there and they would give us bottled water or bottles of tea, whichever we preferred.

* * *

I thought the university room looked like a very plain lecture hall with not many rows of auditorium seats. Jerry offered to help the custodians who brought in folding chairs, but Ye told him it was not necessary. To preserve 'face' the school had to help us with the essentials.

Somehow the news spread. We started class only thirty minutes late, but the room was filled to capacity. This room had air-conditioning that groaned as it worked to overcome the heat of the day.

The team rotated short bursts of textbook instruction, language games, and we sang every class theme song. Trudy led stretches and isometric exercises. Our students taught us the eye exercises they did in their classes each school day. Their exercises with facial acupoints relaxed eye muscles.

Students do so much close work, they need to reduce eye strain.

These exercises came from ancient practices of traditional Chinese medicine. These exercises are supposed to protect vision by stimulating blood circulation around the eyes, relaxing eye muscles, and reducing eye strain. The Chinese government has promoted these eye exercises for over sixty years to prevent myopia in children. Eye exercises are a habit among Chinese primary and secondary school students yet myopia continues to increase.

We adapted to the change, but I felt tension wondering if this would last longer than a couple of days. If anyone else on my team had this concern, they didn't show it.

At lunch Jim asked if he and Ye could go to the town square for the afternoon.

I saw Danielle hesitate, but she knew if Jim was with Ye, he would be safe. She agreed.

The afternoon rest time passed quickly. Back in the auditorium we settled into our mishmash of activities. Students did not complain. They gave attention and effort to every task and practiced listening and speaking in partner and small group activities.

Students left with sighs at six. We had tried to make the hours a mix of sight, sound, motion, and written activities. At the end of the day only Solomon lingered. He was our tallest student with a look of a young Mongolian warrior, the gait of a heron, and the eldest son of a camel rancher. Solomon approached Jerry and asked, "Will we learn baseball tomorrow?"

"If they allow us to use the center area at the middle school. It's big enough to practice the game."

Solomon said, "Jim showed me and Ye how to toss the whiffle ball and hit it. I have been practicing."

Jerry put his hand on Solomon's shoulder and said, "I hope you hit a home run."

We were talking to one another as we left the university grounds and did not notice immediately when a large black car pulled up alongside us. It stopped. A driver in a short sleeved white shirt and dark trousers stepped out. "Hotel ride," he said.

The old distrusting me, the one who kept people at a distance felt shocked as we smiled and got into the car. My warm-hearted team thought this a wonderful surprise, but I questioned what was shifting in me to feel oddly at ease with this.

Life was different here. With all the construction, I saw thick dust in the streets where work continued on the pipes. But there was no caution tape around the open trenches as there would have been at home.

At the hotel, the promised multiple thermoses were waiting. Not even minutes after we returned, Jim and Ye showed up.

"The superintendent sent someone to find me." Ye told us. "He would like to play tennis again this afternoon if Ms. Danielle and Mr. Jerry feel they can do that after a full day of teaching."

Danielle and Jerry agreed. They would change quickly for the rematch with the superintendent. Jim went along again to be their cheering section, and Ye to help with translating.

Trudy and I took naps. Although the auditorium room had been air-conditioned, the changes and effort to be even more lively and entertaining in teaching tired us. It felt good to relax having made it successfully through the day. I don't think we would have slept if we knew how many more unexpected changes were ahead.

* * *

Before we learned how Jerry and Danielle did in playing tennis, Ye told us, "The school has arranged a trip to Helan Mountains for this Saturday. The superintendent was happy to give you this news."

I nodded, but Trudy spoke up, "You can tell us about that after you tell us who won the tennis games."

"They split again," Jim added. To Ye he said, "Are there bears in the mountains?"

"Not aggressive ones," Ye responded. "If people stay on the paths, there is no danger." We adults stood still and quiet. Jim continued probing. "Wolves? Are there wolves? I know wolves are important in stories in Nei Menggu."

"Wolves avoid people. Bears too." Ye said. "More difficult are the ticks. The mountains have many ticks, but the school will probably give you some repellent."

"So now you're letting us know all the dangers ahead of time?" Danielle asked. "Do they have poisonous plants?"

"Some that are bad for animals, but I don't think so for people. Mosquitos at night but we will be on a day trip. We will be back in the Left Banner before dark."

"Are the paths dirt and rocks, like a hiking trail?" Jim asked.

"Most paths have a pressed hard surface, some sections have black top, and there are stairs up the steepest part of the high mountain."

"Stairs? Up to a mountain top?"

"Yes, but only from the west side, a more gradual slope. The mountains are not like those in the Gobi. They are old with thick forests. I went there as a child with my father. We went to the top of the mountain. It will be good to see it again, with you."

* * *

"I'm glad I was in the classes today. They were mostly fun. When I got bored, I had the Chinese workbooks to do." Jim told us before we started to eat our supper. Ye looked happy.

"I loved the way all the students participated in the activities. They are patient, listen well, and enter in with such enthusiasm." Trudy added.

"I love to hear their singing," Danielle said, and I agreed.

"They don't realize how they naturally harmonize." Jerry said.

"I am thankful for all of you. For an unexpected day, it was a good day. Let's pray." Keeping hands low around our round table, we held hands. We didn't bow our heads. We looked at one another. Jerry said conversationally, "Thank you Lord for your help this day and for this food. Amen."

Chapter 24

Classes, Baseball, Day Trip, and Stones

I n the evening on Tuesday, any teachers interested in learning basics of baseball met on the grounds of the middle school. Jerry and Jim showed them how to create the lines and bases. They also helped our students to learn about the players and positions on a team. Everyone had an opportunity to try tossing up the wiffle ball and trying to hit it with the large plastic wiffle bat. Then they had the experience of receiving a pitch. Jerry and Jim took turns as pitchers.

It was no real surprise to us that on Wednesday we had to still meet in the university. We did learn that on Thursday we would probably be back at the middle school. At the end of the day, Solomon asked Jerry. "Tomorrow, we will play a baseball game?"

"Yes, Solomon. That's the plan." Jerry answered.

"Thank you, Mr. Jerry. Goodbye." Solomon's long strides took him in the direction of the town center.

Back at the hotel, we realized the water outage had dragged into its third day. Danielle joked that if we ran out of water, we could just go move into one of the luxury private dining rooms upstairs in the restaurant. Ye and Jim played a game on Jim's handheld Nintendo Lite while they waited for Jerry. They would soon leave for the school to meet whatever students showed up for baseball.

We all felt thankful to have air-conditioning. Outside heat wrapped us like an unwanted hooded poncho. I couldn't believe our students, Jerry, Jim, and Ye were excited to play baseball this evening, but they were. Hopefully, no one would collapse from heatstroke. Trudy and I stayed at the hotel to work on class plans for the next week. After an hour, Trudy said, "I need to take a nap. I'll be back in a little while."

With the rare time alone, I clasped my hands and prayed for continued health and abilities to serve well in this SEP. I said, "I place my team and our plans in your hands. I can't keep everyone healthy and guarantee success with students. In your mercy, help us to touch lives in positive ways."

I never liked feeling helpless or dependent. It was important to do research, to have answers. Being in this foreign culture so far from the familiar rhythms and options of home took away any layers of illusions I had about control. I had not come to China to feel less control, but I had to face that I was not in charge here. I had the title of team leader and the most experience in teaching, but I realized I faced lessons in being dependent on God, my team, our hosts, students, and this community. Could accepting dependence be a crucial lesson in the understanding of layers of myself?

My team didn't know how I felt, nor did Ye. Only Jerry knew how I struggled with being vulnerable, with not having a clear picture and control. I could face waiting for something I really wanted. Delayed gratification had been a lesson my father ingrained deliberately for anything my brother or I wanted. So waiting I could accept but not surrender. Each day, activities, interactions, and waiting to see more, to learn more, to understand more squeezed me into feeling as if I was being reshaped.

* * *

"You should have seen them running those beanbag bases!" Jim burst into our living room looking like an alien creature covered with dust and sweat, red faced, his blonde hair darkened to honey by sweat. "Mr. Jerry had them act out some plays and practice positions of where to run and where to stand. Some of the ladies in your classes still had their shoes with heels on! How could they think they could play baseball in heels, even if they weren't high heels? Anu didn't wear heels. She was ready with some good gym shoes. She's little and fast."

Jerry looked only slightly less sweat covered than Jim. Jerry looked happy when he told us, "Solomon made the first home run. He hit the wiffle ball farther than I guessed a wiffle ball could go."

Like a little sportscaster, Jim added, "All the students there shouted at him to keep running, first base! Second base! Third base! Home! Run home! And guess what? Anu hit a double. She probably could run fast even if she had shoes with heels!"

They were both so energized by the baseball interactions that consciousness of the water limitations didn't bother them. Like the rest of us, they would use the tall thermoses of water that had been delivered to our rooms. Baseball teaching and playing stayed as the main topic.

Our whole team could tell the classes enjoyed baseball.

We heard them speaking English with enthusiasm about baseball. We heard them practicing baseball vocabulary and expressions: In the ballpark, out of the ballpark, batting 1000, throw a beanball, a big hitter, big-league, bush league, a brand new ballgame, brush-back, a charley horse, cleanup hitter, closer, cover all the bases, cover one's bases, curveball, double header, down to the last strike, down to the last out, ducks on the pond, extra innings, first base, grand slam, home run, grandstanding, hardball, heavy hitter, hit out of the park, It ain't over till it's over, knocked out of the park, leadoff hitter, left field, major league, minor league, ninth inning, off base, on deck, out of left field, out of one's league, pinch hit, play ball, in a pickle, rain-check, relief pitcher, right off the bat, screwball, shutout, singles, softball, spitball, step up to the plate, strike, strike out, strike out swinging, swing and miss, swing for the fences, switch hitter, third strike, three strikes, touch base(s), triple play, wheelhouse, whiff, a whole new ball game. They applied these accurately.

In the time for conversational English practice, Jerry drew diagrams to teach students the basics of the game. He showed photos of some of the most famous baseball players and explained their outstanding skill. Wednesday, Thursday, and Friday, at 5:30 pm, using the wiffle balls and bat, plus bean bags for bases, Jerry and Jim guided any interested students through the basics of baseball. We were amazed at the women who still had shoes with heels who wanted to take their turn at bat, and if they got a hit, ran with delight to the bases.

* * *

On Saturday morning we left the hotel a few minutes after six to walk to the school. I was surprised Ye did not look more tired because after the full day of his constant help, he had gone to the internet café again very late to check his email. Jerry and I were asleep when he returned.

We arrived at the school at 6:45, and a full-size bus arrived at seven. Our students who had been chosen to go along on the trip to the Helan Mountains were a mix representing the homerooms. The choosing had come through a random lottery selection of names submitted as able to take the day trip. No sense of being superior appeared. They were excited, laughing, carrying snacks, phones, and the ubiquitous tin cannisters filled with water and green tea leaves.

None of this happy gathering was a surprise, but there were two surprises. Principal Chimeg and VP Guo would ride in the typical large black sedan administrators liked to use. It wasn't a surprise to see administrators choose the comfort of a car over that of a big bus, but I felt disappointed not to have more time with the two administrators. They had seemed most approachable in the little school van they shared with us on the ride from Yinchuan to the Left Banner. Ye noticed my quick flash of surprise and a frown.

"There needs to be a car, Ms. Virginia." Ye told me. "If someone gets hurt or ill, they can be taken to help in the car."

"Thank you Ye. I am glad to know they have such a considerate plan." I jumped to conclusions too quickly. Restraining this quick judgment of others stood as another lesson I seemed to need to relearn frequently.

The other surprise arrived in a small gray car. It was Gladys and Sally. Glady's husband dropped them off to join the special day trip. My whole team shouted hello and hurried to welcome them.

After enthusiastic greetings, Gladys said, "Thank you for thinking of me and praying. Your God seems to hear you. My mother-in-law improved more rapidly than anyone expected. She was able to improve enough to come back to the Left Banner with me and Sally. She is comfortable in our home."

Slowly we walked to where the bus students were already boarding. Jim and Sally sat behind the bus driver. Jerry and Ye were across the aisle from them. Danielle and Gladys sat behind the two children. Trudy and I sat behind Jerry and Ye.

I heard Jerry ask, "Ye, when you and your father went to the Helan Mountains, how did you travel there?"

"We took a bus, but it took more hours because we traveled from Wuhai."

The scenery changed over the miles from flat and dry with different levels of dunes and barren mountains to looking more like scrub. New hills developed that had bushes and after more miles and curves we saw the Helan Mountains.

They bristled with spruce forests, lush green on the top with glimpses of rugged peaks. Even wildflowers appeared in some of the grass along the road. The colors could have been a sample palette for greens, deep shades of brown, and hints of purple. The sky was blue with only small white clouds.

The Left Banner, its nearby mini-towns, and outpost stores and farms disappeared as we zoomed south and east over miles. When no view of the desert remained in sight, we saw a turn off the highway that led into a wide parking lot. The bus pulled in and parked with one smooth turn. The driver opened the doors, but no one moved.

Gladys said, "VP Guo will come and speak to us."

VP Guo appeared quickly and stood in front beside the driver. He spoke in Chinese and Gladys translated for us. "This is Guangzong Temple, built by Tibetan Buddhists two or three thousand years ago. It was torn down in the early days of our Revolution but rebuilt in the 1980s. It looks now as it did long ago."

I thought Ye looked quickly at Jerry as VP Guo mentioned the destruction of this temple in the revolutionary changes in China. I expected this time of destruction had come up in the early morning conversations about the Cultural Revolution under Mao, the Red Guard, and the Gang of Four. Their morning walks and discussions would never work in any other environment while we were in China.

People exited the bus with excitement evident in eyes, voice, and motions. Only after we were off the bus and our cheerful students hurried to the temple did I notice Ye had stayed beside Jerry. Jim and Sally dashed off toward the temple following a group of teachers that included Solomon and Anu, the baseball champions. I had noticed that Anu had great energy in her personality and actions. Other students enjoyed her company. I guessed her students would feel the same and be glad to have her as a teacher.

"Let's go," I said to Jerry and Ye. "We'll be the last ones to get to the temple."

I took a step, smiled at them, but stopped after carefully looking at Ye. "What is it, Ye?" I thought of Ye going to the internet café late last night. "Did you get bad news last night?"

A laugh like a falling leaf escaped him. "Good news. I

passed the English test with a high score. I have been given a choice of two top universities."

"That's wonderful!" I said, but at that moment I saw in Ye's dark brown eyes a shimmer of tears. I kept my voice low. "I get tears in my eyes too when I get really good news."

Ye blinked to clear his eyes. "It is sad news too. I must return home to meet with officials, complete registration details, and have an interview with representatives before I make my choice. I will need to leave tomorrow."

"Tomorrow?"

"An appointment Monday morning means I must take the bus on Sunday."

I took Ye's left hand in my right and Jerry's right hand in my left. "We are happy for you, but this is a shock. We will miss you more than words can say." I hoped he believed me.

Ye said, "Don't tell Jim today."

"Good idea. Let's enjoy this day together." Jerry said as we all walked toward the temple. He added, "Jim doesn't fully understand the achievement and effort you put into a year to prepare to retake the exam, Ye. He will know he should be happy for you, but he will miss you."

We had reached the wide rows of steps up to the temple. Ye stopped and said, "Gladys thanked you for talking to God. She thinks the God you pray to heard your prayers and answered them for her. How did you know to ask for her to come back now when I would have to leave?"

"Ask for her, now? No. How could we?" I spoke quickly to Ye. Our students were calling to us to come and see this room, to look at the prayer wheels, to go to the room of the huge Buddha. Their happiness rose like the kites so popular in Chinese culture. They urged us forward, distracting us from this heart wrenching news.

"Ye, we didn't know when you would leave. We have

215

tried not to think about you leaving us. Jim cares about you as a friend and big brother. Living with us, sharing all the experiences, having you with us has been a gift. You were outstanding as a helper in 2004. You're stronger in your skills now."

"Ye, you've done well. You will go far. Your country is fortunate to have a young man like you." Jerry said.

And then students came to surround us. They moved us up onto the main level of the temple carrying us with their excitement, interest, and enthusiasm. We moved through the main hall of Guangzong temple with its inlaid jewels, brass, glazed tiles. The splendor of this restored ancient site barely registered. Of all the sights we saw on this Saturday day trip, the outstanding temple registered the least because we tried to absorb the idea of losing Ye.

I let myself be carried by the momentum but felt like my heart had stayed at the foot of the stairs. Jerry seemed to do the same. We noted the glowing smooth saffron color tiles, prayer flags of blue for sky, white for air, red for fire, green for water, and yellow for earth fluttered along roof lines and surrounding prayer wheels. Silk banners drifted from painted poles and wooden columns in all the rooms we could see. The sight of them fluttering reminded me of waving goodbye.

Our students made sure we went to the great hall to see the massive Buddha on the lotus pedestal. Lamps with golden flames scented with sandalwood stood out amid the prayer wheels. These cylindrical tubes held mantras about merit, karma, and well-being. People would spin the wheel and recite mantras. The largest prayer wheels had a rod to help act as a handle for turning the wheel.

Although the point was to view and appreciate this ancient place of worship, I felt like each step was part of a countdown. Ye would be leaving us and we had two more weeks to work. Gladys's return with Sally pleased Jim, but what would he think when he realized Ye would leave?

We didn't talk as we walked back toward the bus. Our students, Danielle, Trudy, Gladys, Sally, and Jim moved quickly ahead of us, laughing and talking. Outside I kept a pleasant smile on my face. Inside I'd gone still, deep into emotional protective mode. I needed a distraction to avoid tears.

About the time I noticed people going toward a long low building far from the temple but beside the parking lot, I asked, "Is that a toilet?"

"Yes," Gladys answered. "We should use this one. I do not think any we will see for the rest of the day will be in as good condition as this one."

Jim and Sally still stayed together, friends reunited. While I watched them, I wished Jim would turn back, speak to Ye, stay close to him. It didn't happen. Sally's return had pulled his focus in a different direction.

Before we boarded the bus, we thanked Principal Chimeg and VP Guo. The next section of the ride had more curves and ascended. We went around a mountain and were high enough to see a hazy view of Yinchuan in the distance. I looked at Jerry and Ye sitting and staring out the big bus windows. What were they seeing in this moment? What were they thinking?

Again the bus turned into an area for parking, but the size here catered to cars. Parking seemed tighter on this mountain side. Unlike parking at home, no posts or fences surrounded the area that had a steep drop.

VP Guo appeared in the bus again. He told us, "We have stopped to see the rock paintings. Some people think they are only 3,000 years old but other scientists have said they could be 10,000 years old."

**One of many rock paintings on the
Yinchuan side of the Helan Mountains**

Gladys had moved back easily into her role of translator. She hadn't even met Ye before she left. Didn't she wonder about the identity of this young man who sat beside Jerry? Then I thought, she has probably heard all about Ye from Principal Chimeg, VP Guo, and even people in the Left Banner. Ye had traveled daily through town, frequently with Jim as his shadow. I could hardly look at Ye. Pressure behind my eyes made me scrunch my brow and blink.

Everyone exited the bus to go as close as possible to the pictographs. Our students pointed out the human figures, masks, hunting scenes, the round Sun God, and animals. Experiencing these images so close that we could almost reach out to touch them felt like a charge had been laid on us to learn more about the people of this part of the world.

Though my emotions were in conflict, I was thankful not to feel rushed to move along. I sensed a lesson here to stop rushing through each day. Appreciating the action, interactions, surprises, wonders, and even the frustrations that filled the days could combine with staying thankful. That was the healthy outlook for me and the team. I hoped our students and hosts felt this too.

We boarded the bus for our last stop, a picnic lunch and time on the mountain trails back across the border in Nei Menggu. The power and majesty of the Helan mountains as part of the border between the two provinces was only matched by the Yellow River that also marked part of the border. Jim, looking out the windows, announced, "I'm going to the top of the mountain! Are you going to the top too, Ye and Mr. Jerry?" They agreed they would try.

This next parking lot had plenty of space. Beyond the parking area we saw broad patches of grass and trees where picnic tables had enough space for our whole group. The day was clear, and the mountains' green forested beauty appeared like a boast from the hand of the Creator. I never expected such depth of forest growth so close to the Gobi.

We left the bus, and I knew I must continue to hide the sadness I felt. This day should be special for everyone on this trip. I hoped it would be for Ye. What a different mix for him from memories of his trip here as a child with his father to this school trip with a foreign team who had depended on him every day.

I thought about the glowing walls at the temple, of imposing Buddha made of stone, of prayers twirled in wheels, of the ancient messages in rocks we had seen. But what dominated my thoughts now was that Ye would leave us. I would gather thoughts of Ye like smooth round stones, gathered and stacked as special marks of something of sacred value.

Chapter 25

Seen and Unseen Dangers

A park stretched on and up beyond the picnic tables and on all sides of the parking lot. Nothing seemed totally flat here. Thick bushes and grass of different heights and blade shapes also lined the park. I remembered what Ye had told us about ticks and resolved to stay out of the grasses and away from the bushes. Our whole group seemed interested in starting up the path that would go to the top of the mountain rather than picnicking.

I wouldn't have known the kinds of trees, but Danielle did. She pointed out other plants too as we ascended the gradual rise. We came to a narrow gorge, but a solid wooden bridge crossed this. On the other side after maybe a quarter of a mile we came to a picnic area and steps. The steps were stone and went up more steeply than the path.

With alacrity and obvious delight, our students surged forward up the stairs. VP Guo was in their midst. Jerry, Ye, Jim, and Sally were in the lead group. Principal Chimeg lingered. I asked her, "These stairs look like marble slabs on top of rocks." Gladys had stayed beside me.

"They are," she answered.

"Do the steps go all the way to the top?" I asked.

"I have not been to the top, but I think that is true."

"Who puts a staircase of marble and rocks all the way up a mountain?"

"I don't know who decided it, but because of the stairs, even people who cannot climb can go up this mountain."

"Let's go," Danielle said. "I will never get this opportunity again, so I'm going to climb steps until I can't."

Up we all went. Anu had stayed near me. She put her hand on my elbow as if to steady me on the steps, one after the other. My right leg was shorter than my left leg. Stairs could be awkward when I had to walk up or down many in a row. I started counting the steps but views into the woods, out over the scenery distracted me. I had fallen behind Danielle and Trudy.

All I could say for sure is that after at least two hundred steps we came to a rest area. Backless stone benches and a couple of round top stone tables were in the clearings on each side of the stairs.

"Let us continue," Anu encouraged me. "Do not stay here now, Ms. Virginia."

I wanted to sit and rest, but with Anu urging me on, I continued. The stairs were not tall, but when we got to the next clearing, I insisted, "You go on. I'm resting here."

Years before I worked with Amity, I'd been told I would need to have surgery on my knees, total replacements. I had not done any treatment yet, no cortisone or anything else. Now even on low steps, the continuing hundreds of them made me decide not to continue. Going down steps could be as difficult as ascending.

On the bench, I relaxed and took a deep breath of the mountain air. As I tried to absorb the environment, I wondered if Jim and Ye would be the first to the top of the mountain. I thought about these mountains bordering two provinces of northwestern China. All the people with us today spoke at least two languages, so had knowledge of crossing borders in communication. Ye had crossed borders of understanding westerners more than by learning English. His living with us had undoubtedly shown him more than we would know.

Laughter interrupted my meandering thoughts. Female students who had climbed the steps in medium heeled shoes were coming back.

"*Nihao*," I called to them. "Have you been to the top of the mountain?"

They giggled, and one said, "No, Ms. Virginia. It is far."

"Some people are racing to the top," another woman said.

"Who is racing?"

"Mr. Jerry, Ye, Jim, and Sally. They will make it to the top. Anu is trying but is far behind them. She is talking too much to go faster." They laughed. "In English, she is talking."

"I think Sally and Jim will win," another student said.

"We are going to walk down slowly. Would you like to walk with us?"

I stood carefully and stretched. "Yes, thank you."

* * *

Sally and Jim made it to the top of the mountain first. Ye, Solomon, and a few other young men were next. Jerry and Danielle were third and after that no one was so far ahead to stand out as a winner in the race to the top.

Back at the base of the mountain path there were more tables and benches. We had lunch there from baskets the bus driver, Ye, VP Guo, Solomon and some other students carried from the back of the bus to the tables. *Baozi*, spring rolls, dumplings watermelon, kimchi, and in a bowl, beef that had been marinated in chilis, garlic, soy, sesame, and some sugar. They warned Jerry to avoid that dish. He happily heeded the warning. I ate a little and kept watching Ye. He moved with his usual calm, but his eyes flickered over the group as if to memorize everything and everyone.

"What was it like at the top?" I asked.

"The steps kept it from being a hard hike. We could run up the steps," Jerry told me.

"You could. Not me."

"It's steep!" Jim assured me. "There's edges with no rails. You could fall off."

People congratulated Jim and Sally on being first to make it to the top of the mountain. Jim accepted with an enthusiastic *xie xie*. Sally blushed and said little.

By the time the leisurely picnic finished, people were glad the park had a WC. "Why call it a WC?" Trudy asked about the small wooden building that had one entrance for women and one for men. "WC is not a Chinese word or abbreviation."

I explained. "Remember the British had long influence here. In England they say water closet, WC, for toilets."

Jim heard us and asked, "Why water closet? Because people pee there?"

"Not exactly. Early bathrooms had toilets about as big as a closet with a tank of water above the toilet bowl. People pulled a chain, and water ran down into the toilet causing it to flush. There are still toilets like that. Lots of tourists around the world know WC stands for a toilet. I've seen the WC sign in more than a dozen countries."

"Come on," Jerry said to Jim.

"Are you going in first, Mr. Jerry?" That had been our practice in remote WCs. We had Jerry go in first in all the rural places to see the conditions. He would come out and warn us. But now, Ye passed Jerry and went in first. In seconds he was out. "Maybe, Jim and Jerry, you can find a big bush and use the outdoors. This place has poor conditions."

The PRC had more people than jobs, but I had never seen clean toilets in rural areas. In cities and in developed rest stops by tolls, the WCs might appear clean, but rarely did we see sinks for washing hands. Everyone carried their own little packets of toilet paper.

I noticed that the female teachers had wandered in different directions. I went to the WC and pushed open the hinged door to the toilet. There was a dirt floor with a hole in the ground, and of course some people miss the hole. Danielle camped a lot. She'd cope. Trudy as a nurse and non-camper would be appalled, but she'd manage.

As soon as possible, we walked fast and far away from the toilet building. Whatever Sally and Jim had chosen to do, they'd gone in different directions. But now we saw them racing in and out of the picnic tables and benches. They still had so much energy in the late afternoon. They ran to the edge of the parking area near a hill.

Suddenly we did not see Jim. He been in sight, and then he vanished. We heard him shout. Then he gave loud cries. Sally stood at the edge of the bushes as if frozen. Everyone headed toward her and the bushes where Jim had disappeared.

In the next instant Jim leapt into sight still shouting in pain. Sally started to cry. Teachers in our group came from all directions rushing toward the low part of the hill where

Jim now stood streaked with bits of the foliage; a red rash becoming visible on his face, arms, and legs.

Every bit of Jim's skin that was not covered by his T-shirt, shorts, and socks had a rash. It was turning an unnatural angry red. Principal Chimeg, VP Guo, Jerry, Solomon, and Ye rushed to Jim.

Ye took hold of Jim first. He spoke sharply to everyone in Chinese. VP Guo and Solomon ran to get something from the bus. The rest of those near Jim backed away carefully. Ye pulled Jim up and out of the bush. Jerry and Ye brought Jim to the path. All Jim's exposed skin seemed to change to blisters on red patches while we looked at him.

"Oh my God! What is it?" Danielle asked without snatching Jim away from Ye.

Chapter 26

Who Knew?

Sally ran to her mother and clung to her waist, eyes wide with fear. Principal Chimeg called out something to VP Guo. He rushed to the bus and reappeared carrying a First Aid kit and a tall bottle like a gallon size jug.

Jim cried out a sound that mixed pain and embarrassment. He stood on the path with his arms held out away from his body. Jerry stood near him with his hand on Jim's back.

Ye turned to our students and gave some instructions with urgent authority. We saw a half dozen students hurry off toward the higher level of the path. They were looking for something alongside the path in the grass and bushes.

Anu and Solomon were first to hurry back with leaves and bunches of scruffy grass. Others arrived clutching more handfuls of the same two-toned grass. Ye took these and began to rub Jim's face, neck, arms, hands. Then he knelt and using fresh clumps of the grasses rubbed Jim's legs with the plants.

VP Guo also brought bottles of something. Now that Ye

had used the grasses on Jim's skin, VP Guo offered the bottle. Ye opened it. VP Guo took gauze from the first aid kit and gave that to Ye. With the liquid soaked into gauze, Ye wiped over the redness and blisters.

Jim stopped crying, He spoke through gritted teeth when he said, "It stings."

"That is good," Ye told him.

Danielle stepped forward. She sounded calmer now than I felt. "What is it? What did Jim fall into?" Her voice shook with her motherly alarm.

The teachers around us murmured in tones of concern and guesses. Ye told Danielle, "I do not know the English name. It is a plant. I once touched it when I hiked with my father. My hand instantly burned. It itched, and these blisters came out. My father found these grasses, the same as Anu and Solomon have given me. My father rubbed these over the blistered skin. Then he put the medicine on it that Mr. Guo has provided."

Ye wiped that liquid over all the irritated skin on Jim's face, arms, and legs. Trudy asked, "What is the liquid? Alcohol? Calamine?"

Ye said, "I don't know it in English. The itching and burning was fierce. They faded over time. A warm shower will make the blisters shrink, but the feeling of a burn took a few days to disappear. When we get back, I will get a paste to help heal him."

"Baking soda paste? Maybe." Trudy said to Danielle and put an arm around Danielle's shoulders.

It was such an abrupt, scary, ending to an otherwise amazing day. We had started in a place of worship thousands of years old, ancient messages in rocks, gorges, narrow bridges, cliffs, and a stairway to a mountain top. And now a plant that left welts and blisters.

The students started boarding the bus, and VP Guo told Jim he was brave. I felt grateful for these words of theirs and the generosity to us and the students. Our students could not have afforded this trip without the school's help. The admission fees for each of the sites had been paid by the school.

As the students started boarding the bus, Principal Chimeg and VP Guo went to their car. Jim's accident had not required them to use their car as an ambulance. What would they have done if Ye had not known what to do? Yinchuan had the nearest large hospital.

Talk and napping created a low background murmur on the ride back to town. I hoped Jim's misadventure had not spoiled the day for anyone else. Sally sat with Gladys on the ride back so Jim could lean against his mom. Sometimes I heard his sniffles as he tried not to cry.

At the hotel, Ye spoke again with VP Guo. Then told us, "VP Guo knows where to get the paste for Jim. He will bring it soon. Ms. Danielle can put the paste on Jim after he has a shower."

Danielle and Jim stayed in their room during dinner time. We brought their food to them. Ye asked for a container of the strawberry sherbet for Jim. We all went with Ye to see Jim. His smile was good to see as Ye handed him the surprise treat.

"I cannot thank you enough," Danielle said as she gave Ye a hug.

Later that night in the dark of our room, when I snuggled close to Jerry, he whispered. "Tomorrow we will have this suite to ourselves, but we will all miss Ye. I will almost feel guilty having so much space to ourselves here. Some of the teachers described their rented rooms to me and they sound like barely more than cells. I am very thankful Ye could stay with us."

I nodded and said, "Ye has done far more than Gladys could have done. She lives here and has family and school responsibilities here. I am happy for her that her mother-in-law is doing so much better, but Ye is amazing. Who knew his memory of that awful blistering plant when visiting the Helan Mountains as a child would rescue Jim from misery today?"

Jerry laughed softly into my hair, "Who knew Ruby's cousin would find Trudy's bag in Shanghai airport? Who knew the Christian student you met in 2004 would guide us in Beijing for super full days? Who knew it would rain on bone dry earth? Who knew that with the sun and the rain we'd see a rainbow from the Yellow River to the Left Banner? Who knew Ye would arrive to step in when Gladys had to leave? Who knew Ye and Jim would be like brothers? Who knew Gladys could arrive back the day before Ye had to leave? Who knew?" He yawned and laughed. "You do make me laugh. I love you."

I stayed still. His chuckling faded into sleep.

Who knew? I whispered thinking of the answer. Who was I becoming through these multiple God-incidences? I knew that I should try to figure out what events like today taught me, not just about other people, but about me. I expected to stay awake longer thinking and analyzing, but I fell into deep sleep.

Sunday morning, Danielle came to our suite early, a little after six. Jerry and Ye were still out walking.

"I'm going to stay back here with Jim this morning."

"That's fine, Danielle.'

"Jim slept restlessly. Sometimes he cried in his sleep. He's sleeping soundly now."

"What's that about Jim sleeping?" Trudy asked as she joined us. Did that thick paste on his skin help much?'

"Yes, we coated all the area that blistered after he took a shower. He said it felt good. I expect it will dry up the remains of the blisters and the red rash. We have enough to coat his skin again after he gets up."

"We can bring some breakfast back for you two."

"Ok. That will be good. Thanks."

They both started to leave the room, so I spoke up. "Danielle, Trudy, we have big news we didn't tell you yesterday. We wanted Jim and both of you to just enjoy the day. Jerry and I only heard the news from Ye at the start of the day trip."

"What? What is it?"

"Ye is leaving today. He passed his test with a high score and has follow-up interviews and appointments on Monday in Wuhai."

* * *

Four of our students showed up at the church, and they were surprised at the warm welcome they received. They too were escorted to the rows down front where we sat. They spread out among us. It was the easiest access we'd had to translations whispered to us through the service. Ye sat on the end of our row nearest to the center aisle, Jerry to his left.

I thought Ye seemed more remote than he had on other Sundays. Was it because we had enough other translators today? Did it bother him to feel easily replaced? Was he emotionally preparing for his leaving today? Was he bothered by something he'd talked about with Jerry this morning? Who knew?

Walking back to the hotel our quartet, Trudy, Ye, Jerry, and I did not chat as much as usual. I wondered if our thoughts were focused on looking back at these first full weeks with Ye or ahead at the two weeks without him. Inside I felt an alarm not just because he would leave, but because I wondered what his absence would reveal about the whole team.

"Would you like to go to see Jim as soon as we get back?" I asked Ye.

"Yes. I will see him. If he wants to eat in his room during lunch, I can keep him company. I can talk with him. My bus leaves at three."

Back at the hotel, Trudy, Jerry, and I sat in our living room waiting. We prayed for Jim and Ye to find peace with this change, for healing of Jim's skin, for Ye to know he was truly more to us than a translator and helper.

"Jim will eat in his room," Ye said as he stopped in our living room. "I will stay with him. Ms. Danielle will go with you."

"Does he seem better?"

"I think so. He did not cry when I told him I must leave. He stayed quiet."

Jerry said, "Jim will miss you as we all will miss you, but differently. You have been like a big brother to him. He admires you. You and Jim are young enough that you will both travel more in your lives. Maybe you will meet again. Maybe one day you will come to our country."

Danielle showed up in the doorway. "We can go to lunch. I will bring something back for Ye and Jim. They are going to talk and play games until I return with their food."

* * *

"Do you and Mr. Jerry still plan to come to Wuhai?" Ye asked as we walked with him to the bus stop.

"Yes." Jerry responded quickly. "Virginia and I will. We asked the others if they wanted to see Wuhai, but they said they needed a quiet weekend to rest and plan for the last week. You know they are not full-time teachers like Virginia. This has been an adventure and challenge for them, but they really wanted to do this volunteer program and learn about China."

"You teach too," Ye said with a smile. "Especially on early morning walks."

A bus, not as comfortable looking as the one we had for the Helan Mountain trip, turned a corner. Ye asked, "If you come to Wuhai on Friday, I will still be there. By then, I will have made the school decision. The next week I will leave for the university to meet with an advisor and other students."

"Friday will be a half day, so yes, we plan to take a bus to Wuhai then."

A couple with small suitcases joined us at the bus stop. The bus slowed down. We were near the boarding door.

Ye asked, "Are you sure you can take the bus to Wuhai? The bus between these distant towns is not like a city bus. Because of stops it is not as fast as going in a car. The trip may take five or six hours to bring you to Wuhai"

"Jerry and I have taken buses in many countries. We took several different kinds of buses in Beijing. Don't worry about us."

The couple boarded ahead of Ye. We hugged him and said, "See you next weekend."

"I will meet you at the Wuhai bus station," he said. "Other friends will come too."

We stood back watching him get on and walk down the center aisle. He settled into a seat near the window on our side. The bus started and we waved at him. He returned the motion.

"I've only known Ye a short time, but I feel like I knew him before we met in person because of everything you told me about his help for your team in 2004. Now, after two weeks with him, it almost feels like saying goodbye to a family member."

"I agree." My emotions moved like a cart with no brakes on a roller coaster.

Jerry asked, "Are you nervous at all about taking a bus by ourselves here in Nei Menggu. It's very different from Beijing and Nanjing?"

"We'll be fine. Gladys or Anu or Solomon or anyone of our students can help make sure we get on the right bus. Then we just have to stay on it until we are in Wuhai. I may not have been there for two years, but I know I will recognize Wuhai, even the outskirts.

"I'll email Ye our arrival time. I'll send it to some of the other teachers who have kept in contact with me. It would be terrible to be just hours away from seeing them and not get to Wuhai. I promised that if you came to China with me, I'd bring you to Wuhai."

* * *

Monday morning my team and I arrived at school at 7:30, and Jim was with us. He rode his scooter alongside us rather than pushing past us and circling back as had been his habit when Ye walked with us or jogged alongside Jim.

As we set out supplies we needed for the day, I saw Gladys walk by my room. I called out, "Gladys, may I speak with you?"

"Of course, Ms. Virginia."

"Is your mother-in-law still doing well?"

"Oh yes, she is amazed at the strength she feels. We are grateful for her health. Thank you for your concern."

"I wanted to ask you too, when might it be a good time to let Principal Chimeg know that Jerry and I would like to go to Wuhai next weekend. The school has no field trip planned. I think a free weekend works well before we start our last week of work here. Danielle, Trudy, and Jim will stay here and be glad for the free time. I promised Wuhai friends that if my husband ever came to China with me, I would bring him to Wuhai to meet them. This next weekend with no set plans will be a good time to make the trip."

Gladys looked wide-eyed in surprise.

"But how will you get there, to Wuhai, Ms. Virginia?"

"We plan to take the bus. Ye said it goes back and forth two times a day."

"A bus? Out of here? To Wuhai?"

"We'll pay for it. We've taken many buses in our travels, even in China."

"That's not the difficulty, Ms. Virginia. You and all your team are the responsibility of Principal Chimeg and this city. Your safety is the first concern." Gladys had a tone that told me she did not like the idea of us taking a bus to Wuhai.

"Ms. Virginia, this week a tv station from our city, and one from Ningxia, plan to come and interview you and your team. They will follow you around for part of a teaching day. People in this province and Ningxia and others will know more about you. Everyone will recognize you. We have few channels, but people watch the local news. People who can watch television will learn about you, see you. If you are on a bus, and someone who does not like Americans recognizes you, there could be danger. It would be a better plan when the Amity program has concluded, to visit your friends in Wuhai."

"Gladys, we have flight tickets and a schedule that will take us to Shanghai when we leave here. The Amity workers will gather in Shanghai for a couple of days. Jerry, Danielle, and Jim will fly back to the United States after the Amity meetings in Shanghai. I am staying a week longer to do presentations at a school in Shanghai. Trudy is staying to keep me company. Shanghai is far from Inner Mongolia. Once I leave this province for the Amity meetings and teaching in Shanghai, I cannot come back before my flight home. I won't have the time or money to do that."

"Ms. Virginia, I can see you have given this thought and chosen a time you thought would be free time. Principal Chimeg has full responsibility for you and your team's safety. She does not know the Wuhai people except for the young man, Ye, who helped with translating."

I quelled my frustration and anger. Gladys had no idea how much more Ye had done than translate. Inside me, a haboob, the wild desert dust storm, churning like a low tornado, gripped my guts. I couldn't let that show. Chinese lose respect for anyone who shows temper if they do not have the excuse of being drunk or the reason of saving face.

"Ms. Virginia, Principal Chimeg will not think it is safe for you to take a bus to Wuhai while you are here, under our care and protection. I will tell her your wish, but please expect to hear her concern about you leaving here on a bus."

With great difficulty, I kept a calm expression. Gladys had honestly told me what she knew and what she guessed.

Her estimation of the principal's response sounded definite. I expected she was right. My thoughts rushed and jumbled as I tried to figure out how to change Principal Chimeg's mind. I thought about my *'Who knew'* conversation with Jerry. *'Who knew,'* moved in my mind to large letters 'NOW WHAT?'

Chapter 27

A Little Help from My Friends

O ur third Monday morning went well in spite of the turmoil I felt due to my conversation with Gladys. In the normal school year, ping pong tables were set up in the school's courtyard area. The sixth-grade level would return in our last week. As new students, they would have a week ahead of all the other students to adapt to the school's schedule. In break time they could play ping pong.

Would this be distracting to our program? A bit, but they would have classes in the long low building we did not see easily. Our students were teachers from schools that had ping pong tables and basketball hoops in the school yard for breaks. Jim, who did not have his full earlier energy, seemed much more like himself when he appeared with Sally to say they had played some ping pong.

The sun and heat rose while our morning classes wound down. The van would take us back to the corner by the restaurant. I was chatting with Anu, about to leave the classroom, when Principal Chimeg and Gladys appeared at the door.

Anu greeted them and turned to me, "See you later, Ms. Virginia."

"Yes, Anu. See you later." When she departed, the principal and Gladys entered.

"Ms. Virginia, Principal Chimeg wanted to make sure you knew that the Yinchuan reporter and camera people will be here to talk with you and film your team tomorrow morning. Since you are the team leader, they will want to talk with you first."

"I will be happy to talk with them. My team also knows this will take place tomorrow. Any of them will do their best to give answers to questions from the news people." Principal Chimeg nodded and smiled even without a translation from Gladys. Again, I wondered how much English she knew.

Gladys continued. "Wednesday, our local television station would like to follow your team through a day. They chose Wednesday because they have heard how all four classes gather in the auditorium for special activities."

"That makes sense." I looked at the principal as much as Gladys when I responded. "Wednesdays do have a good variety. Do they know how crowded the auditorium will be? Usually, television work requires special cameras."

Gladys talked with Principal Chimeg who smiled again, spoke, and Gladys translated, "Principal Chimeg explained the space. They will be able to do the filming. Will Ms. Danielle allow Jim to be interviewed?"

"You will have to ask her that." Again the principal nodded before Gladys translated anything. Now seemed like the time to ask about the weekend.

"Gladys, have you explained to Principal Chimeg that Jerry and I would like to see our friends in Wuhai this coming weekend?"

Immediately, Principal Chimeg spoke to me in Chinese. After a couple of heartbeats, Gladys said, "She is sorry that will not work out because of concern for your safety. You and your team will be known all around the Left Banner after tomorrow and Wednesday." Gladys looked sorry but also relieved.

I nodded. I would not argue. Inside I tried to remind myself I was not in control of anything in any day. I only had times of thinking I was. Who knew we'd encounter this roadblock in getting to Wuhai? I'd pray for a way to get to see those friends.

"How is Jim?" Principal Chimeg said slowly but clearly in English. She and Gladys had stood very still, as if waiting for a repeated plea or argument from me.

"He is doing much better. His skin is healing well. This morning he enjoyed having Sally as company on their scooters and playing table tennis. Our schools do not allow much time for a lunch break, so there is not time for the students to relax by playing a game like table tennis."

Whether she understood me fully on her own or not, I couldn't tell. She spoke rapidly with Gladys who said, "The superintendent has called Principal Chimeg and he would like to have tennis again with Mr. Jerry and Ms. Danielle, Thursday after the school day."

"We will talk at our lunch time, and I will let you know their answer this afternoon." They said *xie xie*, turned and walked to the path that went to the new administration building.

Jerry and Danielle agreed to play tennis, and I passed that news along to Gladys when we returned to our classrooms at 2:45. Anu stood in the background but came to speak to me when Gladys left.

"Ms. Virginia, I want to know if you and your team will

share emails so that we can still ask you questions and stay in contact when you leave China."

"Yes. We will be happy to do that. Come inside the classroom and we can exchange contact information." While I wrote mine, Anu asked, "Did you go to the internet café instead of resting today?"

I had not told anyone but Jerry that I had gone to the internet café and sent an email to Ye about the Principal's concerns about our safety. Jerry agreed that alerting Ye early to this change was important. It wasn't just Ye we would miss seeing.

Emily, the head translator for my 2004 team, and others who had kept in touch through email would know from Ye that my husband had come with me to China. I avoid making promises as much as possible because when I promise something, I intend to keep that promise. I had told my Wuhai hosts, students, and friends that if my husband ever came with me to China, I would bring him to Wuhai so he would meet them and see their city.

I answered Anu. "Yes. I did. I do not nap every day. My team rested, even Jim."

"One of the people in Mr. Jerry's class saw you there."

"And he talked about it with other students?"

"Everything you do, you or any of your team is interesting to us," Anu replied. Then more students started arriving. Again I had to compartmentalize and focus on an afternoon of talking about global educators, their beliefs, and practices. Classes enjoyed comparing the ideas of Montessori, Dewey, Piaget, Gardner, Escalante, and others with their present educational practices and ancient methods of Confucius. Still Ye and Wuhai came into my mind.

Ye knew our hearts. He would let friends in Wuhai

know Jerry and I had hoped to see them. At the conclusion of the afternoon classes, while Jerry, Danielle, and Jim gave the students more practice in baseball, Trudy and I went to the computer room in the administration building. Trudy preferred using computers there because the room was clean and cool. Neither of us did any random searches.

Trudy wanted to send and receive news with her family. I wanted to see if Ye had accepted that Jerry and I would not see him in Wuhai. Honestly, I hoped Ye might have an idea for overcoming the obstacle with our school hosts.

His response appeared shortly before Trudy and I left the computer lab.

> Ms Virginia,
> Do not worry. I have talked with Principal Chen and Ms Emily. They are excited to see you. Soon you will hear better news, I think.
> your friend, Ye

* * *

Somehow our students quickly learned about the television crews coming to visit. On Wednesday they arrived early or on time and milled about in the best outfits we had seen on them. Teachers in China said they dressed plainly for school. Frequently they wore only two or three outfits alternating them over the entire school year.

Schools did not want students to think about a teacher's fashion choices. They needed to focus on studies. Special days and occasions when they were not in their classrooms, our students dressed in special outfits. "You're dressed to the nines," Jerry said to them. They smiled because this idiom they knew from the wide study of English idioms in China. We could not tell them for sure where the idiom came from, but in the 19th century to the nines meant to the highest level or to perfection.

The Yinchuan crew spent time in each classroom filming teaching and interactions. They were professional and fast. When we reached the long lunchtime break, they took the opportunity to have interviews with teachers. With permission from the moms, some minutes of Jim and Sally playing table tennis were filmed.

Principal Chimeg gave the lead reporter a list of the students who were representatives from towns across the rural Gobi. Short interviews happened with these individuals. As quickly as the news team arrived, they were gone. I was not surprised when we returned for the afternoon session to see our students back in their everyday casual plain clothing.

Excitement surged again on Wednesday afternoon, and the dressier outfits appeared again when we gathered as one big class in the main auditorium. The local Left Banner news sent two reporters and a couple of cameramen to film the afternoon session. Each homeroom class stood and sang their class theme song. They also sang and did the ASL motions to "My Heart will Go On."

I felt shivers of emotion. The motions of the classes together had syncopation as if they had practiced together for months. They sang out with a vibrancy that revealed teachers could show strong emotion. The news filmed the whole afternoon session.

The reporters asked questions of us and the teachers who were the SEP students. The first question asked us to speak briefly about a teacher who had made an impression on our lives. The second question asked about goals in teaching. The third question focused on what was enjoyable about teaching when there were so many different responsibilities and no high pay.

We had a role play of an American coming to the Left Banner to learn the language and culture by homestay immersion. The teachers also presented a role play of a student as a class clown trying to avoid having his teacher call his parents. Everyone laughed, even the film crew. The teachers did a good imitation of student actions and excuses. The role play that provoked the most laughter was of a Mongolian, a Chinese, and an American having a conversation layered with English idioms. The applause and laughter made a strong ending to our afternoon.

* * *

Thursday seemed quieter without the excitement of reporters and a film crew. The day included a few long hours, but overall it flew by. We concluded at 5:30 when Gladys told us the van had arrived to take us back to the hotel since Jerry and Danielle would play tennis again with the superintendent.

Jim went along with his mom and Jerry when the car returned to take them to an outdoor tennis court. They returned at eight-thirty. Jim sat in our living room with Trudy and me while we waited for the tennis players to shower and dress before we all went to dinner.

"They didn't win sets today." Jim said. "The superintendent and his partner won the sets, but it wasn't a slaughter. At the end, the superintendent said something to Pastor Jerry in English. He said, I wish you a good weekend with your friends. What do you think he meant? Doesn't he know we are all friends? And he said it in English? Do you think he knows English or used a little because Gladys didn't come to the indoor recreation center with us?"

Trudy and I exchanged glances. If I said anything as an explanation, I'd only be guessing. Maybe tomorrow Principal Chimeg would have some news for us about our last weekend.

"I don't know, Jim, but maybe someone can explain that to us tomorrow."

As we walked to dinner, we enjoyed the coolness of a clear evening and eighty degrees. Danielle commented on how amazing it was to feel that eighty was comfortable. Jim reminded her, "That's twenty-six here, Mom. Forty Celsius is one hundred Fahrenheit. If it was eighty here, we'd be dead."

We laughed at his calculation and entered the restaurant. To our surprise, Gladys and Sally were there beside the table where we usually sat. My immediate thought was not just happiness for Jim, but a hope that we might find out what the superintendent's English sentence to Jerry and Danielle meant.

Friday afternoon at 1:30, Jerry and I each had a small suitcase. I had a fanny pack too, just plain black. I wore it with the strap over my shoulder instead of around my waist. Trudy, Danielle, and Jim waited with us. We'd had lunch right after our morning classes concluded. Now we waited in the hotel lobby.

Principal Chimeg sent a message through Gladys that she would meet us at 1:30 to greet the friends who came from Wuhai at the hotel address. A car would arrive to pick us up and take us to Wuhai for the weekend. Gladys did not give any information about how this arrangement had occurred, but her discomfort with us leaving on this trip had not disappeared.

Was it '*face,*' I wondered. Had she or Principal Chimeg felt a loss of face because Jerry and I were now going to Wuhai? Did they feel concern for their town and school wondering if I and my team would ever want to come back and visit them? Speak of them as friends?

At almost the same moment, two black cars arrived. Principal Chimeg and VP Guo emerged from their Mercedes sedan. From the other larger Mercedes Tourer, Emily, the head of the English department at my Wuhai host school emerged. Behind her Thomas, one of my former students appeared. We all stood together sharing greetings, formal and serious in tone.

With her height, Principal Chimeg looked dignified and svelte in her dark blue suit and white blouse. She did most of the talking at this meeting. VP Guo was not as tall as the principal, but he too looked more formal than usual in a suit, white shirt, and tie.

Emily looked like she must have had a lovely vacation recently. Her dress, a simple A-line, a tropical hibiscus pink color. I knew from email exchanges with her since 2004 that she and her husband liked to visit places near the sea on vacations. Emily often won trips as prizes because her students earned high scores on the exams. Her district gave a variety of prizes to teachers in every school who had students with outstanding test scores.

Emily's glasses in oversized tortoise shell frames made her eyes look large. She carried a shoulder bag that matched her creamy white and top-quality leather shoes. Emily had been surprised in 2004 when none of the women on our team carried a handbag. Quality handbags seemed like a professional essential to many female teachers. Face. Emily had no shyness in establishing hers.

Thomas, dear Thomas, looked the same as he had in 2004. A tall Mongolian and dedicated teacher, he had taught my team to sand surf. His black framed glasses seemed like a Clark Kent attempt to disguise his strengths because he had the height and muscles of an athlete.

This meeting by the cars seemed set on establishing power base dynamics. Principal Chimeg was younger than Emily, but I did not think Emily felt in any way less than the principal. If Emily wanted to be a principal, she could be, but she loved teaching. VP Guo was Chinese, older than Thomas, and had an administrative position. Still, Thomas gave a formally polite greeting without showing any hint of subservience.

After the conversation in Chinese that no one interpreted for us, Emily and Thomas turned toward Jerry and me. We introduced them to the rest of our team. Jim spoke Chinese to them. "*Wǒ jiào jímǔ, jīnnián shí suì, hěn gāoxìng rènshí nǐ.*" My name is Jim. I am ten years old. It is nice to meet you.

"You speak Chinese well young man." Emily said.

"If our students were in school, I'd want you to come with us so they could be inspired to speak English as well as you speak Chinese," Thomas told Jim.

"Ye taught me," Jim said proudly. Emily and Thomas exchanged a quick glance. Then Thomas said, "Ye has taught you well."

We said goodbyes. In the large black car, Emily said, "Sit facing the driver. That's more comfortable. We don't want you to feel car sick by riding backwards." She and Thomas sat on the seat opposite us with their backs to the driver.

"Emily, Thomas, it is a super surprise to see both of you and to travel with you to Wuhai. We did not want to have you, or anyone, make the trip here. We had planned to take the bus."

Jerry said, "I have heard a lot about both of you from Virginia's time with you in the 2004 SEP. Thank you for all you did to help that teaching time be a success. She has longed for me to meet the people of Wuhai. You are very special to her. I thank you too for providing the transportation for us."

"We remember Virginia well. It would have been a pity if she had been this close to Wuhai and not had a chance to visit us for even two days."

"Our hosts here, like you, were concerned for our safety and comfort," I said not wanting to speak negatively about the Left Banner. "They did not want us taking a bus and having no clear idea of who would meet us except for Ye. Did he tell you how it worked out for him to be our translator for a couple of weeks?"

"He did. He was honored to stay with you and be of help." Emily added.

"He sent me an email on Monday that said, Don't worry because he talked to you, Emily, and to Principal Chen. I didn't know what would happen, but Ye seemed sure we would be able to visit Wuhai."

Thomas said, "Ye recognizes much more than many young people his age. He knew who to call. Our principal knows the Superintendent here, but our principal does not play tennis."

I looked from Thomas to Emily as the process of our trip fell into place.

Emily smiled and said, "Ye understands the power of friends."

Chapter 28

Reflections in Flavors of Wuhai

We did not even pass the bus station when we arrived in Wuhai. The driver took us to the main gates of my 2004 host school. A guard opened the iron gate and smiled in welcome.

"There's the sculpture where many pictures were taken with the Amity team and teachers here." Thomas said.

"Yes, Virginia has those in a photo album at home. It is great to see these now with her and you. Thank you again for this chance to visit." Jerry said.

The car took us around the four-story classroom buildings. Neither Jerry nor I commented on the low bathroom building on the left that I had described to Jerry. It was the first time and place where I had encountered a trough toilet.

Further to our left, the exercise equipment and the rubber synthetic track could be seen. Beyond that the wall separated the school grounds from a street and houses of old neighborhoods. My eyes found the road that led up to the beautiful home of Emily's parents. It had been the most lovely and peaceful family home I had visited in Wuhai reflecting the partnership of sixty plus years of marriage.

The car made another turn to the right. Now we faced the dormitory where I had stayed in 2004. The modern administration and science building were on our left. The old barracks that had been on the right were gone. A beautiful garden with benches and paths for meandering through flowering bushes and young trees filled the space just as Principal Chen had envisioned.

We got out. The dry heat immediately replaced the coolness we had felt in the air-conditioned car.

"I need to get home now, but I will see you at dinner tonight," Thomas said. He shook hands with Jerry, nodded to Emily and me, and walked toward the narrow alley on the side of the dorm building. I remembered the alley that ran alongside the dorm building with a gate at the end. It opened to a narrow street full of shops and apartments.

We walked toward the dorm. The wide patio and stairs still looked like polished white stone. I had often seen the housekeeper and her assistants working to keep the area clean, no easy task with all the dust. The air blended the scent of flowers in the garden, scents of life, cooking from small shops on the street behind the dorm building, and the clear air that came when the sky was visible and blue.

A cafeteria took up most of the first floor of the dorm. In front of the center doors stood the head housekeeper. I recognized her instantly. She waved and smiled.

"She has told the story of her first conversation with you many times," Emily said with a smile. "But you are also remembered because of your consideration and kindness to the staff."

I clasped the housekeeper's hands. She grinned and asked, *"Ni chi le ma?"* Did you eat? I knew enough Mandarin Chinese to answer her, *Chi le ni ne.* I did eat, and you?

She laughed and said, "*Hao tan*," good talk.

Jerry had already heard this question in greeting in the Left Banner, and even from Naomi back when we were in Beijing. Did you eat? Now it would be part of his special memories of China too.

I nodded and introduced her to my husband saying, "*Zhè shì wǒ de zhàngfū.*" I hoped I said this is my husband, correctly. He knew the story of what I'd said incorrectly to her back in 2004. My poor wording had caused her to smile and giggle for days.

She nodded to him, welcomed him, then led us and Emily to the second floor. We entered the hallway and stopped at the first room on the left.

"This is the room I had in 2004," I said as the housekeeper unlocked the door and then handed me the key. In 2004 it had little furniture other than two twin beds and a bedside table.

Now the room had a bureau, desk, lamp, and two straight chairs. "*Xiè xiè,*" I told the housekeeper. She nodded happily and left.

"You don't mind staying in the dorm this weekend?" Emily asked.

"Not at all. Jerry will enjoy the exercise equipment and track early in the morning."

"Ye told me that. He said he would come meet Jerry at 5:30 each morning. Principal Chen has approved that plan.

* * *

The weekend whirled by with a big dinner but not the formal ceremonial kind. Ye had learned and shared that Jerry did not like those. Ye, Emily, Kent, and Kent's younger sister Autumn who was also an English teacher, but not at this host school, took us to a restaurant near the city square. I recognized Autumn. But I would not have remembered her English name without Kent's help. Seasons, flowers, and nature were popular as Chinese names for women.

"We'll enjoy walking in the square tonight after dinner," Emily announced as we got out of the large black car.

"Is this your car or the school's?" Jerry asked. Then he looked momentarily flustered as if worried he had been too direct. I had told him the Chinese were direct in asking questions but would avoid saying a direct, no.

"My husband likes this smaller sedan. It belongs to him. I don't drive. My husband is provided a car due to his work."

A great surprise appeared as we stepped inside the restaurant that had the decorations of the Mongolian region. Principal Chen and twenty of my homeroom students from 2004 came forward to greet me and to meet Jerry. We went to a room on the second floor of the restaurant that had enough round tables and chairs for thirty people. Emily told us that with great difficulty the menu had been chosen. Everyone had favorite dishes they wanted us to try. Of course they included the essentials, Emily added.

"Essentials?" Jerry asked.

Autumn explained, "Sweet, from something natural, like fruit, must be a part of a full meal because it improves moods. Bitter improves digestion. Sour helps the stomach cope with greasy food. Salt brings out flavors, and spicy warms the body."

The meal had many courses served on small plates and in bowls less than half the size of what commonly appeared in portions in the United States. We had Chinese and Mongolian dishes. Jerry impressed people with his use of *kuaizi* and ease in picking up a bowl to drink broth. Because spicy dishes were so strong with chilis, he could recognize them and say, *Bù là.*

The Chinese have a traditional belief that everyone should walk at least a hundred steps after a meal. Our group went to the Wuhai city square after our dinner time walked a hundred steps in a few minutes. The night air was a comfortable temperature in the mid-seventies.

"Our square is more than half as big as Tiananmen Square," Thomas said.

On this warm night children darted in and out of the light fountain spray. The square had more colorful fountains and games than it had had in 2004, more food carts, and it still had music. Our group walked together about halfway across the square. Then novelty carts, time, or meeting other friends caused some of our group to say goodbye.

"Look, there is the new pastor in our city," Terry said. "I have not met him yet. That must be his wife and daughter with him, but I don't know the other person."

They were walking toward us. I said, "Terry can you introduce us to him? Then you can meet him too and tell him you are a member of the church."

"That is easy. You two are the only foreigners in the square. He is already staring at you. He will want to meet you. Come with me."

Terry led us to this young pastor. She spoke in Chinese to him, and he responded, looking at us while he talked.

"His name is Samuel, and he is happy to meet you. This is his wife, Ruth, and his daughter, Deborah. All Bible names. This other person is Ying Yue. She is a friend of the family but has been away in Beijing earning a master's degree in English."

"I am pleased to meet you," Ying Yue said clearly. "Pastor

Samuel does not have English. He has wanted some help with translations of questions he has about the city. Wuhai is different than where he lived near Nanjing. He wishes he had some people here like those he learned with in the seminary."

"We were in Nanjing, and I have a friend who teaches at that seminary." I said. Pastor Samuel and his wife were surprised and suddenly Chinese and English flew in both directions with two able translators, Terry and Ying Yue.

Ying Yue stared at Jerry. "I do not go to church. Pastor Samuel told me as we walked, he wished he had someone older who knew the Bible well. I do not know the Bible at all. How amazing and lucky to meet you here!"

We went toward a low marble wall that was a good height for a seat. For the next fifteen minutes, Samuel asked questions that Jerry tried to answer briefly. Ying Yue did the translating. Terry sat patiently, interested in the conversation, and helpful when a Bible word Ying Yue had never heard needed translation.

In my peripheral vision, I saw Emily waving at us. A few of my class members from 2004 stood with her.

"I'm sorry but we have to leave." I said.

"May we exchange email?" Pastor Samuel asked Jerry.

Jerry agreed, but neither man had any personal card. I had paper and pen in my little fanny pack, so I wrote the information for both of them. Ying Yue asked if she could exchange email with me, so that was shared too. After *zai jians*, we hurried to Emily.

Emily smiled and said to Jerry, "This is where Virginia heard the song in English, *My Heart Will Go On*." It came over the loudspeakers here in the square.

Jerry replied, "She has made that her theme song for many situations, especially for teaching in China."

"We all knew the song, but enjoyed it most singing sign language motions," Autumn added. Emily led us to where her husband's driver and car met us at ten.

"You will have a short night I think," Kent said as she held the car door for us.

* * *

I did not get up when Jerry left for the track at 5:30. He told me later that Ye was already there waiting for him. Later we met more Wuhai friends at a café style restaurant within walking distance of the school. From that breakfast we walked to the town park that had the museum about geology and gem rocks. Once again, Ye used his expansive and rare vocabulary about rocks to take us through the museum.

At lunchtime, a van for twelve people showed up at the park, arranged by Thomas to take us to the Yellow River and the site of the dam that would create a huge lake behind it. We saw the start of the bridge expanding across the river. While we stood and stared, Thomas joined us. With enthusiasm and pride he told us of the progress in city plans beyond the bridge and dam. "There will be technology museum, cultural museum, and special center about calligraphy. Did you know Wuhai has been called a city of beautiful writing?"

We didn't know that about the city, but we admired calligraphy we had seen. Though the day was hot, we had bottled water and enjoyed the leisurely pace of the walking tour. Wuhai would double in size. By mid-afternoon people mentioned how good it would feel to have a nap, and we went back into the city

At the school Emily said, "Tonight many of your students will join us at a restaurant that has hot pot."

* * *

"I feel almost guilty at leaving Danielle, Jim, and Trudy back away from this." I said to Jerry as we descended the steps in front of the dorm. We walked into the garden area, through it and around the classroom buildings. We were supposed to meet Emily at the main gate.

Jerry said, "Everyone is glad you came to visit and brought me to meet them. They are wonderful warm hosts."

"They are friends to me. These days are flying by. When we get back, the days will go by fast too with responsibilities of review, tests, presentations, and closing programs."

"And I remember you said those last days are bittersweet." He stopped and turned me to face him. "Ginny, have you figured out yet why you felt such a pull to return to China?"

"No, but I do feel more peaceful by seeing these Wuhai friends again. And learning about the differences—just a few hours south in the Left Banner—gives me more cultural insight. I feel like there is a lot more to learn. I wonder how our students will feel when we leave."

"Yes, I think we will see our students with fresh eyes when we know we will leave them and maybe never see them again," Jerry added.

"I don't like thinking we will never see any of them again. They work so hard for very little. Does it ever hit you that we know our students have classrooms of fifty or more students, low pay, challenging lives, and yet continue teaching with energy and care? I want them to know they can touch the future through their work with students and feel hopeful and valued."

Jerry gave me a quick kiss, took my hand, and we continued walking to the front gates. He asked, "Have any of the Left Banner students stood out to you as much as the friends you've made here in Wuhai?"

"A few. But I think the two years of exchanging email with Wuhai people built our friendship. I'll have to wait and see who keeps in contact."

"They will probably realize, just like the Wuhai teachers, that you can mentor them in English strategies through email exchanges, and I know you have sent books to more than this Wuhai host school."

"I haven't thought as much about the Left Banner students today as I have about Danielle, Jim, and Trudy. I hope they have a good weekend. We'll all be so busy this week. It is hard to believe in less than a week we'll be in Shanghai."

"Have you heard more from the principal of the school in Shanghai where you will do English activities?"

"Not recently, but she knows I won't be in Shanghai until late this Friday night. The hotel where the Amity debriefing is has a business center. I can check emails there. I could probably call her. She says she only has a little English, but you know that is typical Chinese modesty. She could be fluent."

"Will Trudy go to school with you each day?"

"That is up to her. She's the oldest person on our team and we have a hotel in a location where she can walk and see museums and malls if she wants to. I'd be glad to have her come with me to the school. It is modern and well supported by the government because of its demanding courses, especially in languages and sciences. In our country it would be called a magnet school."

"You love all of this don't you? Learning and teaching in another culture."

"I do, but I feel like there is something more than teaching that draws me here ."

"What?"

"I wanted to discover that by coming back to work with the SEP in another remote area. I think I am seeing something about myself and what this culture gives me in challenges that I need, but it's like blurry vision. I need to figure it out. It's about something in me that needs a challenge to realize how much I need to depend on God's lessons for me.

"I've also been wondering if, like Ye coming to us, I am supposed to be meeting someone to help them along with a need I don't know about. I am trying to take more time for reflection than I did in 2004, but I am still looking at the lessons that can affect the rest of my life, choices I need to make."

Jerry looked serious as he said, "You have faced a lot of unusual challenges in your life. And I am probably one of them. I hope it's not that you want to get away from me..."

"No. I love you and I am so thankful you chose to travel to China with me. All our students enjoyed you and learned a lot. Ye appreciated the walking and conversations each day. There's no way to measure how much he learned from those times with you."

"He was a great help, a true gift from God."

"I can see that."

"You know, whether you figure out what was compelling you to return to China or not, you'll probably want to travel to China again," Jerry said with a look as they're serious as the serious Buddha we'd seen inside the Guangzong Temple.

Chapter 29

Out of the Hotpot and into the Church

"T*oono*," Emily said. "In a yurt it rises to an opening in the top. This restaurant is a solid building but inside they have decorated the walls and ceiling to remind people of the *ger* or *yurt* as you call them."

I recognized the wide white round tent. I'd described it to Jerry but felt thankful he could know by experience. Inside, at a rectangular table along the whole back wall of the restaurant were some of my former students familiar enough to recognize them by name. Principal Chen, VP Zhu, Ye, Thomas, Penny, Jeff, Marge, Erdeen, Kent, Autumn, Terry, Jason. We joined them. With room for ten people on each side and one on each end, we could easily reach the three hot pots set on the table.

Everyone tried to give Jerry instructions. They used their English telling us about the round pots of boiling broth kept warm by low level flames beneath them.

"Each pot had two sections, causing them to be called split pots. One has a broth so spicy it can clear your nose and ears. That's the red colored broth," Autumn told Jerry.

"The other side has a flavorful soup but no hot spicy flavor."

Erdeen told Jerry some facts about hotpots. "Once in Mongolia, hotpot was called fire pot. It is said Kublai Khan favored this meal for troops before battle. Hot pot could be made in haste but had nutrition. In the north, hot pot meals warmed the ger, their temporary tent, and the people who enjoyed the meal. Around the hot pot were small bowls with flavorful sauces, crushed chili peppers, sweet ginger, soy sauce, minced garlic, smooth peanut sauce, Chinese vinegar, and sriracha."

Ye pointed out sesame and chive sauce to Jerry as a tasty favorite. Waiters brought heaping platters of meats and vegetables. Noodles already were on the table.

Thomas told Jerry, "People put root vegetables, like yams, into the boiling broths first because they take longer to cook. The meats are thinly shaved pork belly, beef, lamb, and fish. Noodles and vegetables like spinach, leeks, tofu, and mushrooms cook quickly."

My former students enjoyed being teachers to Jerry. Kent said, "Tongs let a person put the raw foods into the pot, root vegetables usually went in first, though meat went in early too. Servings are removed from the pot with serving chopsticks or slotted serving spoons. I will take some out for you."

Jason explained, "A person does not use the *kuaizi* they put into their mouth to take out food from the hot pot. In a person's home with family and close friends, people would use their hands to drop in ingredients. At public places the sharing requires care."

Throughout the dinner I noticed hardly anyone translated for Principal Chen and VP Zhu. I had heard a few English words and phrases from them in 2004, but they could have known more than I chanced to hear. Perhaps it was 'face' again that kept them from speaking in front of these fluent young teachers of English.

We enjoyed this food adventure and the lessons and then came the singing. Principal Chen spoke and Emily translated. "It is a custom in Mongolia to enjoy songs with time together at a meal. Can you sing a song for us? Ms. Virginia did when she first had such a dinner as this. I remember it was about a boy who killed a giant with a slingshot."

Jerry looked at me and I told him, "I sang 'Only a Boy Named David,' because it was short, and I knew it well."

"All right," Jerry said before he sat back and launched into singing the chorus, first verse, and chorus again of "This Little Light of Mine."

When Jerry finished, Principal Chen said, *"Hao."* Then he invited Erdeen to sing a Mongolian chorus. VP Zhu surprised everyone by singing a Chinese song, and then the students sang the national anthem. In Chinese, the fierceness of the words was not apparent to Jerry, but I would tell him later. I learned the anthem in 2004 from my students.

March of the Volunteers
(The 1935 lyrics of the Chinese national anthem in English)

Stand up! Those who refuse to be slaves!
With our flesh and blood, let's build our newest Great Wall!
The Chinese Nation is at its greatest peril,
Each one is forced to let out one last roar.
Stand up! Stand up! Stand up!
We are billions of one heart,
Braving the enemies' fire, March on!

Braving the enemies' fire, March on!
March on! March on! On!

With so much eating, talking, singing, applauding, and talking, it was no surprise that we found it was ten thirty when we arrived back at the dorm. The housekeeper sat on the top step and smiled at us as we approached.

"W *ǎn'ān*," she said.

Jerry and I repeated it back to her. It was a simple good night.

As usual, Jerry fell asleep quickly. I lay awake wondering how Danielle, Jim, and Trudy were doing and thinking about the people here who were so kind and hard-working. I could see changes in the people and the town. They had more assurance, hope, and pride. Wuhai had advanced because of the dam, the bridge, and now with the whole new sections of buildings being constructed and plans for bright styled apartment houses to business streets, recreation areas, museums, parks, and schools. Wasn't this enough? Shouldn't I just be thankful to see these advances in the lives of students and teachers I had come to care about as friends? Now I'd had this second visit to China. How could I ask for more?

* * *

Ye had time again to walk and talk with Jerry on Sunday morning. Jerry said they talked about the licensing of the Three Selves churches in China. They are legal churches because in registering, they identify as being patriotic. They adhere to self-governance, self-support, and self-propagation, which means not evangelizing. They live and exist under the government's supervision and guidance. Ye

263

explained the unofficial churches, the underground churches, no foreigners should visit because these churches refused to be under government oversight. Jerry told me as we got ready to go to the church led by Pastor Samuel, that this morning's walk and talk had been mental and physical exercise for him and Ye.

A few other friends and Ye would go with us to church even though we could have learned enough with just one translator. Kent came to greet us and take us to breakfast. We followed her through the narrow alley, the large now unlocked gate, and into the busy street beside the school.

In a restaurant owned by a family Kent knew, we took a seat at one of the small round tables. Kent's sister Autumn joined us with her husband *Héxié*. I asked what his name meant. Autumn said, "Harmony. And I am thankful he is a man who seeks harmony, but he knows little English." She patted his arm affectionately.

For breakfast we had traditional Chinese choices. Jerry and I chose a small bowl of noodle soup and vegetables that had become a staple for us. Baozi also came to the table, because Kent had heard from Ye that *baozi* was a favorite for my whole group.

As we left the restaurant, I said to Kent, "You should let us at least pay for breakfast for all of us. We've been treated to everything since we arrived."

"Ms Virginia, our school library has more than two dozen English books that you sent. Even with our older students, your Dr. Seuss is popular. Some of our students have been able to read the classics you sent. The teachers who chose books from the prizes at our closing day parties use those books with their classes and with their families.

"We know from the boxes that arrived what it cost for you to mail them. It is our honor and privilege to treat you and any guests you bring to visit us. We are thankful and happy to meet your husband. Thank you for coming back to visit us."

Autumn came up alongside us and said, "Everyone notices you two still have romance. You hold hands when you walk."

Jerry and I were holding hands when she said this to us. Autumn continued, "I have told *Hexie*, I want to hold hands when we walk like you two."

Jerry and I both felt surprised at what people noticed. Had our students in the Left Banner noticed our hand holding and hugs too? I wondered if this should make us more or less likely to hold hands for the rest of our time in the Left Banner.

Ye, Terry, Jeff, and Thomas waited in front of the school for us. They had three of the local pedicabs ready to take us to church. Jerry and I got in one, Ye and Thomas in the other, Terry and Jeff in the third one. Kent and Autumn said they would see us at lunchtime.

I had told Jerry about the little clay brick church building I'd attended in 2004, but the pedicabs took us nowhere near that building. We went almost directly across the city, narrow in width, and came to a new wide avenue. Across this avenue was a building site, and the cabs crossed the avenue and parked. We got out near the door where people were entering the large new building.

"This didn't exist in 2004," I said to Jerry. "No one had wealth in that congregation. How can they afford this?" I asked Thomas and Ye.

"They have a new pastor, a young man. He has led the church to join the Three Self Churches. The Three Self Churches can have some financial assistance for a new building."

Virginia Heslinga

"I had no idea your government gave money to help churches build." Jerry said.

Sunday morning service in the large new Wuhai church

"We want a harmonious society." Thomas said as if this should be no surprise. "Our president, Hu Jintao, wants to handle the religious beliefs and practices fairly."

The inside of the church was not complete. Sunshine gave plenty of light through the tall multi-pane windows. The front platform went almost from wall to wall. There was a pulpit forward at the edge and four chairs set in a row behind the pulpit. A large red cross decorated the wall behind the platform. I looked around dumbfounded at how spacious, bright, and modern this building was compared to the one I had visited in 2004.

The church had enough people to fill the rows of seats. As we stood looking around, people noticed us. Smiles and words of welcome came in waves from some people who recognized me. I saw the older woman who had been the pastor in 2004. She looked happy. I hoped that meant she had not been pushed aside for a new pastor.

And as the pianist started to play music, the pastor and deacons took seats on the platform. The pastor was Samuel. I looked around for his wife. She was seated in the front row next to her daughter.

266

Terry sat beside me and pointed out her father who was one of the deacons. "People are very happy with Pastor Samuel, old and young. You will like his sermon. I will try my best translating for you."

After some announcements, Pastor Samuel looked out over the congregation and said a few words. Thomas leaned toward Jerry to translate, "I see we have some visitors today. You are near our sister Terry. Please introduce our visitors, Sister Terry."

"Please stand as she speaks," Thomas whispered.

After our introduction, I sat down. Jerry stayed standing and said, "We would like to give you a word of greeting from our church in the United States. They appreciate brothers and sisters in the Lord around the world and are praying for the church in China."

Nods, hallelujahs, and amens followed his greeting. *Amen and hallelujah* are recognizable around the world. The service included music, a choir, reading Scripture, a sermon, and testimonies. People in this remote area revealed emotions freely within their church.

Terry leaned toward me and said, "It's rare to have a seminary-trained pastor."

I could see how the congregation listened. In that sanctuary with sun pouring in, I felt a clenching in my heart. This city had changed and expanded in two years, but the bonds here had not withered over time or distance. In this place of worship I saw familiar faces. We all still shared a desire to learn, to be kind, to pray, and to live with purpose.

Glancing through the tall windows, the outside still under construction showed frames of other buildings; some, barely outlined now, looked like they would eventually join. If the government gave money to assist in building a new church, a state approved church, was it only cement and steel they allowed or would something else less benign be attached. What kind of strings might be attached? Would the hope they felt with Hu Jintao's leadership prove reliable?

I had hopes with them as they lived their faith amid national pressures. Would this new young pastor be a leader for good times and bad? Emails had careful wording on some topics and certain subjects were avoided entirely. How would I know how this church continued to grow, and if it did? Why did I feel a need to know and to see them again? What if it wasn't just my own desire to see these people again? What if it was something I was supposed to do for a reason I could not know now?

Chapter 30

Kaleidoscope Week

Emily, Ye, and Erdeen accompanied us back to the Left Banner. We arrived in the late afternoon. The large black car drove into the parking lot behind the restaurant and our three Wuhai friends walked with us to the hotel. I kept thinking this parting would be tough. Who knew if we would ever see one another again? These individuals represented the kind friends who stayed in my mind, heart, and prayers. It seemed cruel to say goodbye without any hope of meeting again on this earth.

The team was waiting in the lobby. Jim ran to Ye and hugged him in an abrupt motion.

"I missed you," he said.

"I have missed you too little brother." Ye smiled, but I could see the emotion of this greeting lay like a weighted mantle. This greeting time was a parting too.

"I am sorry we cannot visit. We must leave." Emily said in her head teacher voice. "Our students will return this week for some special classes. The musicians and athletes are already practicing daily. We hope your last week in the Left Banner will be a strong conclusion, as we had with Ms.

Virginia and the 2004 Amity team." Emily sounded gracious and in charge.

My team and I walked Emily, Erdeen, and Ye to the car. Emily's driver stood waiting by the car. He would have come around to open the back door, but Ye took that job. Jerry and I thanked Emily again for the transportation and the weekend they had arranged for us that included so many 2004 SEP participants and views of Wuhai.

Emily said, "Principal Chen coordinated this when Ye told him you wanted to visit. I am glad you had a chance to see him and thank him before we left today. Mr. Jerry, he enjoyed your song about being light. He will keep that in his collection of stories. You should know one of his favorite stories is about teaching the 2004 team the proper way to eat noodles. He thought you Americans were strangely inhibited about making noise while eating."

Jerry did not look confused. He laughed. Emily looked surprised until he added, "Virginia told me about the slurping up noodles lesson. She is very good at making noise if you give her a reason or a challenge."

Emily smiled and nodded. Then Jerry shook hands in parting, but I hugged each one. I am not a huggy person, but if this was the last time we would ever meet in the flesh, I needed to hug each of these precious people. They had helped me feel so safe and at home with them.

After I hugged Ye, he said, "I hope we will meet again, Ms. Virginia. Will you think about returning, maybe especially in 2008 when we have the Olympics in Beijing?"

"I want to return, probably to work with Amity again, but not in an Olympic year. Crowds will be huge in Beijing, prices will be higher, events like that cause many superficial changes."

"The university I have chosen is a short train ride from Beijing."

"You will do well, Ye." Jerry said.

I said, "Ye, if I can return, I will find and visit you. You can give me a tour of your university. I am sure of it. Jerry and I will pray for you while we are apart. If I cannot return for a few years, maybe I can arrive in time to see you graduate from the University."

Ye said, "*Xie xie*," and entered the car. He shut the door after a last wave at Jim. We stood where we were until their car was out of sight.

"I hope you all got some rest this weekend?" I meant it as a statement, but my words sounded like a question.

"We did get rest, but we also had an English corner Friday night. Last night we stayed in and took our time this morning to get ready for church. Tell us about your weekend." Trudy said.

"First, thanks for doing another English corner. Did many people show up?"

"Many, all ages," Danielle answered. "Now tell us about what you did in Wuhai."

It took me a while to share even the highlights.

"Goodbyes are tiring." Danielle said and hugged Jim to her side.

Jim's voice sounded like he was fighting tears. "I feel sad saying goodbye to Ye. But it was harder to say goodbye to Dad when we left. I miss him."

I felt a shift. Thoughts of home affected all our moods. More than a month in a foreign culture was catching up to us, especially to Jim. He did a lot of work and projects with his dad. Jim knew Jerry well from church activities, but Ye had been a companion and positive distraction from homesickness, more fully than Sally.

271

Had being left on their own this weekend, a quiet time, made all of them miss home more? They'd had a quiet weekend in contrast to ours in Wuhai. Had I made a selfish mistake in leaving them?

Danielle's hugs and Trudy's caring presence helped Jim at this moment. Jerry did well in bringing up baseball plans for the last week of our teaching time. I told Jim I was glad he had learned so much from Ye. I tried to encourage him, noting that in this last week, he and Sally could help the rest of us with some Chinese and in finding certain items in the town.

"Did you eat?" Danielle asked with a laugh. "Before you returned here today?"

"Yes," Jerry explained. "We ate well the whole time. Even today, after the church service, we went to a Korean restaurant. Many of Ginny's Wuhai friends joined us there. I liked the *bulgogi* that was not spicy. Koreans have some really hot dishes."

"What's *bulgogi*?" Jim asked.

I explained, "It's thinly sliced beef marinated in soy sauce, garlic, sugar, and sesame oil. People with us ordered spicy pork, galbi, and spicy grilled chicken. They do like spicy dishes, but you know Jerry doesn't eat those. I think the group enjoyed hearing him say *Bù là.* Did you three eat a good lunch after church?"

"Yes." Danielle answered. "We ate at the restaurant near the park after church. Gladys, her husband, and Sally met us there. They didn't linger because the grandmom was home alone. There was an unusual breeze today and we walked farther across the park than usual. You know that swimming pool we've seen? It has never had water in it in this whole hot summer."

* * *

Our last Monday started totally differently than any others. The first-year junior middle school students were back. Our classes continued, but now loud music poured from speakers at the corners of each building. Even the English teachers who were students in the Amity SEP looked surprised at the volume.

Songs ranged from the tune of Yankee Doodle Dandy to London Bridge is Falling Down and Chinese children's songs like Two Tigers and Planting the Sun. Our students could not sing our class theme songs over the blaring music, nor could they talk and be heard. We moved to activities requiring writing until the school's morning music stopped.

That afternoon, a teacher, Zaya, who had been in my homeroom, appeared at the classroom door. She had a class now and wanted to say thank you for the help I and the team had given her. "You gave me new energy for teaching, and such lovely books." Most all the books we'd brought would be given out at the closing day party, but Zaya's responsibilities would keep her from attending.

"Zaya, we all wish you a wonderful school year."

"I came not only to thank you. Ms. Virginia, please could you come speak to my class briefly right now? They would be excited to meet my homeroom teacher. I have a high-level group, fifty-six students. You can encourage them."

"I can do that," I turned and gave an activity to my students that they could do with a partner. It should fill their time until I returned.

As I followed Zaya to the end of the classroom wing, I asked, "Who is with your class while you came to talk to me?"

"They are working. No one had to be with them."

In a few more steps we could see across to her class-room. I could not imagine leaving fifty-six middle school students alone in the United States and expecting them to keep working while no adult was with them. The students I saw worked quietly, head down, pencils moving. Zaya had not lost control. She showed trust they could carry on in the moment.

"You are an excellent group of students," I said to them as I entered the room.

Zaya followed me in and translated. Now the students had smiles as wide as hers. We had twenty minutes of conversation with their halting English speech and my answers as simple as possible. I would tell Zaya that her students were brave and polite. She exhibited the qualities that would make her an excellent teacher. I hoped she would remember the affirmation on the tough days any teacher faces.

Monday through Wednesday morning went by fast as a blink. We took time to have our last English corners Monday and Tuesday. Wednesday morning a mixture of excitement and nerves invaded each class while we started the presentations that counted as final exams.

In each of our classes we helped by juggling props, scanning presentation plans, and making efforts to help everyone to shine. The main concern was making sure they left with a certificate of successful completion because of attendance, participation, and final projects. Those certificates would be given out on Friday morning and registered with their schools. They would give them a new status.

Wednesday afternoon, our last gathering in the auditorium had a warmup after the lunch break using the class songs; not just the class theme songs, but also the humorous songs they had learned like 'There Was an Old Lady Who Swallowed a Fly,' 'Eensy weensy Spider,' 'Take Me Out to the Ballgame,' 'Hickory, Dickory, Dock,' 'Country Road,' 'She'll Be Comin' Round the Mountain,' 'I've Been Working on the Railroad,' and the sentimental favorite, "My Heart Will Go On." When I heard the classes sing, I felt grateful. A surprising sense of peace filled me because the students seemed relaxed from the stress of concern about earning the certificates.

We had a last role play to help them see a difference between a major event in both cultures, a wedding. We successfully used props we had gathered, bouquets, veil, a pillow for a ring bearer, toy store rings, and one of our Bibles to do a western style traditional wedding. Students in the presentation had a script we had given them.

Everyone present had a part. If they were not the bride or groom, bridesmaids, or groomsmen, ring bearer, the official certifying the wedding, soloist, or reader of a special love selection, or flower girl, they were wedding guests. The wedding reading included the Love Chapter, Corinthians 13. One of our best dramatic readers presented the love chapter. His reading fit the poetry.

[1] Though I speak with the tongues of men and of angels, but have not love,

I have become like sounding brass or a clanging cymbal. [2] And though I have the gift

of prophecy, and understand all mysteries and all knowledge, and though I have all faith, so that I could remove mountains, but have not love, I am nothing.

³ And though I bestow all my goods to feed the poor, and though I give my body

[a]to be burned, but have not love, it profits me nothing.

⁴ Love suffers long and is kind; love does not envy; love does not parade itself,

is not puffed up; ⁵ does not behave rudely, does not seek its own, is not provoked,

thinks no evil; ⁶ does not rejoice in iniquity, but re-joices in the truth;

⁷ bears all things, believes all things, hopes all things, endures all things.

⁸ Love never fails. But whether there are prophecies, they will fail; whether

there *are* tongues, they will cease; whether *there is* knowledge, it will

vanish away. ⁹ For we know in part and we prophesy in part. ¹⁰ But when

that which is perfect has come, then that which is in part will be done away.

¹¹ When I was a child, I spoke as a child, I understood as a child, I thought as a child;

but when I became a man, I put away childish things. ¹² For now we see in a mirror,

dimly, but then face to face. Now I know in part, but then I shall know just as I also

am known.¹³ And now abide faith, hope, love, these three; but the greatest of these *is* love.

Afterwards students asked questions about words and phrases in the Love Chapter. Who wrote it? What book had this chapter? Some students requested a copy. This chaotic emotional last week had collaborative appreciation, intense moments, laughter, care for one another, and a sense of beauty.

We concluded the full gathering early because students wanted to have one last baseball game. More students than Solomon hit home runs now from Jerry or Jim's pitches. They both told me that they aimed for the bats. "Good pitching practice," Jim said.

The baseball mitts we had brought would be part of the prizes people might choose on Friday at the class parties. The Wiffle ball and bat would also stay in the Left Banner. That two-part prize would have to go together.

VP Guo came to let us know we needed to end an hour earlier on Thursday because the local administrators would take us to yet another special dinner. This added time pressure, but we finished the presentations.

In front of their peers, some students chose to give speeches for their final exam. Some speeches made us laugh. Some stirred tears. They all earned our applause. We had briefer times than we wanted for comments. Each presentation had something well done. General applause came from each classroom. We ended at five o'clock.

The van took us back to the hotel. At six we went to the restaurant. Our group included the superintendent, town administrators, Principal Chimeg, VP Guo and his wife, Gladys, her husband, Sally, Jim, Danielle, Trudy, Jerry, and me. We went into the same dining room on the second floor where we had our first ceremonial dinner in the Left Banner. Jim still commented again on the flocked wallpaper, but without the wide-eyed energy of his first experience. Jim had changed. We all had.

The men shared toasts with liquor. We still returned

our toasts with glasses of juice. No one seemed offended. Whenever glasses were raised, I contrasted the dinner experiences in both of my SEP experiences. The main differences were less pressure in ceremonial show and in expectations for drinking liquor.

In our late-night pillow talk, Jerry admitted feeling overloaded from the touring in Beijing, church experiences, cultural training classes, Nanjing's environment and history that contrasted with the Left Banner. He realized he could not have done the SEP well without God's help. Each day had required actions of him in classroom teaching that differed from his work at home. But he also felt he'd been given more than he expected.

"Ginny, I'm not sure I could ever do this again. Could you? Could you come back again and not have the valuable difference of a child's presence? Having Jim along has changed the tone of many gatherings. You've told us how different 2004 was from this year's experience."

I was searching for words for an honest answer. To tell Jerry now that I wanted to return seemed like poor timing. I hadn't told him what I had hoped for from the experience because it had been a jumble in my mind. In these weeks of control and lack of control, leadership and vulnerability were my seesaws. I felt that answers about my life, faith, and choices were within reach now, or would be if I returned.

I turned to Jerry, but before I could share my thoughts, he was asleep.

Friday, the morning included finishing the presentations, a break to set up for the class parties. We had homeroom ceremonies to hand out the certificates of completing the course with excellence, a closing set of speeches in the auditorium, pictures taken by a local professional photographer, and dozens more pictures taken by our students. It was late afternoon before everyone said their goodbyes.

We concluded with laughing, some hugs, many thanks, and goodbyes. Zaya and Anu gave me their email addresses, and I shared mine. Each member of my team had a couple of students who wanted to continue contact. When we left the school, I sensed the relief in Trudy, Jerry, and Danielle. Jim seemed like a tired little boy.

I guessed we felt like pieces shaken in a kaleidoscope tube of activities, expectations, and emotions turning and tumbling. The patterns had changed each day, even in each hour. The kaleidoscope of our experiences had more changeable pictures than the thousand piece puzzle I pictured and tried to put together in my mind back in Massachusetts.

The big picture? Perhaps while resting on the plane before we landed in Shanghai, I could review the times when something went well or something flopped. I needed to see the lessons I had learned.

Jessie and MeiLi would be in Shanghai for the debriefing. Jessie had grown up in California, but she had lived in China for more than a decade. MeiLi had lived in the US for eighteen months at a major university, so she knew small and deep cultural differences.

I would try to talk with them before the debriefing weekend ended. Jerry, Danielle, and Jim would leave Sunday evening. Trudy and I would move to a hotel not far from the experimental school where I would be a guest presenter. I didn't want a totally new teaching experience without having a better understanding of what had wrapped around me in the Left Banner.

Chapter 31

Debriefing, a Meltdown, and Resilience

On the Friday evening three-hour flight from Ningxia to Shanghai for the Amity debriefing, we slept for about an hour. This happened only after Jim went through his review of each class party. He seemed to perk up in evaluating the celebrations.

"Pastor Jerry had the best games, funny, silly, everyone laughed. I liked those and his class did too. Mom's class has lots of people who like art. The decorations they made looked colorful. Ms. Virginia's class had the most music and rhymes. Ms. Trudy's class had the most snacks. But I don't think the people at home would like the party snacks here. Watermelon is okay, but every class had sunflower seeds and hazelnuts. My friends would choose soda. I thought we would have cake and ice cream."

"Your friends, like everyone in our country choose more sugar than people eat here." Danielle commented.

"Everyone got a prize, so they were more like gifts than prizes. Solomon looked happiest when you gave him the wiffle ball and bat as his prize, Pastor Jerry, but the people who chose mitts liked those too. Everybody liked the certificates. I have certificates at home. I didn't know grown-ups liked certificates too." Jim added.

"They remind us of special experiences, of work that matters," Jerry said.

"Thinking about the prizes, I am so glad everyone had a choice and that the leftover books and games can be left with the school. Principal Chimeg and VP Guo appreciated that," Trudy commented.

"I felt adrenalin, I guess all day because of the party, ceremony, photo session, and goodbyes." Danielle sighed and continued. "I really enjoyed my students, but I didn't get teary during the goodbyes. And I'm glad we had at least one mitt per class to offer as a prize option."

Trudy added, "I feel like my energy drained out of my body when we got on this plane."

"We won't have to do a lot for the debriefing days, will we?" Danielle asked.

"Informal meetings, some questionnaires to fill out, and discussions tomorrow morning. In the afternoon some time for a nap or sightseeing or both."

"And we get to hear about where all the other teams were and how their work went?" Danielle asked.

"Yes. It is very interesting to hear presentations on all the places from the teams."

"How much sightseeing are we doing?" Trudy asked while yawning.

"It's up to you. Sightseeing with Amity guides will be after lunch, just Saturday afternoon. Amity will have options and take people around to special sites. After dinner we can take a river ride on the Huangpu River lined with buildings and lights that are world famous. The Huangpu is like the main artery in the city. The price of the ride is reasonable too."

...

"Since I don't think I'll ever get back to China, I want to do the boat ride," Danielle said. "How about you buster?" she asked Jim.

"I just want to go home," he said. He yawned largely and looked out the window. "I thought we'd go home Saturday night, not on a boat ride."

"Sunday evening, Jim." I told him. "You, your mom, and Pastor Jerry will go to the airport late Sunday afternoon. Amity takes you there and makes sure to see you through to the security check. You'll get on the plane and go to sleep. Then..."

"Then we wake up and we're home?" His face suddenly had a broad smile.

"Not quite." Danielle said after she gave him a hug and a kiss. "You will wake up when we land in Chicago. We go through customs, then go to our plane to Boston. And because we are twelve hours ahead of Boston time here, when we get home, we will feel like we have been traveling for two days, but it will be early in our day at home."

"And Dad will meet us," Jim repeated. He didn't care about the time as much as he thought about seeing his dad.

"Yes," Danielle said. They leaned against one another and were asleep in a minute. Trudy, beyond Danielle and Jim, made light fluttery snuffles in sleep. Jerry, beside me, snored.

* * *

Jim's meltdown came Saturday night after we boarded the river boat and found seats that would give us a great view of both sides of the Huangpu River. The skyscrapers and Oriental Pearl Tower glowed with lights that would rouse spirits like a fantasy light show. None of those sights mattered to the ten-year-old with us. Jim was past any touristic interests.

Danielle edged him closer to her while he muttered, "I don't want to go on this ride. I want to go home. I want to see Dad. I want to go home," Jim muttered, tears appearing in his eyes. They spilled and continued. "Mom, I want to go home."

The small ship was packed with tourists out for a delightful evening ride on one of the most famous rivers in China. Now they listened to a child cry with exhaustion and homesickness.

The SEP could have been as miserable as this ride if Jim had felt the homesickness he struggled with now. I felt sad that he felt so miserable, but thankful the meltdown didn't happen until this last evening together. I expected he'd return to his usual good-natured self soon. Resilience. Children had an amazing ability to adapt, to bounce back.

Resilience. I should have that too. I felt the warmth of the night while I listened to Jim sob softly against Danielle. She was such a good mom, no impatience or aggravation toward Jim's meltdown. Beyond his crying we had a background track of Chinese instrumental music piped through the boat. Trudy, Jerry, and I stayed close to Danielle and Jim to shield them as much as we could from stares of the curious.

Jessie and MeiLi had been too busy with teams and staff to have a conversation with me. I didn't pressure them. My inner turmoil would remain mine. Sunday morning we would have a last gathering of all the SEP volunteers for a worship service. Amity staff would spend the afternoon taking volunteers to the airport. I would say goodbye to my team except for Trudy.

We stayed physically close aboard the ship on the

Huangpu while Jim cried against his mother. Although his crying became quieter, it lasted for the boat ride down to the place where the river met the sea and back to the Bund's Shiliupu Warf. He fell asleep in the cab we took to get back to the hotel.

"Jim will be all right." Danielle said, "He rarely has had a crying spell as this. I'm glad he didn't have this meltdown until the end of the trip."

"Jim's been great, Danielle. He did so well through every day. He was a super helper. So much that happened to him could have scared him or frustrated him. He has acted wonderfully as a young ambassador." I said this to her but hoped my words registered with Jim too. "I am thankful he came on this trip. He made it easier, more down to earth, and fun. It was a true gift to have him with us."

* * *

In bed I said to Jerry, "You know what has been the most different this year working as an Amity volunteer?"

"What?"

"Not being alone when I went to my room, having you to talk to, to love, to pray with, to discuss plans with, and to laugh with. I'll miss you this week."

"I believe you, but you always do all right on your own or with me."

"I guess I look like I do, but I've been searching for why I felt such a need to come back to China. I haven't figured out totally yet what in China affects me so that I feel it is changing me in good ways. Do you think there's a bigger purpose I can't see."

"There's always something we can't see. I've been thinking a lot about Jim's meltdown. He just fell apart with no sign of anything like that in all our time in Beijing, Nanjing, Yinchuan, or the Left Banner," Jerry said.

"I know. It's hard to understand except that time is different to kids. He was ready to go home when we left Yinchuan. He thought about his dad and wanted to be with him. That's all he could think about. Kids' emotions are intense and you know how completely they can focus on something they want."

"I agree with Danielle that he'll probably be fine tomorrow."

"And you?" I asked as I snuggled in close.

"I will do what I can to help Danielle and Jim have a good trip home. I'll miss you, but there's a pile of work waiting for me when I get home. You're the one who first told me anyone with a job who takes a break pays a penalty of having more work when they get home."

"It does seem like that often. It's one of the reasons teachers try not to miss days. Writing plans for a substitute and getting back on track after absences are penalties."

"In a week, I'll see you in Boston. I'll be praying for you every day. Are you nervous about presenting at the experimental school?"

"The school will be entirely different than the facilities in the Left Banner. I've heard it is technologically futuristic and has beautiful facilities."

"You said it's like a Magnet School, so I expect the student level will be high, and they'll have high level curriculum."

Jerry hugged me close. "I think you're more resilient than Jim. You'll have a good week."

I never fell asleep as quickly as Jerry did, but I felt safe in his arms, secure enough to keep looking for missing puzzle pieces, to wrestle with emerging from a cocoon of perspectives and desires. I'd seen how being vulnerable made me uncomfortable, but it also made me feel like I was alive.

Relationships seemed to deepen when I felt vulnerable with others. Choosing the unknown over the familiar connected to wanting to grow stronger in new skills. I also knew that courage and resilience grew through facing challenges and overcoming the tough times. Did I have some kind of drive to face difficult situations because moving through them made me feel alive? I wriggled beneath the covers in our air-conditioned room and fell asleep without connecting all the dots.

Chapter 32

Sunday's TGI Friday

The city of Shanghai has more people than the continent of Australia. The neighborhoods ranged from old time Shanghai with its own foods and Shanghainese dialect to an area called the French Concession because it has buildings from the early 19th century built by Europeans in ostentatious styles. Trudy and I stayed in a hotel near the People's Park. In our country it would have been a four-star hotel, and we would not have been able to afford to stay there. In China, with the American dollar in 2006, it cost about twenty-six dollars a night.

Trudy was fourteen years older than me. When we got ready for bed in our spacious room, she announced she was taking all of Monday just to rest. "I saw enough just checking in to know the hotel has plenty for me to enjoy right here, and I do want to sleep in until late morning. I do that at home at least once a week and I haven't slept in more than one day since we arrived in China. If it wasn't responsibilities, it was the experiences and concerns about teaching that kept me awake. This has been the most unusual summer of my life, but I am ready to go home."

In the morning, a car sent from the experimental school took me to the school for a day of talking with classes and a meeting with the language teachers. The entire staff knew English as well as Gladys did. The well-funded school had modern equipment, furnishings, and grounds. I could have conversations about pedagogy with teachers while we sat in garden chairs backed by sculpted hedges. I thought about the teachers of English who were our students in the SEP. I didn't know if they had any idea of the quality and look of a Shanghai experimental school.

Trudy was reading in the lobby when I returned at 7 pm. Traffic in the city matched New York City on a grid-lock day. Trudy looked rested.

"*Ni hao*, did you eat?" she said sounding cheerful.

"I had a delicious light lunch in an air-conditioned faculty room."

"We had air-conditioning in that lovely little restaurant in the Left Banner."

"We did. Did you hear anything from home?"

"I got an email from Danielle. Jim almost knocked Greg over when he rushed into his arms. Jerry told Greg how wonderful Jim had been on this whole adventure. Danielle said Greg was shocked that Jim could speak and write some Chinese."

"I'll check my email after supper. Hopefully Jerry will have sent me news about getting home too. Are you feeling as if you'd like to come to the school with me tomorrow?"

"No. No more schools here for me, but I do want to hear about what you saw and did. Let's go up the room. You can tell me more about the school and what you did when you're freshened up. Then we'll have supper?"

After a delicious supper in the hotel restaurant that had food choices from around the world, we both did an email check and sent some. Jerry's email to me was typically his short telegram style, but he did include a list of his immediate work for the week.

Back in our room, Trudy turned on CCTV.

"Trudy, did you watch CCTV often in the Left Banner?"

"A little, but most days I was so tired, I went to bed pretty early. When I did turn on CCTV, it was good to hear and see newscasters speaking English."

"Jerry watched it in the evening. He missed English from sources other than what we had brought. He was shocked that no stores sold the China Daily in English."

"Danielle said Jim always wanted to watch kid shows in Chinese whenever they were in their room. That's partly how he learned Chinese so quickly."

Trudy and I read for a while and then went to bed. I thought about Jerry. We were a case of opposites attract. He liked familiar routines. If my days were too routine, I felt trapped. Is that what pushed me to take the risk of going to China? Was it my career that pushed me to take risks? Teachers supposedly had control in their classroom, but teachers I knew learned quickly that anything could happen on any day and require changing plans.

Living and working in remote areas instead of a place like Shanghai pushed me to the edges of my understanding, abilities, and comfort. Is that what I needed to know about myself? I thought I needed to acknowledge that I liked or craved intensity in my daily life. Should I feel guilty about that need?

* * *

Tuesday afternoon and Wednesday, Trudy explored blocks around our hotel. Stores and small unique museums easily filled her days. On Thursday, Trudy told me, "I've had enough rest and when you can go with me, I'm ready to see more than what I can walk to. Are you finished with the school tomorrow?"

"I am going for the morning. Let's take that Hop-on Hop-off bus in the afternoon. We can get a ticket that will be good for Friday and Saturday."

We saw everything from the French Concession grand buildings and art galleries to the Bund of European buildings, once banks and global business centers, built along the Huangpu River, and we went up in the Pearl Tower. We visited Madame Tussauds Wax Museum. Trudy was not interested in large museums or historic buildings as much as watching people fly kites near the river or visiting Shanghai's Botanical Gardens. The best part of the garden for me came with a section devoted to flowering plants that attracted butterflies.

Even though we both felt tired from walking in heat and humidity, I felt peaceful watching the butterflies. Trudy thought of them as bugs with wings, so she walked more to read information about the flowering plants.

Black and white, with light tint of gold, butterfly in Shanghai Botanical Garden

I stared at the fragility of the butterflies and thought

about their freedom. This summer, acceptance for transformation had come through hard lessons learned about me, trusting God to provide for needs even before we knew we had a need, friendship, teamwork, risk taking, awareness of face, motivations, even guanxi. I'd learned through the weeks that my resilience developed from challenges. The butterflies went through dramatic changes. They had beauty and freedom after the changes in their environment and bodies. Couldn't I accept and feel this too?

The lives of butterflies were short. In terms of eternity our human lives were too. Every day counted. Everything we could touch counted. Butterflies were vital to pollination and supporting other living creatures. I thought about this as I returned to the hotel.

What would Jerry think if I explained my thoughts about not feeling guilty anymore about needing a different environment and experiences to grow? Could he understand my desire to support other teachers in cross cultural communication and collaborative work? Could he accept that I would want to return to China again because of the people here who inspired me?

In our room for the last night, I asked, "And tomorrow, Trudy? Do you want to go to church in the French Concession? Remember we passed three large churches in that area?"

"I don't know. Maybe I'm like Jim now. Traveling around this city even on the tourist bus is overwhelming. China is overwhelming. If we go to church, we'll be escorted to a special section. That makes me self-conscious. What if they don't have headphones that translate? I think I should just stay here and wait for you. Right now, I want to think about home. I need something familiar, faces, language, food, sounds, buildings."

"We don't leave for the airport until three. Come to church with me. I bet you'll feel better. Think of how familiar it is in our lives to gather with people who love God."

"Can I tell you in the morning if I want to go to church?"

"Sure." I tried to sound calm, as if it didn't matter, but I thought Trudy would feel better for the long trip home, if she went to a morning worship service.

Trudy found that her packing went quickly in the morning. She agreed to go to church with me but did not feel up to walking there. Shanghai has hot steamy mornings in the summer which can be almost overwhelming unless a person can feel breezes from an open space like a river or a park.

People welcomed us as vibrantly there as in any church I'd visited in China. The service followed the order we'd encountered from Beijing to the Left Banner: Music that included singing from congregation and the choir, announcements, Bible reading, prayer, the Lord's Prayer, sermon, reciting the Apostles Creed, and communion.

When we left the church grounds I asked, "Would you like to walk a little bit before we take a taxi? We'll be sitting hours through the rest of the day."

"Okay, but this section frustrates me. It looks like Europe, but all I see are Chinese. What I still crave desperately is American company, food, and beverages."

"Let's walk a couple of blocks. See that big white building ahead? That could be right out of Paris or Brussels. We can walk there, cross the street, and get a taxi back to the hotel."

"And then go to the airport," Trudy said. We began walking.

"You do sound like Jim now, happy to leave."

"And you're not happy to leave?"

"People appreciate education so much more here. They don't pay teachers more here than in our country, but they respect teachers more. I wouldn't want to live here the rest of my life, but I'd be happy to live here for a few years."

"I couldn't do that."

"Neither could Jerry, so I will go back and wait and pray about a chance to return."

"You'll come back again? Really? Will Jerry come back with you another time?"

"I don't know. We'll talk about it."

When we crossed the street, I looked far ahead and thought I had hallucinated a TGI Friday's restaurant. "Trudy! Look down this street. Look on the right. What do you see?" She turned back from searching for a taxi.

The expression on her face was a blend of disbelief and joy. I went back to her and took her hand. We could have skipped like kids down the street.

Inside the familiar chain restaurant, the crowd had as many western looking people as Chinese, and the atmosphere had the classic TGI Friday's American look and fare. Trudy had the meal she'd been longing for, a cheeseburger, fries, and a chocolate milk shake. Between mouthfuls she acknowledged what I had been thinking but resisted saying.

"You know, if I hadn't come to church with you this morning, I never would have had a chance to enjoy this meal. I feel more relaxed now, better able to maneuver through the airport and travel home. Who knew we'd come across a TGI Friday's after church?"

Chapter 33

Homecomings, Progression, and Remediation

Are homecomings ever fully what we expect? As I exited into the main arrival area in Boston's airport I saw Jerry. He wasn't smiling and something about his face looked off kilter.

When he kissed me, I pulled back, and asked, "What's wrong?"

"My glasses got knocked off. I hurried to get out of the car in the parking lot. Bent the frame." He showed me the lopsided frame.

"I'm glad it isn't you off kilter, just your glasses."

"I have been off kilter without you." His words were a corny line, but I didn't mind. He kissed me again and said, "I felt happy all morning knowing I'd see you. Thanks for calling from Chicago."

"We had that slight delay there. I walked Trudy to her gate. She was flying to Philadelphia, then to Atlantic City. Friends will pick her up to drive her home."

"I left in plenty of time to be here when you arrived, but there was construction and a detour. Traffic slowed down. I was afraid you'd come out and I wouldn't be here. I rushed to park the car, and when I jumped out, I turned some way that knocked my glasses off."

We laughed, kissed, and hugged again. When my bags were in the car, he walked to the passenger side and opened my door. As I got into the car I said, "Wow, dating behavior. Thanks."

Now he laughed and went around to get in on the driver's side. "Let's have more dating behavior before I drive home." He pulled me close. Not having bucket seats made access easy.

He started the car for the trip home and asked, "Everything on your flights went well?"

"Yes, and I learned there is going to be a new route, a direct route, Boston to Beijing. The airlines can make it in 12 hours if they fly north. They'll fly over the North Pole and then down to Beijing. I'd do that next time I go."

Jerry stayed quiet while navigating the airport exit and aimed to go through the Ted Williams Tunnel. I guessed he must be thinking about me already mentioning the next time I'd go to China. I hadn't been back in Massachusetts for an hour.

When our route was set and the traffic lighter, Jerry said, "Ginny, do you want to do the Amity program again? You've done it twice."

"Yes, I do, and I don't want to feel guilty about having that desire. If it is not the right time or not right at all for me to go, God can easily stop me. There's no guarantee that China will give anyone a visa, plus lots of other obstacles could arise to keep me here. I think God is the one who has given me this desire to work with teachers and students in China."

Jerry was quiet for a minute. Then he asked, "Did

having your own team work out better, like you thought it would?"

"Yes, but I can see where I could have exercised more consideration for the team, for you, and for our hosts."

"You were a good leader."

"Jerry, right from that missing bag of Trudy's I felt nervous for our group. I am glad God is patient with me. From my first time in China, I should have remembered how even the unpleasant and unexpected difficulties were resolved in repeated God-incidences."

"God took care of problems quickly for us. That doesn't always happen, but I'm thankful it did. Hey, that was a big sigh just now. What are you thinking of?"

"I'm thinking of the people I really care about in China. For now, we can exchange email, but that might not always be the case. We could lose touch with people by having communication cut off."

"You do worry about something happening before it does."

"I know. I need help overcoming that too. And I need to pray more for the friends who have come to mean so much to me. They sure have their own challenges."

"Thinking of Ye?"

"Yes, and others, I've recognized I need to be glad I can carry people in my heart when distances and expense keep us so far apart. What about you? Have you had time to digest your time in China?"

"Since I've been home, I realize I had no idea about how tough English would be for teachers or English because in the Left Banner, they already are speakers of Chinese and Mongolian. Some of them know Russian, and they all know dialects. I often felt slow in comparison, and it was embarrassing that they knew English grammar far better than I do. I wish I had studied a foreign language more years."

The adrenalin rush of traveling home had faded. I probably sounded tired when I asked him, "Have you thought at all about going back?"

"I thought about it, and I guessed that you would want to do the Amity program again. You mentioned it even before Danielle, Jim, and I left. That made me think about whether or not I could do the program again. That heat and Chinese food every day were the toughest parts of the SEP for me. You weren't thinking about applying to work there next year, were you?"

"No."

"And you want me to go with you again?"

"Yes. But I know you like what's familiar, a routine."

"It's funny what I missed. I thought it would be family and friends, but I knew they were back here and praying each day for me, for us. What I missed was cereal, sandwiches on multi-grain bread, and glasses of cold milk."

"They had goat milk."

"Yes. I tried it. You know, after two weeks in the Left Banner, I felt like I had an addiction to reading English words and was going through withdrawal. I never imagined how disorienting it would seem to go weeks without seeing anything written in English. I'd prepare differently if I went again. When did you think you'd apply to work with Amity again?"

"I think it would be too much to go before 2009. We need to save more if we are both going again. The Olympic year will affect the whole country. I think even distant areas will be consumed with following the events. Ye thought everyone would want to come to Beijing."

"We'll see it better and more comfortably on television."

"He's young, plus he's so proud of his country having the opportunity to host the world for the Olympics."

"Would we see Ye again if we went? Go to Wuhai again?"

"I'd try to plan that, but we can't be a team of two, and I still don't feel comfortable with having a team made up of people I don't know. Having you and friends who had a goal to serve made me feel more confident that everyone would do their best."

"Jim did a great job coping until that last night."

"At the debriefing, I did hear that China will stop allowing teachers to bring a child along on the SEP."

"Did Trudy say anything about going back?"

"She told me if she had a year or two to recover, she might do it again. It's always good to have a nurse on a team. I asked her to keep thinking about it. She asked me if I'd plan tourism for the starting week again. I said I would. Xian would be super. Even though I've been there, I'd go again. The Terra Cotta Warriors site had just been planned and marked in 2004, but it wasn't finished. By 2009, the museum and outdoor sites might be completed.

"I also thought about those mountains in the south, the ones that rise up like cones from a fantasy painting. They have mammoth caves and natural bridges. I looked at a map and saw a county area that has a place called Shangri-la in the southern province of Yunnan"

"Isn't Shangri-la a mythical place?"

"I think China has many mythical places. We've seen few of them."

"Guess you haven't thought much at all about the next trip to China," Jerry laughed and reached out to lift my left hand. He took it to his lips and kissed it.

"Is this evidence of absence makes the heart grow fonder?"

"It's all the evidence you get while I'm driving."

"Very funny. I hope in 2009, we can still be romantic role models for whomever we serve with Amity. I never thought of us as a role model for romance, but so many women commented on us holding hands while walking anywhere as being very romantic that I guess it was."

"That probably made it difficult for the men in their lives. The Chinese are more reserved. I don't really think about holding hands when we do. It feels natural. Just like missing you is natural. A big part of why I went along this year is because I missed you so much when you volunteered and were away for all those weeks in 2004."

"Jerry, do you think it's weird that the challenges of being in such a different culture help me feel alert, alive, and even renewed spiritually?"

"Learning to trust God through difficulties usually is renewing."

"Maybe I need to keep going to a different culture to have more lessons in trusting God."

"We can learn more about trusting God here and wait on the timing to return."

"That's a plus and a minus."

"Why?"

"I know waiting for God's timing is best, but I'm not good at waiting."

Jerry smiled and reached his right hand to hold my left hand. "I know you don't enjoy waiting, but you persevere. You've struggled with trust for years, but you also go with your intuition or nudges of the Spirit. I see good changes in you again this year, like you feel more acceptance of yourself and your life. If this is something God is calling you to do, I want you to go and not feel guilty about it. We don't know why He has put this in your heart, but it is clearly a call. I can't say right now that I will go, but I will help you find a team."

He paused again, squeezed my hand and asked, "Are you sure you want to go back?"

I brought his right hand to rest above my heart and said, "Yes."

Appendix: China Spicy
and Salty Vocabulary

NOTE: Pronunciations are approximate. Chinese is a tonal language so not only does the pronunciation matter, but the correct tone also matters. Saying a word even with a simple spelling in a different tone changes the meaning of the word.

· *Aaruul* (ahr-rul): a dairy-based snack made from curds of boiled yogurt
· *Aloo gobi* (uh loo gow bee): potatoes, cauliflower, spices
· *Amity Foundation*: a non-governmental organization (NGO) founded in the mid-1980s by Bishop K.H.Ting with the support of Chinese Christians, to promote education, public health, community development, environmental protection, and disaster relief. It has the world's largest Bible printing company in Nanjing.
· *Baozi* (bough zi): also called bao buns or steamed buns; made of soft white dough kept hot and moist in bamboo bowls and filled with a sweet or savory filling
· *Boortsog* (boort-sog): a Mongolian fried dough that is considered a dessert; like a cookie, it is made from flour,

yeast, milk, eggs, butter, salt, and sugar; also enjoyed as a snack.

· *Bù là* (boo la): not spicy, as from hot peppers and sauces

· *Bulgogi* (bull go gee): a Korean marinated beef dish

· *Buuz* (boatz): large, steamed dumplings filled with meat, onions, and garlic

· *Cha* (chaah): tea

· *Chanasan makh* (chanasan mak): boiled meat, bones, and innards cooked together in salted water that is simmered slowly for hours

· *Chángchéng* (chang chung): Great Wall

· *Dàn* (dan): egg

· *Flying eaves*: Their uplifted corners resemble the wings of a flying bird; help drain water and deflect lightning strikes; often are decorated with gold and green enamel tiles or sculpted with auspicious animals like dragons, cranes, or fish; the curve of the roof, which starts from the ridge and turns up at the eaves, gives Chinese buildings a light and airy feel.

· *Galbi* (kahl bee): a Korean dish of marinated ribs

· *Gao chi* (how chrr): delicious

· *Ger* (gair): a Mongolian temporary tent like a house; also called a yurt

· *Guanxi* (gwan she): a network based on personal relationships, trust, and obligations. Practicing *guanxi* includes exchanging favors to facilitate business deals and social situations.

· *Hâo le ma?* (How la ma?): Are you ready?

· *Huáng Hé* (Hwong Heh): Yellow River

· *Huānyíng* (hwanying): welcome

· *Huānyíng, da jie jie* (hwanying dah jyeh jyeh): welcome, big sister

· *Huānyíng, xiao didi* (hwanying shaow dee dee): welcome, little brother
· *Hushuur* (hoosh-sure): like a Mongolian fast food; similar to small pita bread but crescent-shaped and filled with seasoned mutton; frequently deep-fried
· *Hutong* (hoo tong): narrow alleys found in Beijing and connected to historic houses with courtyards in old residential neighborhoods. A Mongolian word that means 'well' because, like wells, *hutongs* in Beijing share a water source.
· *Kāidāngkù* (kai dang koo): a traditional alternative to diapers in China
· *Khorkhog* (khur-khuhg): barbecue roasted for hours in an enclosed container
· *Kuaizi* (kwaizi): chopsticks
· *Ladetiao* (lahn d'chow): bullfrog cooked in five kinds of chili peppers
· *Lavsha* (lahv-shah): soup with mutton or beef, fat, and homemade eggless noodles
· *Luòtuó* (lowtwah): camel
· *Měiguó rén* (mey gwo ren): Měiguó means America; adding rén makes the word American
· *Miàntiáo* (mee-en tee-ow): Mandarin for noodle
· *Nei Menggu* (nay mung go): the Mandarin name for Inner Mongolia
· *Nǐ de péngyǒu* (nee duh pung yoh): your friend
· *Ni hao* (knee how): hello
· *Palak paneer* (pa luhk puhneer): curry with spinach, onions, cottage cheese, and spices
· *RMB* (ren min bee): renminbi currency of China. It means 'people's currency' in Mandarin. Used interchangeable with 'yuan.'
· *Shagaa* (sh ah gah): a Mongolian word for a sour berry that is bright orange in color

· *Shaji* (sha jee): a Chinese word for a sour bright-orange berry
· *Shūcài* (shoo tzai): vegetables
· *Shui* (shway): water
· *Siheyuan* (sih-hyeh-yuen): a courtyard communal area, often with a garden relaxing area; also a neighborhood formed by the joining of one *siheyuan* to another to form a *hutong*
· *Summer English Program* (SEP): a program designed to offer English enrichment and teaching classes to teachers of English in remote areas of China with the help of volunteers, teachers, and other English speakers
· *Suutei tsai* (sootay-sigh): traditional Mongolian milk tea made with black or green tea; milk from cows, sheep, goats, camels, or horses. A pinch of salt, fried millet, barley, yogurt, or butter can be added.
· *Tài guile* (tie gwey luh): too expensive
· *Tang* (tahng): soup
· *Táoqì* (tou chee): naughty
· *Toono* (too no): the rounded roof rising to an opening in a *ger*/yurt
· *Tsuvian* (tsoo-veen): stir-fried meat and vegetables with hand-cut noodles
· *Xie xie* (she-eh she-eh): thank you
· *Yī dùn fàn* (ee dn fan): meal
· *Youtiao* (yoh tee oh): fried dough sticks
· *Yuan* (yoo ahn): the basic money of China. In the summer of 2006, one dollar equaled almost eight yuan.
· *Zài jiàn* (zai-jee-an): goodbye

Acknowledgments

The person I thank first supports me in more ways than I can list here; my husband of fifty-three years, Jerry. Not only does he work as an alpha and beta reader, but he has taken on household tasks to give me more time to write.

Next, I am thankful for a friend of more than five decades who is an author and cover designer, who also works as a developmental editor, Dr. Gordon Saunders. He grasps the big picture while helping me to analyze the structure, characters, narrative details, and the essential core elements.

Over the years or months in which I work on a book, I am thankful for the family and friends who give encouragement about writing the story in this memoir. I am grateful to each one and to the honesty of evaluation by members of the writing groups, Ashland's 'Must Love Words' and the Zoom group, 'Advancing Writing Endeavors (AWE)' writers. Special thanks to my dear friend, Ruby Huang, whose advice and encouragement helps me see China and its language more deeply. Thank you to copy editor, Carolyn Allard, for affirmation and corrections.

Some people took on the task of reading a full draft, in a month of their own busy schedules, and gave helpful feedback as 'alpha readers.' They told me what didn't make sense, what they wanted to know more about, what distracted them, what connected with some of their own concerns, and what they saw in the story that they hoped would continue in the series. Thank you to Sparkie Ciriacy, Cindy Bradley, Juanita Shade, Sharon Moore, Cindy Mayo, Rebecca Jones, and Jerry.

When the author thinks the story is ready to be shared, 'Beta readers' go through it for readability—considering such things as plot points, fullness of characters, pacing, and details of language. Thank you especially to Lieutenant Fred Lussier, (Massachusetts State Police, ret.), Ann Martin, Anne Marie Lauranzon, and Sparkie Ciriacy for the Beta and ARC reading.

And thank you reader! I appreciate comments and questions from readers. You can email me at virginia@ time2create.info. I respond to all emails.

For some of my published articles, unpublished short stories and writing from Substack and Medium, visit my website https://time2create.info

Virginia Heslinga

Book 3 in the series, '**Did You Eat?'** *China Sharp and Zesty: 2009*, is expected to launch in the spring of 2026.

About the Author

Virginia Heslinga, Ed.D., is Associate Professor of Humanities at Anna Maria College in Paxton, Massachusetts. She is a recipient of the 'Living the Mission Award' which is presented to a member of the faculty who understands and appreciates the importance of educating the whole student and who seizes every opportunity to do so.

For more than fifty years, Virginia has taught in schools—public, private, alternative, home, religious, juvenile detention, and online. She has worked in this country and others with every age group. She has published articles in education journals, written curriculum, plays, and short stories.

In 2023 she released her first full-length book, a memoir about a fire that devastated her family and changed her life, *Grace Interlaced*. In 2024, a Spanish-language version of that book, *Gracia entrelazada* (translated by Dr. Carlos Miranda, Ph.D., MITI), was published. This was followed by her historical novel, *Wounded Dove* (2024), about the life of a family of Danish immigrants in twentieth-century Worcester County, Massachusetts, and their daughter who contracted polio in the New England polio epidemic. The **Did You Eat?** series, starts with *China Sweet and Sour* (2025), which presents Virginia's first experience leaving home to teach in a remote region of China in 2004.

Virginia continues to teach and write from her home in Ashland, Virginia. To contact her use Virgina@time2create.info or visit her website https://time2create.info.

Virginia in the grasslands of central Inner Mongolia.